Vindicating the Founders

Vindicating the Founders

RACE, SEX, CLASS, AND JUSTICE IN THE ORIGINS OF AMERICA

Thomas G. West

ROWMAN & LITTLEFIELD PUBLISHERS, INC.
Lanham • Boulder • New York • Toronto • Plymouth, UK

ROWMAN & LITTLEFIELD PUBLISHERS, INC.

Published in the United States of America
by Rowman & Littlefield Publishers, Inc.
A wholly owned subsidiary of The Rowman & Littlefield Publishing Group, Inc.
4501 Forbes Boulevard, Suite 200, Lanham, Maryland 20706
www.rowmanlittlefield.com

Estover Road
Plymouth PL6 7PY
United Kingdom

Copyright © 1997 by Rowman & Littlefield Publishers, Inc.
First paperback printing 2001

British Library Cataloguing in Publication Information Available

The hardback edition of this book was previously cataloged by the Library of
Congress as follows:

Library of Congress Cataloging-in-Publication Data

West, Thomas G., 1945–
    Vindicating the founders: race, sex, class, and justice in the origins of
America / Thomas G. West.
        p.   cm.
    Includes bibliographical references and index.

    1. United States—Politics and government—1783–1865.   2. United
States—Politics and government—1775–1783.   3. Constitutional
history—United States.   4. Citizenship—United States—History.   6. Right
of property—United States—History.   7. Women's rights—United
States—History.   I. Title.
E302.1.W47   1997
973.5—DC21   97-16791
                                                                                    CIP

ISBN 0-8476-8516-0 (cloth : alk. paper)
ISBN 0-8476-8517-9 (pbk. : alk. paper)

Printed in the United States of America

⊖™ The paper used in this publication meets the minimum requirements of
American National Standard for Information Sciences—Permanence of Paper for
Printed Library Materials, ANSI/NISO Z39.48–1992.

For my father and mother

Irving Parmelee West and
Marjorie Ergmann West

Contents

Acknowledgments

The Claremont Institute for the Study of Statesmanship and Political Philosophy in Claremont, California, commissioned the originals of the chapters on slavery, women's rights, and voting rights. I finished the book while serving as the Institute's Ahmanson Fellow in Religion and Politics in 1995-96. Thanks to Howard and Roberta Ahmanson, to Institute president Larry P. Arnn, and to former vice presidents (now senior fellows) Douglas A. Jeffrey and Charles Heatherly for their generous support and encouragement, in this project and many others. Doug also helped extensively with the editing.

Thanks also to the University of Dallas for funding one semester of my 1995-96 sabbatical and for supporting my work in many other ways.

Through the generosity of Henry Salvatori, Charles Kesler brought me to Claremont McKenna College as Salvatori Visiting Scholar from 1990-92, where I began the research that led to this book—which research, God willing, will soon lead to another.

The first draft of the chapter on property rights was written for a 1993 conference at the Pacific Research Institute through the kind invitation of Program Officer Steven Hayward.

The Earhart Foundation enabled me to take time off from teaching to work on the book through grants in the summer of 1990 and the academic year 1993-94. Thanks to President David Kennedy and Director of Program Antony Sullivan for their support of this and other projects over the years.

Thanks also to the Aequus Foundation for grants in 1994 and 1995 to work on the revisions.

Forrest McDonald, who read the manuscript for Rowman & Littlefield, endorsed the book in spite of our disagreement on the meaning of equality in the founding (see the beginning of chapter 1). I appreciate his generosity, and I acknowledge him here as a leading historian of the founding era. I also thank the publisher's other readers—Burton Folsom and Herman Belz, capable historians both, and Dan Mahoney, one of our ablest political scientists—for their praise as well as occasional sharp criticisms. Steve Wrinn, my editor at Rowman & Littlefield, was always helpful.

Finally, I owe gratitude to other colleagues, friends, and students who responded sympathetically to my arguments: John Alvis, Julie Kessler, John Grant, Jameson Taylor, Jack Paynter, John Marini, Ed Erler, Ken Masugi, Ralph Rossum, Rich Dougherty, and my wife, Grace. Others helped by attacking me: Hiram Caton, Peter Skerry, Rogers Smith, and Edward Chynoweth. Chris Wolfe suggested the title. John Grant, Julie Kessler, and Abbie Erler helped with proofreading, and John Grant with the index.

I studied political philosophy and America in graduate school with Harry V. Jaffa, who has done more than anyone else I know to recover the Founders' understanding of liberty and equality. Almost alone, he has revived serious interest in the principles of the founding, not as historical curiosities of a world that is dead and gone, but as life-giving truths, real sources of political wisdom and health.

As a graduate student I took most of my classes with Harry Neumann, Harry Jaffa, Martin Diamond, and Leo Strauss. At that time and for some years after, I concentrated on Greek and German political philosophy. I always had an interest in America, but I tended to assume that Jaffa and Diamond had already done the main work and that all that remained was to dot *i*'s and cross *t*'s.

Eventually I began to look into the founding on my own. In 1983, William B. Allen, now Dean of James Madison College at Michigan State, asked me to write an essay for one of several Liberty Fund conferences that he and Eugene Miller organized and I attended. (The essay was published as "The Classical Spirit of the Founding," in *The American Founding: Essays on the Formation of the Constitution*, ed. Leonard Levy, J. Jackson Barlow, and Ken Masugi (Westport, Conn.: Greenwood Press, 1988), 1-56.) I am grateful to Bill, Gene, and the Liberty Fund for pointing me toward applying my knowledge of the philosophical tradition to American politics. The Great Books themselves teach that theory is about the real world. We students of political philosophy sometimes forget that. Some of us are tempted to equate political philosophy with the study of texts and nothing but the study of texts. The Great Books are indispensable preliminaries to real thinking, but the thinking itself must be about the world we live in if it is to be our own and not merely transmission of someone else's thought.

Chapter 7 is reprinted with permission from *Loyalty Misplaced: Misdirected Virtue and Social Disintegration,* ed. Gerald Frost (London: Social Affairs Unit, 1997). The chapter appears in a revised version in this book.

Preface

𝒯his book will show that America's Founders well deserve the respect that citizens and schoolchildren still pay them, but which has long been out of fashion among America's elites. The Founders wrote and approved a Declaration of Independence whose central proposition was that "all men are created equal." They set up a government that did what no democracy had ever done before: It combined majority rule with effective protection for minority rights. It enabled a larger number of men and women to live in prosperity and liberty than any other nation has ever done.

In spite of this undeniable success, many of our leading sophisticates today would rather talk about the Founders' failures. Instead of the victories they won on behalf of freedom, we hear loud complaints about their supposed racism, sexism, and elitism. The Founding Fathers, we are told, did not really believe that "all men (and women) are created equal." Washington and Jefferson owned slaves. Women and the poor were excluded from voting. So how can we take seriously the Founders' supposed belief in human equality?

These arguments are well entrenched in the conventional wisdom of our time. They are repeated endlessly in the media and in popular books, by professors and politicians, as in these typical statements:

On blacks: "The sublime principles of the Declaration did not apply to them. They are for whites only." (Writer Conor Cruise O'Brien) The "prevailing opinion of the framers" was that blacks were "so far inferior, that they had no rights which the white man was bound to respect . . . and that the Negro might justly and lawfully be reduced to slavery for his benefit." (Former Justice Thurgood Marshall, the first black appointed to the Supreme Court)

On the poor: They were "defined . . . in a sense as an alien race that had to be held to close discipline." (Yale historian John Blum)

On women: "In colonial society . . . a married woman had virtually no rights at all. . . . The Revolution did little to change [this]." (A college American history textbook)

On voting rights for the poor: "Most states had numerous [property] requirements that had to be met before a man could vote. . . . In general,

xi

the idea of voting rights or any other kind of rights was not something that particularly troubled the Framers." (A college textbook on American government)

On immigration and citizenship: The Founders' willingness to consider national origin in naturalization and citizenship policy was "quite obviously . . . inconsistent with the ideals of liberty and equality professed in . . . the nation's 'Creed.'" (Yale political scientist Rogers Smith)

In sum: "The American Revolution produced no significant benefits for American women. The same generalization can be made for other powerless groups in the colonies—native Americans, blacks, probably most propertyless white males, and indentured servants." (Feminist historian Joan Hoff Wilson)[1]

It is surprisingly easy to show that these claims are false. We will see that the Founders believed that members of these supposedly "excluded groups" really are "created equal." (By the term "Founders," I mean those who served in notable public offices from about 1765 to 1800, especially the authors of constitutions, laws, and other important public documents.) We will see that George Washington was correct to call his political convictions "liberal."[2] We will see that the Founders were sincere in their professions of the rights of humanity and their commitment to popular government. We will also see that their actions were consistent with their opinions. The Revolution clearly improved conditions for blacks, women, and the poor.

Other "excluded groups" could have become the theme of additional chapters—for example, Indians and religious minorities. Here, too, the Founders come off much better than we are usually told. I chose to focus on blacks (and other racial minorities), women, and the poor because those are the groups most often mentioned in the typical criticisms of the Founders. Relations between the races, between the sexes, and between haves and have-nots are at the forefront of today's debates over justice and public policy.

In spite of the constant criticism of the Founders over the past several decades by textbooks and scholars, most Americans still respect the founding as great and noble. I will show that there are good reasons for that once nearly universal opinion, now often dismissed as simple-minded patriotism—or evil patriarchalism. This does not mean that the founding had no defects. But some of what we disapprove in their policies arose from necessary concessions to passions and interests that they could not tame (as in the case of slavery). We will also see that they had strong reasons to believe that what we easily condemn as antifemale (such as laws against easy divorce) arguably secured the equal rights of all better than today's alternatives. Some of these reasons are now being rediscovered on the cutting edge of the latest social science research. As for the Founders' principles, we will see that they were sincerely held and conscientiously implemented. Their policies and institutions were sensible if imperfect means by which the equal rights of Americans would be secured within the limits imposed by an imperfect human nature.

Here are some of the conclusions reached in this book:

On slavery: Every leading Founder acknowledged that slavery was wrong. Slavery was legal and practiced in every state in 1776; by the end of the founding era, more than a hundred thousand slaves had been freed by the outlawing of slavery in seven of the original thirteen states or by individual acts of manumission, especially in the South. Most important, the ground for the eventual total abolition of slavery was laid in the establishment of the equality principle at the center of the American polity by Jefferson, Madison, Franklin, Hamilton, Adams, Washington, and other leading Founders.

On the poor: Far from being indifferent to the poor, the Founders regarded the protection of private property rights as a necessary means for the poor to escape the kind of subjugation by the wealthy that they had experienced in Old Europe. And far from throwing the needy into the streets, the Founders maintained government-funded "safety net" programs for them. Their property rights and welfare policies, which are often scorned today for their supposed indifference to the poor, were arguably more just and compassionate than ours.

On women: Women were understood by everyone to be included in the "all men" (all human beings) who are created equal. In New Jersey, women voted in elections routinely during the 1790s and early 1800s, for the first time anywhere in world history. This fact, as we will see, is clearly connected to the Founders' equality principle. So also was the idea, which grew during and after the founding era, that women and men have equal importance, but different roles, in the family and society. The best protection of women's rights, in the minds of both the men and the women of the founding era, was the core private association of a free and civilized society: lifelong marriage and the family. The alternatives—permitting no-fault divorce, pushing women into the job market, and legitimizing the treatment of women (and men) as sex objects—were thought to dehumanize and exploit, not liberate.

On the supposedly undemocratic electorate: Far from excluding the poor, the electorate in the founding era was the most democratic of any large nation in history. It included about 85 to 90 percent of free males. Those Founders who defended a property requirement for voting did so, not in opposition to, but on the basis of, the equality principle of the Declaration of Independence. They feared—as we will see, not without reason—that the propertyless poor might become the tools of influential and wealthy demagogues, distorting election results and endangering the survival of liberty. They changed their minds on this point as it became increasingly clear that the poor were not opponents but friends of the rights of mankind, including the right to acquire and possess property.

On naturalization and citizenship: The Founders' policy generously welcomed as equal citizens people from many nations and religions. However, there was a concern that immigrants might come in numbers too large, or from countries too despotic, to assimilate to the American way of life. There was also a concern that newcomers would not possess, or be in a position to acquire soon, the principles and habits necessary for democratic citizenship. Naturalization in early America was therefore limited primarily to those who had been formed by Western civilization. Still, the American way of life was informed by the universal principles of the Declaration. So although the Founders expected most immigrants to come from Europe, their principles made it possible for people of every race and continent to become, in Lincoln's phrase, "blood of the blood, and flesh of the flesh" of the Founding Fathers who came before them.

This book began as a series of short essays on slavery, women, and voting rights published in connection with the Claremont Institute's Salvatori program for high school teachers.[3] When I first started to write, I did not expect my task to be very hard. Many of the typical objections to the Founders are crude and ill informed, and it is easy to answer them.

I had long known that the evidence on the slavery question favored the Founders. What I did not know is that an adequate treatment of the question, including the embarrassing denial of citizenship to most free blacks before the Civil War, calls for reflection that goes beyond the work of those who have preceded me in vindicating the Founders. The same proved to be true of the question of women's rights, which soon led into the Founders' understanding of male and female sex roles, the evidence supporting their views, the question of feminism, and other controversial topics. In several cases—including property rights, women and the family, and welfare—a full and fair treatment of the Founders led to a confrontation between their approach and today's approach. Most of the topics treated in this book, as the reader will see, sooner or later compel us to choose between two competing visions of equality and liberty: the Founders' view, and today's.

This confrontation between what I call the Old and the New Liberalism leads beyond the defensive stance with which this book begins. We are accustomed to put the Founders on trial, to ask why it took so long for Americans to recognize the equal rights of racial minorities, women, and the poor. Eventually, we become aware that from the point of view of the Founders' principles—the principles of the Declaration and the Constitution—the question becomes whether we can justify our departure from the founding. We will see that our easy assumption of moral superiority rests on shaky ground.

The scholarship informing this book is meant to be factual and objective. It tries to present a historically accurate picture of the Founders' real views and policies. But the truth does have implications that bear on the choices facing us today. I have not shied away from those implications.

Jefferson thought that the chief value of studying the past is

> rendering the people the safe, as they are the ultimate, guardians of their own liberty. . . . History by apprising them of the past will enable them to judge of the future; . . . [I]t will qualify them as judges of the actions and designs of men; it will enable them to know ambition under every disguise it may assume; and knowing it, to defeat its views.

Jefferson was describing the kind of history that Thucydides and Winston Churchill wrote: loyal to the truth but not afraid to distinguish between justice and injustice, honor and villainy, greatness and degradation. That is the kind of scholarship to which this book aspires.

1

Slavery

The Declaration of Independence announces that "all men are created equal." Yet by the end of the founding era, writes historian Peter Kolchin, "slavery in the Southern states emerged . . . largely unscathed. Indeed, . . . the slave population of the new nation in 1810 was more than twice what it had been in 1770."

How should we understand the fact that America's founding generation failed to abolish slavery? Does it mean, as Kolchin says, that America's origins were "unfree"? If so, Abraham Lincoln was wrong to say in the Gettysburg Address that America was "conceived in liberty, and dedicated to the proposition that all men are created equal." Was the Founders' "sense of justice" flawed, as Thurgood Marshall, the first black appointed to the Supreme Court, complained? Was the founding a failure?[1]

There are three leading charges against the Founders in the dominant scholarship of our time, and in the textbooks that follow that scholarship. This chapter will show that all three are false.

The first charge is that the Founders never really believed that all men are created equal. Scholars who promote this view admit that the Founders spoke the language of equal rights. They deny that the Founders meant what they said. In a widely publicized 1987 speech, Justice Thurgood Marshall said that in spite of their occasional noble words, the "prevailing opinion of the framers" was that blacks were "so far inferior, that they had no rights which the white man was bound to respect . . . and that the Negro might justly and lawfully be reduced to slavery for his benefit." Conor Cruise O'Brien's 1996 book on Jefferson agrees:

> It is accepted that the words "all men are created equal" do not, in their literal meaning, apply to women, and were not intended by the Founding Fathers (collectively) to apply to slaves. Yet it is also accepted that the expectations aroused by this formula have been a force which eventually changed the meaning of the formula, to include women and people of all races.

Some conservative admirers of the founding agree that the Founders' view of equality did not condemn slavery. Historian Forrest McDonald writes, "The words equal and equality, as used in the eighteenth century, did not necessarily imply a conflict with the institution of slavery."[2]

The second charge is that the Founders believed that all men are created equal, but they did not know what that meant. In this view, it is conceded that the Founders believed in human equality. But they are said to have remained largely ignorant of what equality means. Historian Richard Bushman writes, "The significance of the Declaration's fundamental principles came to be understood only as American history unfolded."[3] In other words, the Founders' words were more radical than they knew. They condemned slavery (and other forms of inequality) without quite intending to.

Current scholarship's third contention is that the Founders believed that all men are created equal, and they understood very well what that meant; they then betrayed their own principles, with open eyes. According to this accusation, they knew that slavery was wrong but refused to do much about it. In a leading high-school textbook, Edmund S. Morgan of Yale writes: "No great imagination was needed to see wider implications in Jefferson's axiomatic statement of human equality. Its relevance to black slavery was inescapable. . . . But Americans were not yet ready to face up to the racial meaning of their egalitarian creed. No Southern state provided for the legal abolition of slavery. Jefferson himself continued to hold slaves throughout his lifetime." In an even harsher critique, historian Paul Finkelman concludes that Jefferson committed "treason against the hopes of the world" because he was unable "to transcend his economic interests and his sectional background to implement the ideals he articulated."[4]

Did the Founders Believe Blacks Are "Created Equal"?

The first two of the three views just mentioned are the easiest to refute. The evidence against them is overwhelming.

All the Founders, even those who defended slavery, knew well that blacks are human beings. Hardly anyone claimed that slavery is right in principle. Each of the leading Founders acknowledged its wrongness.

Let us begin with the words of Harvard historian Samuel Eliot Morison, from his *Oxford History of the American People*, which has sold many thousands of copies since it was first published in 1965. He asked, "Did Jefferson think of blacks when he wrote, 'all men are created equal'? His subsequent career indicates that he did not; that in his view blacks were not 'men.'" Morison's formulation is evasive. He does not actually say that Jefferson believed blacks were not men. Morison was a competent historian. He knew very well that at the very moment Jefferson was writing the Declaration, he was not only "thinking of blacks" but writing that blacks *were* men. This passage appeared in Jefferson's first draft:

> He [the king of Britain] has waged cruel war against human nature itself, violating its most sacred rights of life and liberty in the persons of a distant people who never offended him, captivating and carrying them into slavery in another hemisphere. . . . Determined to keep open a market where MEN should be bought and sold, he has prostituted his negative for suppressing every legislative attempt to prohibit or to restrain this execrable commerce.

Morison's procedure is typical of many critics of the founding. By intentionally omitting a crucial piece of evidence (Jefferson said that blacks were men), they cause the reader to imagine something that the historian hints at but never actually says (Jefferson believed blacks were not men).[5]

Morison says that Jefferson's "subsequent career indicates that he did not" believe slaves to be human beings. Let us see. In 1779, Jefferson proposed a law that would have provided for gradual emancipation in Virginia. In Congress in 1784 he proposed a law, which came within one vote of adoption, that would have banned slavery from the entire Western territory of the United States. In 1787 he published his widely read *Notes on the State of Virginia*, which contained in Query 18 the most eloquent denunciation of slavery written by anyone in the founding era. In 1807 President Jefferson publicly supported the abolition of the slave trade, urging Congress to "withdraw the citizens of the United States from all further participation in those violations of human rights which have been so long continued on the unoffending inhabitants of Africa." Throughout his life, Jefferson expressed his opposition to slavery in numerous private letters. In light of this "subsequent career," one can only wonder what depths of hostility (to Jefferson in particular or the Founders in general) would lead a capable historian like Samuel Eliot Morison to leave his readers with such a false impression about the author of the Declaration of Independence.[6]

In the years since 1965, Morison's hint has become orthodox doctrine among many scholars. Gordon Wood, widely regarded as the leading historian of the political thought of the American founding, asks: "What was radical about the Declaration in 1776? We know it did not mean that blacks and women were created equal to white men (although it would in time be used to justify those equalities too). It was radical in 1776 because it meant that all white men were equal."[7] Surprisingly, Wood was actually trying to *defend* the Founders with this statement. He was saying that the Revolution at least included poor white males. Wood's critics would not grant the Founders even this much. For them, the Revolution was not only antiwomen and antiblack but also antipoor. Both Wood and his critics take it as a given that blacks and women were excluded from the Declaration. Such is the state of the debate within the historians' guild.

Historian Jack Greene argues that the Founders really believed in liberty only for those who had the capacity to have dependents. Since slaves obviously lacked this capacity, Greene concludes, "The philosophy of civil rights championed by the American Revolutionaries was thus not . . . betrayed but fulfilled by their failures to abolish slavery and adopt a more inclusive definition of citizenship." Greene is unable to reconcile his odd opinion with the Founders' constant assertion that liberty is a natural right, a gift of God that *all* human beings are born with and of which *no one* may rightfully be deprived—whether he has the capacity to have dependents or not.[8]

Views like Wood's and Greene's are popularized in textbooks like John Garraty's *The Story of America*, written for eighth-graders: "By the first of his self-evident truths in the Declaration of Independence, . . . Jefferson certainly meant that *only free men were created equal.* Jefferson believed that for free men there were certain inalienable rights, God-given rights that no just government could take away for any reason. How could he, a slaveholder, claim that liberty was a God-given right of 'all men'?" Garraty, like Morison and Wood, is regarded by many as a leading historian. Yet in his telling, the Declaration becomes nearly incoherent. That is because Garraty confuses unalienable rights (possessed by everyone, whether or not the law acknowledges it) with legal rights (possessed only by those favored by the law). Garraty's Declaration says that only those recognized as free by the law deserve to be free ("only free men were created equal"). If Garraty were right, then the Declaration not only excludes black slaves; it justifies every form of government that has ever existed, however tyrannical. When Stalin ruled the Soviet Union, his subjects had fewer legal rights than Southern slaves. Only Stalin was free. If only free men are created equal, as Garraty's version of the Declaration has it, then no one in the Soviet Union except Stalin had an unalienable right to liberty! Like Morison, Garraty never mentions any of the massive evidence contradicting his assertion that Jefferson and the Founders excluded slaves from "all men."[9]

Contrary to what one would expect from these quotations, all the leading Founders affirmed on many occasions that blacks are created equal to whites and that slavery is wrong. Here are a few examples:

- George Washington: "There is not a man living who wishes more sincerely than I do, to see a plan adopted for the abolition of it."

- John Adams: "Every measure of prudence, therefore, ought to be assumed for the eventual total extirpation of slavery from the United States. . . . I have, through my whole life, held the practice of slavery in . . . abhorrence."

- Benjamin Franklin: "Slavery is . . . an atrocious debasement of human nature."

- Alexander Hamilton: "The laws of certain states . . . give an ownership in the service of Negroes as personal property. . . . But being men, by the laws of God and nature, they were capable of acquiring liberty—and when the captor in war . . . thought fit to give them liberty, the gift was not only valid, but irrevocable."

- James Madison: "We have seen the mere distinction of color made in the most enlightened period of time, a ground of the most oppressive dominion ever exercised by man over man."[10]

How Americans Came to See That Slavery Is Wrong

We have shown that the leading Founders said that blacks were human beings and that they said that enslavement was unjust because it denied blacks their natural human right to liberty. But did they really know what they were saying?

Earlier we quoted Richard Bushman: "The significance of the Declaration's fundamental principles came to be understood only as American history unfolded."[11] Bushman implies that the Founders did not understand their own principles. This view allows us to think well of them—up to a point. From our later eminence of enlightened wisdom, we graciously excuse them for a bigotry they could not help. After all, we assume, their minds were hopelessly imprisoned by their time.

This assumption is one of *our* typical prejudices. It discourages us from trying to understand the Founders on their own terms, as they understood themselves. As we will see, we distort the past when we impose on it our easy assumption that slavery would have been abolished immediately if the Founders had understood the full meaning of the right to liberty.

A glance at the years leading up to 1776 and independence will show that the Founders were not merely mouthing the equality doctrine.

Regarding the slavery question, we may call this period "the opening of the American mind."

John Jay was an early governor of New York and the first chief justice of the Supreme Court. He summarizes the change of opinion in America during the founding era:

> Prior to the great Revolution, . . . our people had been so long accustomed to the practice and convenience of having slaves, that very few among them even doubted the propriety and rectitude of it. Some liberal and conscientious men had indeed, by their conduct and writings, drawn the lawfulness of slavery into question. . . . Their doctrines prevailed by almost insensible degrees, and was like the little lump of leaven which was put into three measures of meal.[12]

The whole Revolution was an antislavery movement—for the colonists. The political logic of the Revolution pointed inexorably to the eventual abolition of slavery for the blacks as well.

"Those who are taxed," wrote John Dickinson in 1768, "without their own consent, expressed by themselves or their representatives, are slaves. We are taxed without our own consent, expressed by ourselves or our representatives. We are therefore—SLAVES." Britain had denied the right of the colony legislatures to rule. That was the nub of the quarrel. The Americans said there must be no taxation (and no laws) without representation. In 1775 the Continental Congress declared that Americans "find nothing so dreadful as voluntary slavery" and are therefore resolved "to die freemen, rather than to live slaves."[13]

Why was slavery such a bad thing? Eleven years before independence the Massachusetts Assembly had resolved, "That there are certain essential rights of the British constitution of government, which are founded in the law of God and nature, and are the common rights of mankind . . . and that no law of society can, consistent with the law of God and nature, divest them of those rights." One such right is that "no man can justly take the property of another without his consent."[14] When Britain refused to listen to the appeal to the British constitution, the colonists were compelled to turn entirely to "the law of God and nature" and "the common rights of mankind," universal principles inherent in human nature.

Bushman is right to this extent: Americans did come to understand the meaning of their principles more fully as the Revolution proceeded. But with respect to slavery, they knew by the end of the founding era exactly what their principles meant. The more they based their arguments on the natural rights of *all* men, and not just the rights of Englishmen, the more the Americans noticed, by the same logic, that enslavement of blacks was also unjust. For slavery by definition "takes the property of another without his consent."

Some Americans had spoken out against slavery from the start of the quarrel between Britain and the colonies. In a 1764 publication endorsed by the Massachusetts legislature, James Otis said, "The colonists are by the law of nature freeborn, as indeed all men are, white or black." John Jay stated the problem vividly: "That men should pray and fight for their own freedom and yet keep others in slavery is certainly acting a very inconsistent as well as unjust and perhaps impious part." In 1776 the house of representatives of New York, a slave state, formally resolved that slavery is "utterly inconsistent with the avowed principles in which this and other states have carried on their struggle for liberty."[15]

Even in the South the idea began to take hold. In 1775, residents of Darien, Georgia, went against the grain of the rest of their state by declaring slavery an "unnatural practice . . . founded in injustice and cruelty, and highly dangerous to our liberty (as well as our lives), debasing part of our fellow creatures below men, and corrupting the virtue and morals of the rest, and is laying the basis of the liberty we contend for . . . upon a very wrong foundation." In 1787 two Virginia counties asked the state legislature to abolish slavery, saying, "The glorious and ever memorable Revolution can be justified on no other principles but what doth plead with greater force for the emancipation of our slaves, in proportion as the oppression exercised over them exceeds the oppression formerly exercised by Great Britain over these states."[16]

The slaves themselves appealed to the natural rights argument. In our time, the principles of the Revolution have been denounced as "white" or "Eurocentric." It is true that a tiny minority of European philosophers, who opposed the convictions of most whites of their day, first published those principles to the world. But whoever may have discovered them, American whites and blacks alike came to believe that the rights of mankind, like the laws of gravity discovered by Newton, were not some ethnocentric ideology but God's own truth. In a 1774 petition to the government of Massachusetts, one group of slaves said:

> [W]e have in common with all other men a natural right to our freedoms without being deprived of them by our fellow men, as we are a freeborn people and have never forfeited this blessing by any compact or agreement whatever. . . . But we were unjustly dragged by the cruel hand of power from our dearest friends, and some of us stolen from the bosoms of our tender parents. . . . We therefore beg . . . that we may obtain our natural right, our freedoms, and our children be set at liberty at the year of twenty-one.

Vindicating the Founders

Men of all races had held slaves throughout human history, and slaves had often revolted for their freedom. But even the slaves had not doubted the right of some men to enslave others. They just did not want to be slaves themselves. The American slaves' protests of the 1770s were the first in history to condemn slavery as an inherently unjust institution on the ground that all human beings are born free.[17]

Were the Founders Prejudiced against Blacks?

John Garraty writes, in his textbook *The Story of America*, "Nearly every European person in America of the 1770s was in some ways prejudiced against Africans by today's standards."[18]

Two things must be said in response to this claim. First, it is at least an exaggeration. Many people, some of them prominent, believed that blacks have the same natural abilities as whites. Second, the leading Founders understood that the blacks' right to liberty does not depend on whether people believe them to be inferior to whites, or even whether they actually are inferior as a group.

Franklin and Hamilton held views that are close to our own. After a visit to a school for black children, Franklin wrote: "[I] have conceived a higher opinion of the natural capacities of the black race than I had ever before entertained. Their apprehension seems as quick, their memory as strong, and their docility in every respect equal to that of white children." Hamilton's judgment was the same: "Their natural faculties are probably as good as ours. . . . The contempt we have been taught to entertain for the blacks, makes us fancy many things that are founded neither in reason nor experience."[19]

More important, in his *Notes on the State of Virginia* Jefferson makes clear that the inferiority question is irrelevant to natural rights. Based on his observations of slaves, he argues, "as a suspicion only," that blacks "are inferior in the faculties of reason and imagination." He admits that this opinion "must be hazarded with great diffidence," for Jefferson knows that "their condition of life," not their nature, is at least partly responsible for their lesser accomplishments. In spite of his "suspicion," Jefferson was able to write on the subject of slavery, later in the same book, "I tremble for my country when I reflect that God is just: that his justice cannot sleep forever."

In a letter written some years later, Jefferson explained why his doubts about the mental abilities of blacks did not affect his view of their rights as human beings:

> Be assured that no person living wishes more sincerely than I do, to see
> a complete refutation of the doubts I have myself entertained and
> expressed on the grade of understanding allotted to them by nature, and
> to find that in this respect they are on a par with ourselves. . . . *[B]ut*
> *whatever may be the degree of talent it is no measure of their rights. Because Sir*
> *Isaac Newton was superior to others in understanding, he was not therefore lord*
> *of the person or property of others.*

The decisive point here is italicized. Blacks are human. That is enough to
secure them equal human rights. Greater intelligence does not give a more
intelligent man (Newton) a right to enslave others. Nor does it give a more
intelligent race (if one exists) a right to enslave a less intelligent race. The
inferiority of one race to another has no bearing on their natural rights as
human beings.

Benjamin Rush, a Pennsylvania signer of the Declaration of Independence, once responded to a slavery advocate in the same way: "But suppos-
ing our author had proved the Africans to be inferior . . . : will his cause
derive any strength from it? Would it avail a man to plead in a court of justice that he defrauded his neighbor, because he was inferior to him in
genius or knowledge?"[20]

Of course prejudice against blacks was not always accompanied by an
enlightened sense of their just rights. The widespread belief in black inferiority no doubt helped to reconcile many to the continued existence of
slavery. Edmund Randolph, a prominent politician of the founding era,
penned this bitter passage in his 1810 *History of Virginia* (discussing the
beginnings of slavery in the 1600s):

> Nor yet were they [blacks] suspected, as in the arrogant and impious
> philosophy of this day, to be in the lowest grade of human existence. The
> . . . violent heats of summer, and the overwhelming indolence of white
> men, most of whom came hither with the allurement of amassing gold
> without toil, beget a suspicion that those circumstances were [the real
> reason] the inhabitants purchased these Negroes as slaves and spread
> over the character of our country colors more indelible than the sable
> skin which served as a pretext for their unnatural debasement. The poi-
> son from this small event will be seen to diffuse itself in a variety of
> destructive shapes [over the later history of Virginia].

The belief in racial inferiority was an important "pretext" for slavery.
Further, as Yale historian Edmund Morgan rightly argues, the degradation
of blacks also promoted a sense of equality among Virginia whites, rich and
poor alike. From this truth Morgan infers an untruth: that Virginians'
"belief in republican equality . . . rest[ed] on slavery." Morgan admits that

the Founders "had the decency to be disturbed by the apparent inconsistency of what they were doing." In spite of this admission, Morgan insists that Virginians professed "an unbounded love of liberty and of democracy *in consequence of the mass* of the people, who in other countries might become mobs, being there nearly altogether composed of their own Negro slaves" (my emphasis). Nowhere does Morgan address the fact that the leading Virginia politicians not only "had the decency to be disturbed" by slavery but also condemned it in the strongest terms. Nor does Morgan address the fact that no leading Virginia politician justified slavery as a necessary condition of freedom. That argument was indeed made later, by John C. Calhoun and other pre–Civil War Southerners. But during the founding era, Virginians like Washington, Jefferson, Madison, and Randolph refused to flinch before the stark contradiction between slavery and the principles of their country.[21]

Actions against Slavery

We have answered two of the three charges commonly made against the Founders. We can say with confidence, first, that the Founders believed that blacks are fully human; and, second, that they knew well what this meant: slavery in every form violates the right to liberty.

The third charge against the Founders is harder to meet. Did they, in the words of historian Paul Finkelman, commit "treason against the hopes of the world" when they failed to abolish slavery?

We will answer this charge in several stages. The first is to see what actions against slavery actually were taken by the founding generation. We will show that for large numbers of blacks, the Revolution did lead to freedom. We will then turn to the factors that slowed and eventually stopped the abolition movement of the founding era.

To repeat: at the beginning of the Revolution, slavery existed in each of the thirteen original states, and the slave trade with Africa was carried on without constraint. Official actions aiming at the abolition of slavery began in 1774, before independence was declared, and this movement achieved substantial victories over the next thirty-five years.

The growth of slavery was quickly limited by reducing or abolishing the slave trade. Delegates to the first Continental Congress in 1774 pledged to stop the importation of slaves into America. By 1798 every state had outlawed slave importation. South Carolina renewed the slave trade in 1803, but Congress abolished the trade altogether in 1808.[22]

During the founding era, eight states proceeded to abolish slavery, either gradually or immediately. (Like almost all public policy, slavery was then regulated by state governments.) Abolition came quickly only in states where few slaves were held. The first to forbid slavery in its constitution was Vermont in 1777. Court cases and the actions of town governments ended slavery in Massachusetts and New Hampshire in the 1780s. In the other Northern states, abolition came harder. Pennsylvania passed the first law for gradual emancipation in 1780. Rhode Island and Connecticut followed in 1783 and 1784. After long struggles, New York and New Jersey finally did the same in 1799 and 1804. Abolition began so late in New Jersey that eighteen slaves still living were counted in the census of 1860, on the eve of the Civil War.[23]

New York's gradual abolition law, writes historian Arthur Zilversmit, "implicitly recognized the connection between abolition and the principles of the Declaration of Independence," as "evidenced by the fact that the act would take effect on July 4, 1799." The preamble to Pennsylvania's emancipation law made the tie explicit:

> We conceive that it is our duty . . . to extend a portion of that freedom to others, which hath been extended to us, and release them from that thralldom, to which we ourselves were tyrannically doomed. . . . It is not for us to inquire why, in the creation of mankind, the inhabitants of the several parts of the earth were distinguished by a difference in feature or complexion. It is sufficient to know that all are the work of the Almighty hand.[24]

Textbooks are virtually silent on the substantial abolition movement undertaken by individuals in the South, where slavery remained legal. Delaware, Maryland, Virginia, and North Carolina changed their laws to make it easier for owners to emancipate slaves. In 1776 the number of free blacks in America was very small. The first census, taken in 1790, counted 27,000 free blacks in the North and 32,000 in the South. Because of the much larger slave populations in the South, by 1810 more Southern blacks had won their freedom through individual manumissions than northern blacks had through manumissions and abolition combined. In that year the census reported 78,000 free blacks (and 27,500 slaves) in the North, but 108,000 free blacks (and 1.2 million slaves) in the South. Delaware owners freed their slaves in such large numbers that it amounted to a near abolition. By 1810, 76 percent of Delaware blacks were free; in Maryland, free blacks numbered a substantial 23 percent.

In spite of these numbers, historians today often disparage the importance of private manumissions. Paul Finkelman admits that "thousands" of slaves won their freedom in this way (in fact, many thousands of manumissions must have contributed to the 108,000 free Southern blacks in 1810), but he goes on to say, improbably, that "very few large slaveholders" were "willing to sacrifice [their] personal wealth for the principles of the Revolution." Who then, we must ask, were the owners of these thousands?

Some states also freed slaves who fought in the Revolutionary War. About five thousand slaves from every part of America except South Carolina and Georgia won their freedom in this way. This process began slowly, but it naturally accelerated in response to the British promise (motivated by a desire to weaken America) of freedom for slaves who became Tories, as many eventually did.[25]

Alexander Hamilton unsuccessfully proposed an emancipation plan of this kind for South Carolina when he served on General Washington's staff during the war. He wrote to John Jay, at that time president of Congress: "An essential part of the plan is to give them their freedom with their muskets. . . . [F]or the dictates of humanity and true policy equally interest me in favor of this unfortunate class of men."[26]

At the federal level, Congress passed the Northwest Ordinance in 1787, forbidding slavery in the territory where the future states of Ohio, Indiana, Michigan, Illinois, and Wisconsin would be formed. This law proved to be of crucial importance to the end of slavery in America. Lincoln mentioned it frequently in the 1850s as a sign that the Founders opposed the expansion of slavery. In the 1860s these states, along with the original Northeast, formed the core of the coalition that elected Lincoln president, fought the Civil War, and abolished slavery nationwide.

Congress did permit slavery in the Southwestern Territory (the future states of Kentucky, Tennessee, Alabama, and Mississippi). This region had been claimed by seaboard slaveholding states and was ceded to the national government with the expectation that slavery would continue. North Carolina had made it an explicit condition of its cession that "no regulations made or to be made by Congress shall tend to emancipate slaves." This was generally regarded not as an endorsement of slavery expansion but an acceptance of it where it already existed.[27]

Although no Southern state abolished slavery, there was broad agreement that slavery was wrong. Proposals for abolition were presented to the Virginia legislature in 1778 (Jefferson authored it) and again in 1796 and to the Kentucky constitutional convention of 1792. Societies for abolition were established in Delaware and Maryland, whose legislatures debated abolition in 1785 and 1786.

Southern courts of law before the 1840s generally took the position that slavery violates the natural rights of the blacks. Slavery may be legal, the courts held, but that does not make it just. For example, the Mississippi Supreme Court held in 1818: "Slavery is condemned by reason and the laws of nature. It exists and can only exist, through municipal regulations, and in matters of doubt, . . . courts must lean *in favorem vitae et libertatis* [in favor of life and liberty]." In 1820 the same court said that the slave "is still a human being, and possesses all those rights, of which he is not deprived by the positive provisions of the law." In the early years of the nineteenth century, most courts of other Southern states where records exist agreed with this presumption of freedom. Slaves whose masters took them to free states or territories were sometimes able to win their freedom in Southern courts in this way.[28]

Even where slavery remained legal, the doctrines of the Revolution led to reforms that recognized the slaves' humanity. Historian Lawrence Friedman reports:

> In North Carolina, in 1774, the punishment for killing a slave "willfully and maliciously" was a year's imprisonment; and the murderer was required to pay the owner the value of the slave. In 1791, the state's legislature denounced this law as "disgraceful to humanity and degrading in the highest degree to the laws and principles of a free, Christian, and enlightened country" because it drew a "distinction of criminality between the murder of a white person and of one who is *equally an human creature, but merely of a different complexion.*" Thereupon, by law, it was murder to kill a slave willfully and maliciously.[29]

An observation made by John Jay in the letter quoted earlier deserves emphasis. Prior to the Revolution, political opposition to slavery was slight. Therefore, abolition in the founding era was mostly a consequence of the logic of Revolution principles, which many felt a conscientious duty to fulfill. After all, the same proslavery interests existed before and after the founding. Yet it was only afterward that the limitation and abolition of slavery occurred.

John Adams was not altogether wrong when he said that opposition to slavery in Massachusetts came from "the multiplication of laboring white people, who would no longer suffer the rich to employ these sable rivals so much to their injury." Self-interest is always at work in politics. But there are some times when higher motives overcome low ones. Adams's cynical remark does not explain why the movement toward emancipating slaves and restricting the growth of slavery took hold all over America just when Americans began to articulate with increasing clarity the principle that all men are created equal in the fundamental right to liberty. The main inspiration for opposition to slavery in Massachusetts came not from workers fearing black competition but from the moral convictions of politicians and their constituents who were persuaded that the principles of the Massachusetts bill of rights—the principles of the Declaration—apply to all human beings. Here was one of those outstanding moments in politics when self-interest is to some degree overcome by moral conviction in the formation of public policy.[30]

The third charge against the Founders was that they failed to abolish slavery. Our answer, to this point, has been: they limited and eventually outlawed the importation of slaves from abroad; they abolished slavery in a majority of the original states; they forbade the expansion of slavery into areas where it had not been previously permitted; they made laws regulating slavery more humane; individual owners in most states freed slaves in large numbers. In light of all this, it is a gross exaggeration to speak, as Kolchin does, of "the unfree origins of the United States."[31] Freedom was secured for the large majority of Americans, and important actions were undertaken in the service of freedom for the rest.

Slavery in the Constitution

Critics of the Founders often target the Constitution of 1787 as a document indifferent to, or even favoring, slavery.

The Constitution's compromises with the slave interests are sometimes said to be so wicked that the Constitution deserves little or no respect. Historians like Paul Finkelman, echoing the most extreme abolitionists before the Civil War, condemn the Constitution as "a covenant with death." In a 1987 bicentennial address, former Supreme Court Justice Thurgood Marshall said, "Nor do I find the wisdom, foresight, and sense of justice exhibited by the framers particularly profound. To the contrary, the government they devised was defective from the start."[32]

These are powerful accusations. If they are true, Americans' admiration for the Framers of the Constitution—celebrated in patriotic songs and speeches throughout American history—must be tainted with racism. If they are false, as will be argued here, today's critics have unfairly slandered a noble achievement.

Most of the Constitution's Framers knew, and many said, that slavery was wrong. For example, at the Convention, Gouverneur Morris said that the African slave trade, "in defiance of the most sacred laws of humanity, tears away his fellow creatures from their dearest connections and damns them to the most cruel bondages."[33]

However, powerful interests supported slavery, especially in the deep South. Representing those interests, some delegates to the Convention demanded major concessions to slavery. To some extent they got them.

How are we to understand this unhappy fact?

The slavery question was the most divisive at the Convention. Madison correctly noted that "the real difference of interests lay, not between the large and small, but between the Northern and Southern states. The institution of slavery and its consequences formed the line of discrimination." There was little that opponents of slavery could have done about slavery at the Convention unless they were willing to risk breaking up the union. That is what some Southern delegates threatened if their demands on behalf of the slave interest were not met. Among other things, these delegates held hostage one of the most important powers of the federal government, the power to regulate commerce. In the best defense I have seen of the view that the Constitution was a pro-slavery "covenant with death," Finkelman is compelled to admit that "sectional interests caused by slavery" were "a major threat to the Union" at the Convention. He shows how doggedly certain Southern delegates to the Convention insisted on protections to slavery. Finkelman thinks the Southern states would have approved the Constitution without its concessions to slavery. But his own evidence shows that the Southerners did not view their concern as a small matter. It is clear that the Southern delegates, and the Southern states, were not likely to have approved the new Constitution unless they were convinced that the free states would leave the solution to the slavery problem to each state to decide for itself. The compromises gave them that confidence.[34]

In the short term, slavery was bound to continue, with the Constitution or without. If liberty *for anyone* was to have a future in America, the indispensable first step was a stronger national government on a democratic basis. Even the Anti-Federalist opponents of the Constitution admitted this much. Abolition would have to wait.

The problem with Finkelman's analysis is that it does not properly consider the context of the writing of the Constitution of 1787. To understand why the delegates acted as they did, it is necessary to remember that it was not the problem of Negro slavery that led to the calling of the Convention, but a threat to the liberty of all the citizens.

After the British recognition of American independence in 1783, it was by no means clear that the basic rights of even the white population were going to be secured under the governments then in place. Surveying the growing political disarray of the "present crisis," Washington feared for the future of self-government. "[I]t is yet to be decided," he said, "whether the Revolution must ultimately be considered as a blessing or a curse: a blessing or a curse, not to the present age alone, for with our fate will the destiny of unborn millions be involved." These fears were echoed by leading Americans, North and South. The near-collapse of the national gov-

ernment, with the national humiliation, weakness, and injustices that followed, is analyzed in the first twenty-two papers of *The Federalist*.[35]

In light of this sense of urgency, felt by all leading Americans in the
1780s, the plight of the blacks understandably receded into the background
as a national issue. Besides, if the union had collapsed, as it was on the verge
of doing by 1787, it is probable, as *Federalist* No. 5 argues, that the Southern
states would eventually have formed their own confederacy. In that case the
growth of a movement that could legitimately do anything about slavery—
such as the Republican Party of the 1850s—would have been impossible.

Frederick Douglass, the leading black spokesman against slavery during the Civil War era, favored continuation of the union, even with slavery,
for the same reason. "My argument against the dissolution of the American
Union is this: It would place the slave system more exclusively under the
control of the slaveholding states, and withdraw it from the power in the
Northern states which is opposed to slavery. . . . I am, therefore, for drawing the bond of the union more closely, and bringing the Slave States more
completely under the power of the Free States."[36]

The Constitution's Framers compromised on the slavery question, in
three main provisions. But even these provisions are by no means as
proslavery as they have often been said to be.

First, the Constitution counted three-fifths of the slaves toward the
population that determined representation in Congress and electoral votes
for presidential elections. This was a significant concession to the slave states
because it gave voters in those states greater weight in the federal government than they would have had if slaves had not been counted at all. This
provision is widely misunderstood today. Here is how UCLA law professor
Kenneth Karst, a severe critic of the Founders, understands it: "Each slave
was to count as three-fifths of a person. . . . The problem of race relations
in America has always revolved around the question whether nonwhites are
or are not to be treated as complete persons, as the equals of whites." Karst's
remark contains two errors. He uses "nonwhites" as if it were the equivalent of "slaves"; yet even in 1790 many blacks (sixty thousand, or 8 percent
of the total) were free, and they were therefore counted as whole persons,
the same as whites. Second, Karst seems to be unaware that at the Constitutional Convention it was Southerners, not Northerners, who said the
slaves should "stand on an equality with the whites" in the determination
of the number of a state's representatives. Northerners argued that it was
wrong "to give such encouragement to the slave trade as would be given
by allowing [the Southern states] a representation for their Negroes."[37]

Second, the Constitution prohibited Congress from outlawing "[t]he
migration or importation of such persons as any of the states now existing

shall think proper to admit" until the year 1808. But was this really a proslavery provision? After 1808, Congress was free to abolish the slave trade, as it did. The guarantee of the trade applied only to the "states now existing." Clearly, this was a grudging, temporary concession to the slave interest. As part of the compromise leading to this provision, the South Carolina and Georgia delegates supported the clause granting Congress control over commerce with foreign countries and among the states, which implicitly included commerce in slaves. In the Missouri debates of 1819-20, Northerners in Congress began to discuss using the commerce and migration clauses to limit or abolish slavery. Southerners disputed this reading, but the Constitution's language supported it.[38]

From the point of view of some Framers, the slave-trade clause had a stronger antislavery character than appears to us. It had not yet been understood how rapidly slaves were multiplying within America. James Wilson said what many Northerners believed, that this clause laid "the foundation for banishing slavery out of this country."[39]

Third, the Constitution provided that runaway slaves would be returned to their owners, even if they escaped to free states. This might seem unambiguously proslavery. But consider the language of the fugitive slave clause: "No person held to service or labor in one state, under the laws thereof, escaping into another, shall, in consequence of any law or regulation therein, be discharged from such service or labor, but shall be delivered up on claim of the party to whom such service or labor may be due." Here, as everywhere in the Constitution, the words "slave" and "slavery" are carefully avoided. Madison wrote that the Convention "thought it wrong to admit in the Constitution the idea that there could be property in men." In this clause the original expression, "legally held to service or labor," was changed when it was objected that the expression "legally" seemed to favor "the idea that slavery was legal in a moral view." The language adopted was meant to show no approval of slavery but only an acknowledgment that it exists and will remain for the time being.[40]

Some writers, not content with attacking the Constitution for its actual compromises with slavery, make up provisions that are not there. Karen O'Connor and Larry Sabato's leading college American government text, for example, states that "the Constitution denied blacks the right to vote."[41] This is totally false. Many blacks voted during the founding era and afterwards in several states.

We acknowledge that the Constitution did give substantial protection to slavery. We also admit that if the Constitution is read in isolation from the principles of the Revolution, it is possible to see it as an unprincipled "bundle of compromises." "Liberty and Slavery—opposite as

Heaven and Hell—are both in the Constitution," wrote Frederick Douglass in 1850. It is even possible to read it as a proslavery document, as critics like Thurgood Marshall and Paul Finkelman do, following the interpretation shared by Southerners and extreme abolitionists during the pre–Civil War period.[42]

The original intent of the Constitution, however, cannot be understood from its text alone. The document was produced by a group of statesmen who generally agreed on the principles of government. In *The Federalist*, Madison said that the Constitution was grounded on "the fundamental principles of the Revolution," namely, "the transcendent laws of nature and of nature's God" and "the rights of humanity" announced in the Declaration of Independence. In this light, the slavery provisions of the Constitution must be read as concessions to a brute fact rather than as affirmations of the rightness of slavery. Most Americans, North and South, who voted for ratification held this view of slavery.[43]

Most Founders knew well that the practice of slavery was ultimately at war with the principles of liberty. One or the other would eventually have to give way. A delegate from Maryland, a slave state, said: "Slavery is inconsistent with the genius of republicanism, and has a tendency to destroy those principles on which it is supported, as it lessens the sense of the equal rights of mankind, and habituates us to tyranny and oppression." Jefferson, in a famous passage in *Notes on Virginia*, agreed that slavery promotes antidemocratic habits and principles:

> The whole commerce between master and slave is a perpetual exercise of the most boisterous passions, the most unremitting despotism on the one part, and degrading submissions on the other . . . The parent storms, the child looks on, catches the lineaments of wrath, puts on the same airs in the circle of smaller slaves, gives a loose to his worst of passions, and thus nursed, educated, and daily exercised in tyranny, cannot but be stamped by it with odious peculiarities. The man must be a prodigy who can retain his manners and morals undepraved by such circumstances.

George Mason, a Virginia delegate, made the same point, without Jefferson's eloquence, at the Convention.[44]

The Constitution protected slavery. But it did not stand in the way of any state that wished to abolish slavery. Congress could cut off the slave trade after twenty years. Congress could cut off the spread of slavery to new states and to the Western territories. Congress could regulate interstate commerce in slaves. The Constitution was not the problem. The problem was the absence of political will. If a majority of Americans had favored it strongly enough, the end of the spread of slavery, and its abolition, could have been achieved much earlier than it was, without changing a single word of the Constitution. We will soon see why it was not.

Ralph Abernathy, a prominent civil rights activist of the 1960s and 1970s, wrote:

> There can be no pure memory of an American Revolution that published a declaration that liberty was a right accorded to "all men" and then created a Constitution that specifically prohibited blacks from enjoying that right. The only logical conclusion that modern blacks can draw from such circumstances is that their forefathers were not regarded as "men" by the white founders of this country.[45]

Abernathy was wrong. The Constitution did not "specifically prohibit" blacks from enjoying their rights. They were certainly regarded as "men" in that document. (Even the slaves were called "persons.") The Constitution allowed states to have slavery, but it did not "prohibit blacks from enjoying" the right to liberty. Otherwise the states could never have passed their emancipation laws. Many thousands of free blacks enjoyed their right to liberty under the Constitution before the Civil War. The rest won their liberty through a war fought under its authority.[46]

Prudence, Expediency, and Morality

Were these concessions to slavery immoral, as Finkelman and Marshall assume? O'Connor and Sabato's textbook *American Government* explains the prevailing view in this way: "Whereas earlier the Declaration of Independence had so eloquently proclaimed that 'all men are created equal,' the delegates to the Constitutional Convention put political expediency before the immorality of slavery."[47] In this view, the only moral course of action was uncompromising opposition to slavery, period. Anything less was mere "expediency," in which considerations of right are supposedly sacrificed to self-interest.

This opposition between morality and expediency is the framework in which Americans have been taught in recent decades to think about politics. If a politician is uncompromising and pure, if he pursues the right goal without regard for consequences, he is thought to be *moral*. If he is willing to accept a lesser evil to avoid a greater one, if he takes circumstances into account in deciding what to do, then he is thought to be merely *expedient* and therefore morally tainted.

A better perspective from which to judge the morality of the Founders is implied in this passage from historian Donald Robinson in his *Slavery in the Structure of American Politics*:

> It is probably fortunate that abolitionism as a movement of consequence in America was still far off in the future, for if Samuel Adams and John Jay and Benjamin Franklin and other Northern politicians had forthrightly criticized slavery in the early 1770s, American history would have developed far differently. To begin with, there would have been no Association of twelve colonies in 1774, and certainly no "Unanimous Declaration of the Thirteen United States of America."[48]

In other words, if the Founders had done what O'Connor and Sabato think they should have done, there would have been no union, the South would have been free to develop slavery without restraint, and the eventual abolition of slavery might never have occurred.

The American Founders understood political morality not in terms of right intentions but rather in terms of just results. For them, moral principles give us the goal or end, but prudence (sensible judgment) must determine the means. After the Declaration sets forth the principles of political right, it says, "Prudence, indeed, will dictate that governments long established should not be changed for light and transient causes." A government that violates in some respects the principle of consent or protection of rights may be tolerable as the lesser evil, if the alternative is likely to be worse. The job of the prudent statesman is to determine the right course in a world in which the immoderate pursuit of moral perfection will more often lead to misery and terror than to justice and happiness.

When Lincoln was a young man, he said that the Founders established "political institutions, conducing more essentially to the ends of civil and religious liberty, than any of which the history of former times tells us."[49] From the point of view of the Declaration's principles, Lincoln was right, in spite of the fact that slavery was still thriving when he said that. Slavery was a terrible injustice. But it would have required the abolition of government by consent to eradicate it during the founding era. Immediate freedom for the minority would have ended freedom for the majority.

The totalitarian impulse at work in Marxist communism is the imprudent, immoderate, and *therefore* immoral demand for the abolition of human evil on earth. That impulse presupposes that human beings can overcome all significant natural, divine, and human limits. Human will, or historical progress, is believed to guarantee this dream. All obstacles to the dream must be ruthlessly thrust aside, no matter what the cost. As he explained in *On the Jewish Question*, Marx had no patience for American democracy, because he was convinced that it would never liberate human beings from the reign of selfishness.

The same utopian fervor was at work in the abolitionism of the 1830s and 1840s (at the same time that Marx began to advocate communism in Europe). Yet abolitionism is the moral stance most often approved by today's scholars. The abolitionists were impatient and shrill. They antagonized the vast majority, North and South. Instead of advancing the cause of abolition, they promoted Southern intransigence and Northern disgust with antislavery opinion. The leading abolitionist, William Lloyd Garrison, demanded not only the immediate end of slavery but (like Marx) "the emancipation of our whole race from the dominion of man, from the thraldom of self, . . . from the bondage of sin." Garrison had nothing but contempt for moderation: "On this subject, I do not wish to think, to speak, or write, with moderation." "I wash my hands of the blood that may be spilled."

If the Constitution really was a "covenant with death," as Garrison maintained, then one should escape it as quickly as possible. Therefore Garrison called for the secession of the North from the South. Had his advice been followed, the North would have lost all influence over the South. Garrison was proud of his commitment to justice; but the Founders would have said that his approach led to injustice. As Frederick Douglass pointed out, Northern secession would have placed "the slave system more exclusively under the control of the slaveholding states." Slavery would have persisted much longer than it did. The first modern nation based on a "scientific" theory of a master race might have been the Confederacy, and not Nazi Germany.[50]

The Incomplete Founding I: Emancipation versus Selfishness

In spite of the undeniable advance of liberty during the founding era, slavery was not ended. To this extent the critics are right. They, and we, are entitled to ask: Why did the abolition movement of the founding era stop short? What thwarted the political logic of the Revolution?

In one sense, the question is easy to answer. Human beings are imperfect. They are rational but also passionate animals. There will always be a gap between moral principles and actions. In the case of slavery we have, in Jefferson's words, "the interesting spectacle of justice, in conflict with avarice and oppression."

In a passage quoted earlier, Ralph Abernathy said, "The only logical conclusion that modern blacks can draw from such circumstances is that their forefathers were not regarded as 'men' by the white founders of this country." Abernathy finds it incomprehensible that someone might believe in a moral truth ("slavery is wrong") and not act on it ("slavery must be abolished immediately"). But this happens every day in small ways. Most Americans believe that cruelty is wrong. Yet most of us have been cruel on many occasions to people we do not like. Sometimes we regret it and feel guilty. More often we barely notice. A family that freed its slaves was likely to endanger its own livelihood. The temptation to keep them was great, even for those who knew it was wrong.

Even in the North considerable support for slavery persisted throughout the Revolutionary period. We have already seen how hard it was to pass abolition laws and how slowly abolition took place even after these laws were passed. John Jay explains:

> That those who know the value of liberty, and are blessed with the enjoyment of it, ought not to subject others to slavery, is, like most other moral precepts, more generally observed in theory than observed in practice. This will continue to be too much the case while men are impelled to action by their passions rather than their reason, and while they are more solicitous to acquire wealth than to do as they would be done by.

Or, as Lincoln put it more simply, it is "the same old serpent that says you work and I eat, you toil and I will enjoy the fruits of it."[51]

Sometimes this age-old conflict between passion and reason is rationalized in the language of crude selfishness. In regard to slavery, this language was sometimes, but not often, heard during the founding era, as in Charles Cotesworth Pinckney's speech at the Constitutional Convention: "South Carolina and Georgia cannot do without slaves. . . . [T]he importation of slaves would be for the interest of the whole union. The more slaves, the more produce to employ the carrying trade; the more consumption, . . . the more of revenue for the common treasury." John Rutledge was even blunter: "If the Convention thinks that North Carolina, South Carolina, and Georgia will ever agree to the plan, unless their right to import slaves be untouched, the expectation is vain. The people of those states will never be such fools as to give up so important an interest."

There was even the rare but ominous assertion, which did not prevail in the South until much later, that slavery is a positive good, not just a necessary evil. Madison denounced some representatives in the first Congress for flirting with this position: "The gentlemen from South Carolina and Georgia are intemperate beyond all example and even all decorum. They are not content with palliating slavery as a deep-rooted abuse, but plead for the lawfulness of the African trade itself."[52]

Selfish interest sometimes led men to misunderstand their own principles. In 1785 six Virginia counties petitioned the state legislature, objecting to any emancipation of slaves "on the ground that the Revolution had been fought to preserve liberty and property." These Virginians, and other slaveholders who shared their view, forgot that the right to property flows from—is part of—the natural right to liberty. If there is no natural right to liberty, there can be no natural right to property. If all men are rightfully free, they all may keep the bread they earn with their own hands. Therefore there can be no right to property *in slaves*.[53]

The Incomplete Founding II: Emancipation versus Survival

Let us be blunt. The problem was not just selfishness. The Founders believed that the immediate abolition of slavery *would have been unjust*. On the face of it, this appears to contradict the equality principle. Let us see.

Political scientist Herbert Storing is the author of an outstanding defense of the Founders against their critics. However, Storing remarked that the Founders "do not come off so well" in one respect because the principle of individual liberty "contains within itself an uncomfortably large opening toward slavery." I believe Storing is right about the "opening" but wrong to criticize the Founders on that account. We are dealing here with a genuine, not a false, moral dilemma.

This is sometimes called the "deep-rooted abuse" or "necessary evil" argument. Patrick Henry, slavery's great defender at the Virginia ratifying convention, admitted his seeming inconsistency in clinging to slavery "at a time when the rights of humanity are defined and understood with precision in a country above all others fond of liberty." Yet, he said, "As much as I deplore slavery, I see that prudence forbids its abolition."

Jefferson gave this argument its most memorable expression when he said, "We have the wolf by the ears, and we can neither hold him, nor safely let him go. Justice is in one scale, and self-preservation in the other." Jefferson meant "self-preservation" quite literally. Throughout his career he was firmly antislavery in principle but just as firmly opposed to the social and political integration of free blacks. He gave this reason:

> Deep rooted prejudices entertained by the whites; ten thousand recollections, by the blacks, of the injuries they have sustained; new provocations; the real distinctions which nature has made; and many other circumstances, will divide us into parties, and produce convulsions which will probably never end but in the *extermination of the one or the other race*.[54]

Such fears are dismissed today as insincere or irrational. In his critique, Finkelman does not bother to give a serious response to Jefferson's worries about a war between the races. Yet many intelligent antislavery observers of the American scene before the Civil War agreed with Jefferson. After his visit to America in the 1830s, Tocqueville feared that "the most horrible of civil wars" would occur if slavery were abolished, terminating "perhaps in the extermination of one or other of the two races." The novelist James Fenimore Cooper agreed: "The time must come when American slavery shall cease. . . . The struggle that will follow, will necessarily be a war of extermination."[55]

Race war became a horrifying reality for the founding generation in the Haitian revolution of 1791–1804, and it was an ever present fear after that. According to a recent historian, chaos "gripped the island" in those years. Whites and blacks alike were "responsible for the cruelest acts against one another." Blacks used "as their standard 'the body of a white infant impaled upon a stake.'" When Dessalines took over at the end of the revolution in 1804, he invited all the whites who had not yet fled or been killed to come forward for pardon. He murdered them all. "Not a white was left in Haiti after these massacres." American newspapers of that time estimated that one hundred thousand whites and sixty thousand blacks lost their lives over thirteen years of struggle. Americans saw in Haiti their own possible future.[56]

The terrible crimes inflicted by American blacks and whites upon each other since the Civil War—including many thousands of murders—suggest that although the fears of Jefferson, Tocqueville, and Cooper may have been exaggerated, they were not altogether unreasonable. Nor has America seen the end of racial strife.

Under the wrong circumstances, the liberty of the slaves might have ended the lives of citizens as well as slaves. But liberty and life are two of the inalienable rights of the Declaration of Independence. This means that neither continued enslavement nor immediate emancipation would have been simply right, because both choices involved a deprivation of rights. The Declaration could not resolve this conflict. In the South before the Civil War, the stronger party, the body of free citizens, dealt with the problem by the continuation of slavery.

The equality principle itself justified the continuation of slavery to this extent. Of course, it would also have justified a bloody rebellion of the slaves against their masters. Jefferson alluded to that justification and that possibility—one that might lead to the "extirpation" of the masters—in a famous passage from his *Notes on Virginia*, part of which was quoted earlier:

I tremble for my country when I reflect that God is just: that his justice cannot sleep forever: that considering numbers, nature, and natural means only, a revolution of the wheel of fortune, an exchange of situation, is among possible events: that it may become probable by supernatural interference! The Almighty has no attribute which can take side with us in such a contest.[57]

But slavery could only be right in this limited way if its wrongness was admitted and people did their best to work toward eventual emancipation. After the last public debate on slavery, in Virginia in 1831, most Southerners gave up this effort and repudiated the principles of the Declaration.

The Incomplete Founding III:
Emancipation versus the Conditions of Citizenship

The threat to life was not the only reason for the Founders' concern about immediate abolition. Even if the problem of violence could be overcome, the question remained: Should the ex-slaves be given citizenship and political equality?

After the Civil War, when the former slaves began to be oppressed once again by their former masters, the Fourteenth and Fifteenth Amendments granted them citizenship and voting rights. But before the Civil War, most Americans, including most of the Founders, opposed black citizenship and political equality. Again, this appears to be another example of raw racism at work, as is commonly believed now. But there is another explanation.

In the first place, we must distinguish between the right to *liberty*, possessed by all human beings, and the right to *citizenship*, which a community gives at its discretion. Lincoln's understanding of this difference was the same as the Founders'. Harry Jaffa explains: "Lincoln did not believe that Negroes had any natural right to citizenship any more than did resident aliens. Citizenship was a privilege which was bestowed upon those whom the community wished, *in their own interests*, to accept as new members. The only political right possessed by free Negroes, implied in the abstract right to freedom, was to leave the country and form political associations of their own, just as the colonists had left Europe to found new political associations in the new world."[58]

Madison opposed emancipation without colonization because of "freedmen who retain the vices and habits of slaves." The result is that "the good of the society" is not "promoted by such a change in their condition." Jefferson agreed: "To give liberty to, or rather, to abandon persons whose habits have been formed in slavery, is like abandoning children. . . . A man's moral sense must be unusually strong, if slavery does not make him a thief. He who is permitted by law to have no property of his own, can with difficulty conceive that property is founded in anything but force." A preacher who had lived among slaves for many years expanded on the observations of Madison and Jefferson: "Feeling and knowing, that their owners regard and treat them as their money—as property only—[the slaves] are inclined to lose sight of their better character and higher interests, and, in their ignorance and depravity, to estimate themselves, and religion, and virtue, no higher than their owners do." Slaves had little reason to develop habits of hard work, self-restraint, or respect for property when the products of their labor were always stolen by others. Consequently, even opponents of slavery feared that if the slaves gained their freedom, they would become, as St. George Tucker wrote, "idle, dissipated, and finally a numerous banditti instead of turning their attention to industry and labor." George Washington agreed: "To set them afloat at once would, I really believe, be productive of much inconvenience and mischief."[59]

For these reasons, it was feared that black citizenship would harm the rest of the community. As one opponent of voting rights for blacks argued, "The natural tendency has been proven by experience, not to be elevation of the degraded, but the deterioration, the lowering, of the better class, towards the standard of the inferior class."[60] The Founders believed that liberty would survive only if the citizens possessed the right habits and beliefs. In general that meant, first, an enlightened understanding of the equal rights of all; second, an appropriate degree of courage or self-assertion on behalf of those rights; third, moderation or self-restraint, including respect for the rights of others. (These conditions of citizenship are discussed more fully in the chapter on immigration and citizenship below.) The ex-slaves generally lacked, or were thought to lack, these qualities, at least in comparison with the other citizens. Perhaps they would eventually acquire them. In the meantime their presence as fellow citizens in large numbers was believed to pose a danger to freedom.

Jefferson's and Madison's opposition to black citizenship was shared by most (but not all) Americans until the Civil War. After the founding era, free blacks tended to be treated as noncitizens. At first, no constitution of any state north of Pennsylvania excluded free blacks from voting, and many blacks voted in those states. Free blacks also voted in the slave states of Delaware, Maryland, North Carolina, Kentucky, and Tennessee. Some blacks definitely were part of "we the people" who made the Constitution of 1787. But this initial pattern did not last. By the time of the Civil War, free blacks were excluded, by custom or law, from voting, jury service, and public schools in almost every state. Some states forbade the immigration of free blacks. All states excluded blacks from their militias, which were understood to consist of the able-bodied adult male citizens of the community. These acts implied that free blacks were something like resident aliens, not citizens, and court decisions increasingly referred to them in this way. On the other hand, blacks in northern New England were treated as citizens, or nearly so.

In spite of these exclusions, the citizenship status of blacks was never quite clear. Obviously, they were not quite resident aliens, for they had no country but the United States. The federal government generally avoided taking a stand on black citizenship when the subject arose. A few blacks got federal passports, implying that they were citizens. Yet the first federal naturalization law (1790) allowed only white immigrants to become citizens. The first federal militia law (1792), in limiting service to whites, seemed to imply that blacks were not citizens of the United States. On the other hand, the Articles of Confederation stated that "the free inhabitants of each of these states . . . shall be entitled to all privileges and immunities of free citizens in the several states," and Congress voted down South Carolina's proposal to insert the word "white" into this clause.[61]

Chief Justice Taney, in the infamous 1857 *Dred Scott* decision, asserted that blacks had never been, and could never be, citizens of the United States. He was wrong. But it was true that *most* free blacks were not citizens.

Today it is assumed that racial prejudice alone was responsible for these exclusions. Historians sometimes wildly exaggerate the views of earlier Americans in order to portray them as mindless racists. For example, in the *Reader's Guide to American History*, historian Marc Kruman writes, "Blacks were seen as incapable of civic virtue, white men as naturally virtuous." Kruman's preposterous claim makes unintelligible the intense early American worries and debates about the absence of virtue among *whites*. Debates over voting rights in states like Tennessee, New York, and Pennsylvania before the Civil War show that the objection to black citizenship was based on *observed* differences in conduct, not just racial prejudice. Free blacks, as a group, did not behave as well as others (although of course many individual blacks were exemplary). Historian Leon Litwack reports:

> New York Negroes constituted one thirty-fifth of the population but contributed one-fourth of the state's convicts; and Pennsylvania Negroes made up one thirty-fourth of the population but supplied one-third of the prisoners. "Already our prisons and poor houses are crowded with blacks," a Pennsylvania state senate committee reported in 1836. "The disparity of crime between the whites and the blacks . . . is . . . distressing to every friend of humanity and virtue."

Litwack argues that this disparity is explained by the exclusion of blacks from juries, government office, and white society generally. But whatever the explanation may be, differences between white and black conduct were widely acknowledged even by those who favored black voting rights, as well as by black leaders. A Pennsylvania supporter of black suffrage said that "in their present depressed and uncultivated condition" they were not "a desirable species of population" and he "should not prefer them as a matter of choice." Horace Greeley's prosuffrage New York Tribune admitted that free blacks tended to be "indolent, improvident, servile and licentious."

However, the most convincing testimony on the reality of the problem comes from the blacks themselves. Frederick Douglass, the great black abolitionist, declared in 1848:

> What we, the colored people, want is *character.* . . . [O]ur general ignorance makes [intelligent and educated blacks] exceptions to our race. . . . Character is the important thing, and without it we must continue to be marked for degradation and stamped with the brand of inferiority. . . . [T]hank heaven, [our oppressors] have not yet been able to take from us the privilege of being honest, industrious, sober, and intelligent.

Litwack reports that "since at least 1828, Negro leaders, newspapers, and conventions had been voicing similar sentiments." These black leaders condemned the larger society for its hostility and injustices to blacks, but they held that blacks shared the blame for their debased condition. Obviously the legacy of slavery had much to do with it. Greeley plausibly argued that "all degraded, downtrodden tribes or races" behave badly. But as long as the disparity remained, citizens were reluctant to admit freedmen to equal citizenship.[62]

We conclude that ex-slaves were generally excluded from citizenship for the same reason that Jefferson and Hamilton opposed indiscriminate, massive immigration. As a nation based on the idea of equality, America has been a melting pot. It has taken people from diverse traditions and turned them into freedom-loving and decent citizens. But when their numbers are large, immigrants can change the attitudes of those already living here. The same argument would apply to a large influx of newly freed slaves. States like Massachusetts that had few blacks felt that they could afford to be generous with citizenship. Others were not so generous.[63]

After the Civil War, when the decision was finally made to accept blacks as full citizens, the Founders' principles provided the theoretical foundation. Lincoln's revival of the Declaration in the 1850s had prepared the way. In principle, people of all races can become citizens of a nation based on the idea that "all men are created equal."

Colonization: Just or Unjust?

If slavery was wrong, and if prejudice and perhaps legitimate fears precluded citizenship for blacks, there was still a solution that would have been consistent with the principles of the Declaration. The policy favored by Jefferson, Madison, Henry Clay, Daniel Webster, and Lincoln was colonization.

Speaking as a slaveholding Southerner, Jefferson wrote:

> There is not a man on earth who would sacrifice more than I would to relieve us from this heavy reproach, in any practicable way. The cession of that kind of property, for so it is misnamed, is a bagatelle which would not cost me a second thought, if, in that way, a general emancipation and expatriation could be effected; and gradually, and with due sacrifices, I think it might be.

If the slaves were to be freed, they must live elsewhere. In his *Notes on Virginia,* Jefferson explained the proposal that he had made to the Virginia legislature for gradual emancipation. Children of slaves would be

> brought up, at the public expense, to tillage, arts, or sciences, according to their geniuses, till the females should be eighteen, and the males twenty-one years of age, when they should be colonized to such place as the circumstances of the time should render most proper, sending them out with arms, implements, of household and of the handicraft arts, feeds, pairs of the useful domestic animals, etc., to declare them a free and independent people, and extend to them our alliance and protection, till they shall have acquired strength.[64]

Recent scholars, such as Winthrop Jordan, have derided colonization as "preposterously utopian" or condemned it as "treating Negroes as essentially unequal."

Was it impracticable? The obstacles were certainly great. But Lincoln pointed out during the Civil War that slave owners could have been compensated and travel costs paid for less than the cost of the war. Several thousand free blacks migrated to Liberia before the Civil War. Lincoln thought Central America a more practical location. Would expulsion have been cruel, as Jordan thought? Certainly it *could* have been. On the other hand, as an alternative to the emancipation through violence of the Civil War, it would have been a blessing to many.[65]

The deeper question is whether it was consistent for those who believed in human equality to favor colonization. It was. All human beings have a right to liberty. But a right to liberty does not include a right to live in the country of one's choice, without the consent of those already citizens in that place. The plan to colonize blacks would not have violated their human rights. What defines a *people* is not race, not tradition, not geography, but the free choice of a group of human beings to live together as fellow citizens. The blacks were unjustly dragged to America against their will. But justice required no more than to give them back their native liberty, with appropriate aid until such time as they could live on their own. This could have been done by sending them to a place where they could be their own masters, and then leaving them alone.

The Incomplete Founding IV: Faith in Progress

Beyond the influence of the ordinary selfish passions and the fear that integration would fail, another belief undermined the tenacity of the antislavery men of the founding period. That was their faith in progress. In a letter composed shortly before his death, Jefferson wrote, "All eyes are opened, or opening, to the rights of man," owing to "the general spread of the light of science." In his *Notes on Virginia,* he had predicted that "the spirit of the master is abating, that of the slave rising from the dust, . . . the way I hope preparing, under the auspices of heaven, for a total emancipation." Madison too spoke of "reflections and sentiments that are secretly undermining the institution."[66]

The belief in progress took away the sense of urgency from antislavery men. If, in Franklin's words, "the daily progress of that luminous and benign spirit of liberty . . . is diffusing itself throughout the world,"[67] then emancipation was bound to come sooner or later. Why press it, especially when real victories for liberty—for example, the Constitution and the union it established—might otherwise be endangered?

The Founders were not witless dreamers. Most agreed with Hamilton's sober view of progress in *The Federalist:* "Is it not time to awake from the deceitful dream of a golden age . . . [and to admit that we] are yet remote from the happy empire of perfect wisdom and perfect virtue?"[68] The leading Founders were too sensible to indulge the fantasy that human evil might one day disappear, a notion that we rightly associate more with the French and Russian Revolutions than with the American. But the feeling was strong that liberty and enlightenment would continue to grow and that slavery would die an inevitable death.

Noah Webster expressed this view when he said that "slavery in this country will be utterly extirpated in the course of two centuries, perhaps in a much shorter period, without any extraordinary efforts to abolish it."

In 1790 Devereaux Jarrett of Virginia was "well pleased that a spirit of liberation is prevailing" and expected that slavery would end "as soon as it may be consistent with public and private utility."[69]

The speeches of delegates at the Constitutional Convention show how this belief weakened the resolve of slavery opponents whenever its defenders dug in their heels. Roger Sherman said that "the abolition of slavery seemed to be going on in the United States and that the good sense of the several states would probably by degrees complete it." Likewise Oliver Ellsworth: "As population increases, poor laborers will be so plenty as to render slaves useless. Slavery in time will not be a speck in this country." Even Abraham Baldwin, who vigorously defended the slave trade, said: "If left to herself, she [Georgia] would probably put a stop to the evil." His evidence was the growing belief in equality.[70]

This faith was especially soothing to Southerners who knew slavery was wrong but shied away from the controversy that public advocacy of abolition would stir up. Although it was well known that he arranged for his slaves to be freed upon the death of his wife, Washington had never spoken publicly against the institution. After 1790, Jefferson never did; Madison did so only rarely. They seem to have been tranquilized by the belief that slavery was, in Lincoln's words, "in course of ultimate extinction." Perhaps they should have known better. They simply did not anticipate that the beliefs of American leaders might actually go "backwards" to the view that some men are born with saddles on their backs and others born with boots and spurs. But that is what happened, within a few decades after the founding. "In some trifling particulars," said Lincoln in 1857, referring to the founding era, "the condition of that race has been ameliorated; but, as a whole, in this country, the change between then and now is decidedly the other way; and their ultimate destiny has never appeared so hopeless as in the last three or four years."[71]

The Founders' hopeful sentiments proved to be a delusion. The grim truth was that slavery was already growing rapidly in the South even in the 1780s. The number of individual manumissions, while substantial, never kept up with the natural increase through new births. The slave interest became so strong over the next seventy years that the quarrel over whether to restrict the expansion of slavery nearly destroyed the nation. So much for the automatic progress of the spirit of liberty and enlightenment.

In the end, as Lincoln saw with supreme clarity, there was no escaping the "eternal struggle between these two principles—right and wrong—throughout the world." No amount of enlightenment, no political reform, however just, can exempt America or any other nation from that struggle, because it springs from the permanent nature of human beings, the conflict between good and evil in every human heart.[72] The battle for justice and liberty will never be permanently won. Each generation must fight that battle over again.

The Civil War: The Founding Completed—in Principle

Bernard Bailyn, a leading historian of the founding era, has given an unusually judicious assessment of the Founders' achievement:

> To note only that certain leaders of the Revolution continued to enjoy the profits of so savage an institution and in their reforms failed to obliterate it inverts the proportions of the story. What is significant in the historical context of the time is not that the liberty-loving Revolutionaries allowed slavery to survive, but that they—even those who profited directly from the institution—went so far in condemning it, confining it, and setting in motion the forces that would ultimately destroy it. . . . A successful and liberty-loving republic might someday destroy the slavery that it had been obliged to tolerate at the start; a weak and fragmented nation would never be able to do so.[73]

Bailyn was echoing Lincoln, who opposed Stephen A. Douglas, Chief Justice Taney, and many others who defended the legitimacy of slavery by maintaining the same view of the Founders as the one that prevails today in elite academic circles and in our textbooks. In 1858 Lincoln said:

> [T]he fathers of this government expected and intended the institution of slavery to come to an end. They expected and intended that it should be in the course of ultimate extinction. . . . It is not true that our fathers, as Judge Douglas assumes, made this government part slave and part free. Understand the sense in which he puts it. He assumes that slavery is a rightful thing within itself,—was introduced by the framers of the Constitution. The exact truth is, that they found the institution existing among us, and they left it as they found it. But in making the government they left this institution with many clear marks of disapprobation upon it. They found slavery among them and they left it among them because of the difficulty—the absolute impossibility of its immediate removal.[74]

From this standpoint, "The American Revolution and the Civil War were not merely discrete events," as Harry Jaffa has written. "They constitute the first and last acts of a single drama. The fourscore and seven years between the Declaration of Independence and the Gettysburg Address comprehended the action of a tremendous world-historical tragedy." The slaves were freed, in accord with the promise of the Declaration—but at the cost of hundreds of thousands of lives and the physical destruction of vast regions of the nation. "The successful outcome resembled . . . the end of *Macbeth* or *Hamlet*, when Scotland and Denmark are restored to political health by the pity and terror of a tragic consummation."[75]

At the very moment of the nation's birth, Jefferson's attack on the slave trade was dropped from the draft of the Declaration of Independence, "in complaisance," Jefferson wrote, "to South Carolina and Georgia, who had never attempted to restrain the importation of slaves, and who on the contrary still wished to continue it."[76] That was a fateful precedent. In 1776 the question could be swept under the rug. That would not do for long.

When it became clear that slavery was not going away by itself, Americans faced a choice. They could keep their slaves and reject their founding principles. Or they could affirm their principles and limit the growth of slavery, placing it, in Lincoln's words, "in course of ultimate extinction." In the 1830s the South made its choice. It broke with the founding. In 1838 Senator John C. Calhoun of South Carolina said:

> This [antislavery] agitation has produced one happy effect at least; it has compelled us to the South to look into the nature and character of this great institution, and to correct many false impressions that even we had entertained in relation to it. Many in the South once believed that it was a moral and political evil; that folly and delusion are gone; we see it now in its true light, and regard it as the most safe and stable basis for free institutions in the world.

Against Jefferson and other Southerners of the founding era, Calhoun and the South now insisted that slavery was "a positive good," "an institution indispensable for the good of both races." They denied what the Founders had affirmed, that there was an inseparable link between the Constitution and the equal rights of humanity. Southerners now openly attacked the political theory of the founding. Like today's legal positivists, they would put "natural law" in quotation marks, to show their contempt for any notion of universal human rights. Calhoun asserted that "nothing can be more unfounded and false" than "the prevalent opinion that all men are born free and equal." In 1857 George Fitzhugh wrote that books written by Southerners more than twenty or thirty years earlier "are likely to be as absurd and as dangerous as the Declaration of Independence, or the Virginia Bill of Rights."[77]

Fitzhugh's views were more extreme than those of other Southerners, but he saw more clearly than they the tendency of their position. He criticized equality not only for blacks but also for whites: "The bestowing upon men equality of rights, is but giving license to the strong to oppress the weak. It begets the grossest inequalities of condition." (Karl Marx was making the same argument at the same time in Europe.) "A southern farm," said Fitzhugh with some exaggeration, but also with some justice, "is the beau ideal of communism."[78]

Alexander Stephens, the Confederate vice president, summed up the Southern rejection of the founding in his "Corner-Stone Speech," delivered in 1861:

> Jefferson in his forecast had anticipated this [slavery] as the "rock upon which the old Union would split." He was right. . . . But whether he fully comprehended the great truth upon which that rock *stood* and *stands,* may be doubted. The prevailing ideas entertained by him and most of the leading statesmen at the time of the formation of the old constitution, were that the enslavement of the African was in violation of the laws of nature; that it was wrong in *principle,* socially, morally, and politically. It was an evil they knew not well how to deal with, but the general opinion of the men of that day was that, somehow or other in the order of Providence, the institution would be evanescent and pass away. . . . These ideas, however, were fundamentally wrong. They rested upon the assumption of the equality of races. This was an error. . . .
>
> Our new government is founded upon exactly the opposite idea; its corner-stone rests upon the great truth, that the negro is not equal to the white man; that slavery—subordination to the superior race—is his natural and normal condition.
>
> This, our new government, is the first, in the history of the world, based upon this great physical, philosophical, and moral truth.[79]

Unlike Alexander Stephens, some Northerners, like Senator Stephen Douglas of Illinois, hoped to solve the slavery controversy without directly attacking the Founders' views. Instead, he pretended that the Founders never meant to include blacks in the Declaration. In his debates with Lincoln, Douglas asserted:

> The signers of the Declaration of Independence never dreamed of the Negro when they were writing that document. They referred to white men, to men of European birth and European descent, when they declared the equality of all men. . . . When the Declaration was put forth, every one of the thirteen colonies were slaveholding colonies, and every man who signed that instrument represented a slave-holding constituency. . . . When you say that the Declaration of Independence includes the Negro, you charge the signers of it with hypocrisy.

Douglas's view is echoed and reechoed today in the textbooks read by America's children, as we have seen. Lincoln treated it with the scorn that it deserved. The equality of the Declaration, he responded, applies to all human beings, black and white. Lincoln said that the historical record before the 1850s

> may be searched in vain for one single affirmation, from one single man, that the Negro was not included in the Declaration of Independence. I think I may defy Judge Douglas to show that he ever said so, that Washington ever said so, that any president ever said so, that any member of Congress ever said so.... And I will remind Judge Douglas and this audience, that while Mr. Jefferson was the owner of slaves, as undoubtedly he was, in speaking upon this very subject, he used the strong language that "he trembled for his country when he remembered that God was just."[80]

Lincoln's response to Douglas recalled Northerners to the Declaration of Independence, which he placed at the center of his political rhetoric during the 1850s and the Civil War.

Abraham Lincoln, Stephen Douglas, and Alexander Stephens agreed on one thing: the cause of the Civil War was slavery. Lincoln and the Republicans wished to curb its further expansion. The South demanded its extension westward and southward. The war resolved the question, through Lincoln's Emancipation Proclamation and the Thirteenth Amendment, abolishing slavery in the United States.

We have quoted former Supreme Court Justice Thurgood Marshall's denunciation of the Constitution because of the stain of slavery upon it. Marshall's resentment is forgivable. As Jefferson predicted, there will be "ten thousand recollections, by the blacks, of the injuries they have sustained." Still, we must not forget why the blacks were liberated. For the first time in history, in America during the founding era, and again during the Civil War, slavery was opposed as unjust by the leading men of a country with large numbers of slaves. Lincoln and the Republican party of the 1850s were able to mobilize a national majority against the expansion of slavery only because of the commitment the Founders had made to the proposition that all men are created equal. The Republican opposition to expanding slavery led to secession and civil war. After the border slave states had become committed to the war effort, Lincoln took his earliest practical opportunity to announce the Emancipation Proclamation. From then on, the war for the union became a war to abolish slavery. Hundreds of thousands of whites gave "the last full measure of devotion" in the cause that "this nation, under God, shall have a new birth of freedom."[81] "The Battle Hymn of the Republic"—Julia Ward Howe's popular Civil War song—makes this clear: "As He died to make men holy, let us die to make men free."

The Founders believed that their compromises with slavery would be corrected in the course of American history after the union was formed. Their belief turned out to be true, although the new birth of freedom proved to be less inevitable and more costly than they anticipated. The Civil War fulfilled the antislavery promise of the American founding.

Lincoln was right, and today's consensus is wrong. America really was "conceived in liberty, and dedicated to the proposition that all men are created equal." Under the principles of the Declaration and the law of the Constitution, blacks won their liberty, became equal citizens, gained the right to vote, and eventually had their life, liberty, and property equally protected by the law. But today the founding, which made all of this possible, is denounced as unjust and antiblack. Surely that uncharitable verdict deserves to be reversed.

2

Property Rights

$\mathcal{U}$ntil the twentieth century, most Americans believed that rich and poor alike benefit from government protection of property rights. They inherited this view from the Founders.

In the American Revolution, liberty and property were thought to be inseparable in two respects. In the first place, there must be "no taxation without representation," as the famous Revolutionary slogan had it. When government takes your property without your consent, it also takes away your liberty. To show how the logic of the founding pointed toward the abolition of slavery, in chapter 1 we quoted John Dickinson's 1768 remark: "Those who are taxed without their own consent, expressed by themselves or their representatives, are slaves. We are taxed without our own consent, expressed by ourselves or our representatives. We are therefore—SLAVES." We quote it again here to introduce our consideration of property. For the same reason, Jefferson spoke of property as part of liberty in his *Summary View of the Rights of British America* (1774):

> Still less let it be proposed that our *properties* within our own territories shall be taxed or regulated by any power on earth but our own. The God who gave us life gave us *liberty* at the same time; the hand of force may destroy, but cannot disjoin them.[1]

But there is a second limitation on government control over property. It is not enough to say that government may take a person's property only if the people or their representatives approve it. Even government by consent of the governed should not have unlimited power over the property of its citizens (just as it should not have unlimited power over their other liberties). The "first principle of association," wrote Jefferson, is "the guarantee to everyone [of] the free exercise of his industry and the fruits acquired by it."[2] Government may take a portion of one's property by taxation, but only on condition that government otherwise protects one's right to acquire property.

The "first principle of association" refers to what the Founders called the social compact, instituted by a people who associate together to secure their right to liberty, including the liberty to acquire property. The Declaration of Independence says:

> We hold these truths to be self-evident, that all men are created equal, that they are endowed by their Creator with certain unalienable rights, that among these rights are life, liberty, and the pursuit of happiness. That to secure these rights, governments are instituted among men, deriving their just powers from the consent of the governed.

Liberty, in the Founders' understanding, "protect[s] the exertions of talent and industry and secur[es] to them their justly acquired fruits." This is Hamilton's formulation, but the "fruits of industry" phrase appears again and again in the writings of the founding era. In 1795 the Supreme Court declared, "The right of acquiring and possessing property, and having it protected, is one of the natural, inherent, and unalienable rights of man. . . . No man would become a member of a community, in which he could not enjoy the fruits of his honest labor and industry. The preservation of property then is a primary object of the social compact."[3]

Some twentieth-century scholars, seeking support for their ideology in the founding, have falsely claimed that the omission of the right to property from the Declaration means that it was *not* one of the founding principles. That is what Vernon Parrington said in his widely read *Main Currents in American Thought* (1927), as did Garry Wills in *Inventing America* (1978). Gordon Wood, in his much praised *Creation of the American Republic* (1969), claimed in effect that the Founders of 1776 had no interest in an individual right to private property: "Ideally, republicanism obliterated the individual," Wood wrote. "The extensive mercantilist regulation of the economy, the numerous attempts in the early years of the war to suppress prices, control wages, . . . was in no way inconsistent with the spirit of '76, but in fact was ideally expressive of what republicanism meant." As the Americans of 1776 understood it, said Wood, "republicanism was essentially anti-capitalistic."[4]

Nothing could be further from the truth than these claims. As we have already seen, the Founders generally, and Jefferson in particular, placed property rights at the center of their theory of politics. As Jefferson stated in his First Inaugural address, a wise and frugal government . . . shall restrain men from injuring one another, shall leave them otherwise free to regulate their own pursuits of industry and improvement, and shall not take from the mouth of labor the bread it has earned. This is the sum of good government.[5]

Documents of the founding era frequently asserted that property was a fundamental natural right. The first article of the 1776 Virginia Declaration of Rights reads:

That all men are by nature equally free and independent, and have certain inherent rights, of which, when they enter into a state of society, they cannot, by any compact, deprive or divest their posterity; namely, the enjoyment of life and liberty, with the means of acquiring and possessing property, and pursuing and obtaining happiness and safety.[6]

The constitutions of several other states either quoted or paraphrased the Virginia language, and no state or individual questioned it. The U.S. Constitution of 1787 threw the weight of the federal government behind property rights.

Since the right to property derives from, or is part of, the right to liberty, there can be no natural right to property in another human being. To enslave a person is to deprive him of his own right to property. That is why Lincoln, following the Founders, often spoke of the heart of slavery as the denial of property rights: "It is the same tyrannical principle," said Lincoln. "It is the same spirit that says, 'You work and toil and earn bread, and I'll eat it.'" Speaking of a black slave, Lincoln said: "In some respects she certainly is not my equal; but in her natural right to eat the bread she earns with her own hands without asking leave of anyone else, she is my equal, and the equal of all others."[7]

We will see shortly how the Founders made sure that property rights were defined and enforced in such a way as to make good on this promise.

Besides being a part of one's natural liberty, the right to property is a necessary condition of all other freedoms. Without private property, government would own the churches, printing presses, and factories. Government would be able to dictate the practice of religion, speech, and employment, as it does under communism. For the Founders, property, as Edward J. Erler writes, is "the great fence to liberty."[8]

Today, for example, all rights to electronic broadcasting are owned by the federal government. The consequence is exactly what the Founders would have predicted: radio and television stations are careful not to broadcast political opinions of which government disapproves too much. It is a little-known but important fact that government has actually closed down several radio and TV stations whose broadcasting content was judged politically incorrect. Television station WLTB in Jackson, Mississippi learned that lesson the hard way, losing its broadcast license after attacking civil rights legislation too strongly in the 1960s.[9]

The Textbooks

We saw in the slavery chapter, and we will see in the chapters on women, that modern textbooks and scholars openly attack the Founders' views and treatment of blacks and women. When it comes to property rights, their approach is more subtle. Instead of criticizing the Founders head-on, they denounce capitalism and free markets as they evolved later in American history.

As the critics tell the story, the Founders' principles, combined with economic changes caused by industrialization, led to massive exploitation of workers and consumers by big businesses. These abuses had to be corrected, we are told, by wide-scale regulation of the economy and an abandonment of the earlier system of free markets and property rights.

Late nineteenth-century capitalism in particular is presented "in a rather harsh light," as Robert Lerner remarks in his survey of leading history texts. High-school textbook author Gary Nash labels steel producer Andrew Carnegie and other business leaders of that era "robber barons," in spite of Nash's own admission that Carnegie was an honest businessman. Without any effort to conceal his partisanship, Nash enthusiastically praises Progressive Era regulation as "means of taming powerful special interests" and curbs on "the irresponsibility of big business." Nash does not mention the fact that many thoughtful and well-intentioned Americans during the Progressive Era rejected these reforms as violations of property rights as those rights had been understood since the founding. He also neglects to report that leading historians have concluded that many of the charges against the "robber barons" are untrue.

The term "robber barons" was popularized in Matthew Josephson's *The Robber Barons*, published in 1934. Josephson was a partisan liberal "not expert in either history or economics," according to historian Allan Nevins. Josephson's highly biased interpretation of the late nineteenth century has been refuted by historians on both the left (David Shi) and the right (Burton Folsom). Both have shown that the leading businessmen of that era committed few of the injustices attributed to them. For example, they did not abuse their power "by raising prices and limiting production," as Nash asserts. Companies like Standard Oil actually grew by *cutting* prices and *increasing* production. Kerosene oil used in lamps became affordable for much larger numbers of Americans when Standard Oil reduced its price by more than half after 1870. The worst abuses of the period were committed, not by businesses like Standard Oil operating in the free market, but by businessmen granted special privileges or monopolies by government, such as some of the railroad companies. These problems were not solved but caused by government intervention in the free market.[10]

This same hostility toward property rights colors the textbooks' treatment of more recent events. The teacher's edition of Nash's textbook suggests that teachers "tell students that the 1980s came to be associated with widespread greed."[11] The expression "decade of greed" was actually popularized by Democrats and their sympathizers in the media as a means of discrediting the Reagan administration, which promoted property rights through tax cuts and deregulation.

We will give the critics of property rights their due later in this chapter. But first, let us try to understand the Founders as they understood themselves.

Problem: Equal Rights, Unequal Results

Madison's famous *Federalist* No. 10 shows that the equal right to property will lead to unequal possession of property. He speaks of the "diversity in the faculties of men, from which the rights of property originate."

> The protection of these faculties [that is, securing the right to liberty, including the right to keep the fruits of one's honest industry] is the first object of government. From the protection of different and unequal faculties of acquiring property, the possession of different degrees and kinds of property immediately results.

Madison has in mind such "faculties" as ambition, intelligence, experience, energy, and strength. These lead people into different jobs and professions (leading to different "kinds of property"), and the same differences lead to different levels of income (different "degrees" of property).[12]

For this reason, protecting property seems to amount to protecting the rich. For example, Michael Parenti, a Marxist scholar, writes that the Constitution "was, and still is, largely an elitist document" because of its focus on "securing property interests."[13]

Few scholars are as openly partisan as Parenti. But many of them agree with Parenti about property rights. UCLA law professor Kenneth Karst, for example, writes that "the protection of property and economic liberty" is something that matters only "to people at the top of the heap." Karst and others have therefore concluded that when the Supreme Court of the late nineteenth century spoke of liberty and due process of law to protect property rights, the Court was simply acting, in the words of another law professor, "as an arm of the capital-owning class." In the view of these and many other scholars, the property-rights Court was an enemy of the poor.[14]

Madison admits that a society that protects equal property rights for all will necessarily contain people who are poor, middle-class, and rich. If "all men are created equal," can this be just?

As the Founders viewed the question, either a man enjoys his equal right to freedom or he does not. Either he disposes of his own labor and property or he does not. Whether the person taking one's property is a thief, a medieval aristocrat, a Southern slave owner, a businessman seeking a government subsidy, or a person on welfare who refuses to work, the principle is the same: "you work, I eat."

Yet, as we will see in the chapter on welfare, this was not the Founders' last word. There are people who are too old, sick, or weak to work. Political society, which is organized for the security of its members' lives as well as their liberty and property, rightly responds to these circumstances. Support of the poor through government-funded relief and voluntary charity was therefore part of the Founders' liberalism. However, unlike the welfare policies of today, the policies of that time compelled the able-bodied poor to labor for their sustenance. Only those too weak to work were supported in idleness at public expense.

Besides the case of old age and sickness, there is a second, more serious problem with the argument for property rights. The ground of the right to private property, we have said, is the natural right to liberty, requiring government to "guarantee to everyone the free exercise of his industry and the fruits acquired by it" (Jefferson, quoted earlier). But even if we accept the "fruits of labor" argument, why should that mean protection of the *existing* distribution of property? In reality, this distribution is only partly due to "the free exercise of [one's] industry." It is also partly the product of one's forebears' labor and partly the result of one's own and one's forebears' luck, connections, and possibly even theft or conquest. Jefferson was well aware that the land of Virginia was mostly owned by descendants of those who had gotten it for little or nothing or by royal grant. This is not to mention the question of how much of it was stolen from the Indians. To protect property so acquired, it would seem, is to protect not the fruits of labor but arbitrary privilege.[15]

Besides, in an established political community, all the land is already owned by someone. Those who do not own land are not in the same position to employ their "faculties of acquiring property" as those who already possess property. They do not have the land or the capital. Liberals like Cass Sunstein of the University of Chicago therefore conclude that there is never a "neutral baseline" of property and ability for government to protect. Everyone is born into a world in which property is already unequally divided and given positive government protection. Sunstein infers that all property is fundamentally created by government, either by its support of an existing distribution or by a policy of redistribution. Therefore, he argues, there is no reason for government to assume that the existing distribution of property is just and right. Instead, since a "modest minimum of food, medical care, and shelter is necessary for people who hope to obtain the status of citizens," government should take away property from the haves and guarantee this "modest minimum"—free food, housing, and health care—to everyone.[16]

Locke's Argument for Private Property

Sunstein's objection is anticipated by Locke in his classic discussion of property in chapter 5 of the *Second Treatise of Government*. Locke was the writer whose presentation of the principles of government was most admired by the American Founders.[17] The Founders agreed with Locke's point of departure:

> Man (by being master of himself, and proprietor of his own person and the actions or labor of it) had still in himself the great foundation of property. . . . Thus labor, in the beginning, gave a right of property whenever anyone was pleased to employ it upon what was common.

But "what was common," Locke notes, has long since been divided up among private owners. "[T]he increase of people and stock, with the use of money, had made land scarce." Once that had happened, laws, that is, "compact and agreement, settled the property which labor and industry began."[18]

Locke now confronts Sunstein's challenge: In a world where property is already divided among existing owners, how can people now find opportunity to "employ labor" upon what is no longer common? Locke answers: When land is owned and cultivated by the "industrious and rational," and when laws protect the "honest industry of mankind," there will be opportunities for everyone to produce and acquire. The actual current distribution of land and money is not decisive. The real source of wealth is not external goods but work. Locke writes, "Labor makes the far greater part of the value of things we enjoy in this world: and the ground which produces the materials, is scarcely to be reckoned in as any, or at most, but a very small, part of it." One hardly needs any land or capital at all to acquire wealth. In fact, large landowners can be and, outside of Europe, often are poor. An Indian "king of a large and fruitful territory there [in the wilds of America] feeds, lodges, and is clad worse than a day-laborer in England."[19]

Locke asserts that $999/1000$ of the value of things comes from labor rather than from nature. Labor takes the things that nature provides (dirt and rocks), and it turns them into wealth or things that produce wealth (plows, harvesters, and computers). Not land and buildings, but ideas, entrepreneurial daring, technical expertise, ambition, and hard work are the real source of wealth. The Indian king is "rich in land and poor in all the comforts of life."[20]

If labor is the primary source of wealth *even after all land has been divided among particular owners*, then the actual origin of the existing distribution of property becomes unimportant. This is the real response to Sunstein. Jefferson himself noted that existing property was partly acquired by luck, and John Stuart Mill bluntly pointed out that the original partition of property in modern Europe "was the result, not of just partition, or acquisition by industry, but of conquest and violence." Government protects property, not because the current pattern of wealth and poverty is in all respects just, but because security of property is a promise to the industrious and talented that they will be able to keep what they earn. The *future* security of the fruits of labor, together with the minuscule value of inanimate nature, guarantees that future wealth will correspond roughly to the talents and efforts of those who work, not to the land and property they inherit from their fathers. When the fruits of labor are secured, and talents and efforts are given a wide scope, the overall level of wealth in a society will grow. Locke writes, "He who appropriates land to himself by his labor, does not lessen but increase the common stock of mankind."[21]

Locke would not have been surprised to learn that in late twentieth-century America, common workers would live with central heating and air conditioning, year-round fresh meat and vegetables, a private car or two, television, VCR, stereo, and competent medical care—conveniences unavailable to the wealthiest elites of medieval and ancient Europe. The unequal results of equal rights will be not only tolerable but just—but only as long as the right to acquire is effectually guaranteed to the poor, so that they can earn enough to buy what they need from this "common stock."

In the American Revolution it was well understood that the poor benefit from the right to acquire. A committee of Congress asked General Washington not to exchange Hessian prisoners, because "we think their capture affords a favorable opportunity of making them acquainted with the situation and circumstances of many of their countrymen, who came here without a farthing of property, and have, by care and industry, acquired plentiful fortunes."[22]

The majority of today's scholars are oblivious to the Founders' interest in enabling the poor to acquire property of their own. For that reason, they often find the Founders' approach to property rights unjust and inconsistent with the proposition that "all men are created equal." Historian Richard Bushman, for example, writes:

> The principle of equality lacked the strength to achieve full realization in the face of opposing interests. . . . In theory the Revolution might have effected reforms in the economy. . . . Wherever large amounts of property accumulated, the danger arose of owners dominating their employees, destroying the equality of dominion that was the republican ideal. "Equality of property," wrote Noah Webster, the dictionary man, "is the very soul of a republic."
>
> If carried to its limit, this line of thinking might have radically disrupted the American social order. But the countervailing notion of rights of property stopped the progress of equality along this line. Confiscation of large properties, except for Tory lands, was unthinkable.[23]

It is noteworthy, and typical, that historians like Bushman assume without argument that forced redistribution of large land holdings to the poor is the natural consequence of the "line of thinking" that informed the American Revolution. As we have seen, nothing could be further from the truth.

Consider in contrast Lincoln's view. On the eve of the Civil War, he enthusiastically summed up the Founders' understanding of the link between freedom, the good of the poor, and the right to acquire property:

> I am glad to see that a system of labor prevails in New England under which laborers *can* strike when they want to, where they . . . are not tied down and obliged to work whether you pay them or not! I *like* the system which lets a man quit when he wants to, and wish it might prevail everywhere. One of the reasons I am opposed to slavery is just here. What is the true condition of the laborer? I take it that it is best for all to leave each man free to acquire property as fast as he can. Some will get wealthy. I don't believe in a law to prevent a man from getting rich.

It would do more harm than good. So while we do not propose any war upon capital, we do wish to allow the humblest man an equal chance to get rich with everybody else. When one starts poor, as most do in the race of life, free society is such that he knows he can better his condition; he knows that there is no fixed condition of labor, for his whole life. I am not ashamed to confess that twenty-five years ago I was a hired laborer, nailing rails, at work on a flat-boat—just what might happen to any poor man's son! I want every man to have the chance—and I believe a black man is entitled to it—in which he can better his condition—when he can look forward and hope to be a hired laborer this year and next, work for himself afterward, and finally to hire men to work for him![24]

We conclude that the right to acquire property was understood by the Founders, and by Americans long afterward, as a protection to rich and poor alike. It was a means by which the poor could ascend from poverty to wealth and not, as is so often asserted today, a device to keep them down.

France and Feudalism: How Property Rights Can Unjustly Defeat the Right to Acquire

How should government guarantee the right to acquire property? In Locke's words, "established laws of liberty" must "secure *protection* and *encouragement* to the honest industry of mankind."[25]

For protection, the laws must secure the right to keep what one earns.

For encouragement, the laws regulating and defining property must allow labor, investment, and other productive effort to achieve their just reward.

This point is crucial, but it is not well understood today. We usually think about property rights in the familiar terms of capitalism (property rights are protected) versus socialism or communism (property rights are not protected). But through most of human history, laws have protected the rights of existing property owners—people in the government and their friends—while discouraging the acquisition of property by those who currently own little or nothing. That was the character of feudal law.

Locke wrote that God gave the world "to the use of the industrious and rational, . . . not to the fancy and covetousness of the quarrelsome and contentious." Feudalism favored "quarrelsome and contentious" nobles over "industrious and rational" workers, inventors, and investors. The idle rich stayed rich, while the ambitious poor faced obstacles to acquiring property wherever they turned.

Jefferson saw in France vivid illustrations of this truth during his time as American ambassador in the 1780s. The laws of the Old Regime kept property in a small number of hands. This helps to explain that nation's widespread poverty, which was a contributing cause of the bloody revolution of the 1790s.

In one of Jefferson's letters he listed the legal restrictions that the French employed to keep property in the hands of the favored few. He asked (expecting the answer to be yes):

> Whether the nation may change the descent of lands holden in tail? Whether they may change the appropriation of lands given anciently to the church, to hospitals, colleges, orders of chivalry, and otherwise in perpetuity? Whether they may abolish the charges and privileges attached on lands, including the whole catalogue ecclesiastical and feudal? It goes to hereditary offices, authorities and jurisdictions; to hereditary orders, distinctions and appellations; to perpetual monopolies in commerce, the arts or sciences; with a long train of et ceteras: and it renders the question of reimbursement a question of generosity and not of right.[26]

One must be careful not to mistake this language for that of twentieth-century socialism, which sees no obstacle to government seizure of property for redistribution to the poor.[27] Jefferson's theme is that property belongs to the living, and the right to acquire property should therefore be available to all. Primogeniture (requiring land ownership to pass from father to firstborn son) and entail (requiring the owner to keep the land intact to pass on to his son) limited that right. So also did monopolies and hereditary jurisdictions, which excluded living competitors from freely entering the market. Hereditary offices and titles gave lucrative privileges to people by accident of birth. Jefferson is calling for a legal system that permits everyone to buy, sell, and use his property without asking leave of government, a system that does away with legally mandated special privileges that have no reference to individual achievement.

Observing the consequences of all these French limitations on the free use of property, Jefferson wrote:

> The property of this country is absolutely concentered in a very few hands. . . . I asked myself what could be the reason so many should be permitted to beg who are willing to work, in a country where there is a very considerable proportion of uncultivated lands? These lands are undisturbed only for the sake of game. It should seem then that it must be because of the enormous wealth of the proprietors which places them above attention to the increase of their revenues by permitting

these lands to be labored. I am conscious that an equal division of property is impracticable, but the consequences of this enormous inequality producing so much misery to the bulk of mankind, legislators cannot invent too many devices for subdividing property, only taking care to let their subdivisions go hand in hand with the natural affections of the human mind. The descent of property of every kind to all the brothers and sisters, or other relations in equal degree, is a politic measure and a practicable one. . . . Whenever there are in any country uncultivated lands and unemployed poor, it is clear that *the laws of property have been so far extended as to violate natural right.* The earth is given as a common stock for man to labor and live on. If for the encouragement of industry we allow it to be appropriated, we must take care that other employment be provided to those excluded from the appropriation. If we do not, *the fundamental right to labor the earth* returns to the unemployed.[28]

French nobles with enormous estates had little incentive to put their land to productive use, because they needed to support only themselves. Besides, they were legally prevented from selling land to those who had an interest in using it productively. By keeping most land off the market, French laws also made it expensive where it was available at all. The brothers and sisters of firstborn sons were out of luck, and so were all their own children except firstborn sons. For Jefferson, this was an outrageous violation of natural right because private property is defined in such a way that the poor cannot find work. Confining property in a small number of hands prevented large numbers of the "industrious and rational" poor from putting their natural talents to work acquiring property of their own.

Founding-Era Reforms to Secure the Right to Acquire

Jefferson did not, however, favor forced redistribution, for he declares in his autobiography that it would equally have been a "deprivation of natural right" if Virginia had taken property away from landowners who had inherited large estates.[29] In the letter just quoted, Jefferson wrote:

I am conscious that an equal division of property is impracticable, but the consequences of this enormous inequality producing so much misery to the bulk of mankind, legislators cannot invent too many devices for subdividing property, only taking care to let their subdivisions go hand in hand with the natural affections of the human mind.

Jefferson had an opportunity to act on his view that property in

France should be protected, but only if redefined so as to secure the right to acquire. "During the French Revolution," writes historian Willi Adams, "Jefferson had struck out 'property' in Lafayette's draft of a bill of rights for France and had replaced it by the phrase 'the power to dispose of his person and the fruits of his industry, and of all of his faculties.'" In this way, Jefferson indicated the need for France to follow the American example of abolishing restrictions on the free division, sale, and use of property.[30]

Hamilton, who is often viewed as a "conservative" in opposition to the "liberal" Jefferson, agreed that feudal property rights did not deserve the protection of government:

> certain feudal rights ... once oppressed all Europe and still oppress too great a part of it. ... These rights, though involving that of property, being contrary to the social order and to the permanent welfare of society, were justifiably abolished.[31]

Jefferson might seem to be asking the impossible. What "devices for subdividing property" can legislators invent without violating the rights of owners?

Consider that in our time the preferred response to the problem described by Jefferson in France is land reform. America imposed it on El Salvador in the 1980s as a condition of its aid in the war against communist rebels. Government simply seizes the land of the wealthy by force and gives it to the poor. But that is precisely what Jefferson ruled out as unjust to property owners.

Jefferson and the Founders preferred a solution that followed "the natural affections of the human mind": encouraging or requiring fathers to divide their property among their children and allowing them to develop and sell their property for productive use. They did this by reforming the inheritance laws.

In Virginia at the time of the Revolution, primogeniture prevented fathers from dividing their land among their children in their wills. Entail prevented them from dividing it while they were still alive. Jefferson's most urgent legal reform after the Declaration of Independence was to abolish these two limits on property owners. The end of entail (also called "fee-tail") meant that all titles to land in Virginia would be "in fee simple"; owners could divide it, sell it, or develop it as they pleased. The end of primogeniture meant that property would be distributed more equally among all heirs, male and female. All other states that had primogeniture and entail got rid of them during the American Revolution.[32]

These reforms were inspired by real problems, as Jefferson wrote:

In the earlier times of the colony when lands were to be obtained for little or nothing, some provident individuals procured large grants, and, desirous of founding great families for themselves, settled them on their descendants in fee-tail. The transmission of this property from generation to generation in the same name raised up a distinct set of families who, being privileged in the law in the perpetuation of their wealth were thus formed into a Patrician order.[33]

Jefferson biographer Willard Randall explains how the old order stood in the way of ambitious newcomers:

The huge hereditary estates of eastern Virginia blocked the access of newer arrivals to the rich alluvial soils of the Tidewater and its vital transportation network of rivers. New migrants had to trek into the hardscrabble backcountry where, as land-tenure lawyer Jefferson well knew, they were also blocked from owning their own land by feudal quitrent laws and by greedy speculators who had engrossed much of the west country without paying for it.[34]

The purpose of Jefferson's reforms was to make prosperity correspond as closely as possible to real merit. For him, democracy was a regime in which talent and effort would receive their due reward, instead of being held back by artificial rules and privileges as in European aristocracy. Jefferson wrote:

To annul this privilege, and instead of an aristocracy of wealth (of more harm and danger, than benefit, to society), to make an opening for an aristocracy of virtue and talent, which nature has wisely provided for the direction of the interests of society, and scattered with an equal hand through all its conditions, was deemed essential to a well ordered republic. To effect it no violence was necessary, no deprivation of natural right, but rather an enlargement of it by a repeal of the law. For this would authorize the present holder to divide the property among his children equally, as his affections were divided; and would place them, by natural generation, on the level of their fellow citizens.[35]

Within a few decades, these reforms did help to produce a society in which property was held much more widely and equally, as Tocqueville observed when he visited America in the 1830s. "Owing to the law of inheritance," he wrote, "the death of each owner causes a revolution in property; . . . possessions . . . are continually broken up into smaller fractions." Therefore "wealth circulates there with incredible rapidity."[36]

Behind these and other legal reforms was the desire to secure the right to acquire property while protecting the right to hold it. That is a necessary implication of the equality principle of the Declaration.

Jefferson's awareness of possible tension or conflict between the natural right to acquire and the natural right to hold property was a theme of the earliest American textbook on political science, Nathaniel Chipman's *Sketches of the Principles of Government* (1793). Chipman speaks of "primary rights," among which is

> the right which men have of using their powers and faculties, under certain reciprocal modifications, for their own convenience and happiness. . . . I shall here instance . . . *the right of acquisition.* To the security of this right, certain regulations, as to the modes and conditions of enjoying the *secondary rights,* or in other words, *of holding property,* are necessary. . . . To give to any individual, or class of men, a monopoly, an exclusive right of acquisition . . . is an exclusion of the rights of others. It is a violation of the equal rights of man. Of this nature are all exclusive privileges; all perpetuities of riches and honors, and all the pretended right of primogeniture.[37]

These "regulations as to the modes and conditions of enjoying the secondary rights, or in other words, of holding property" were written into several of the early state constitutions. Maryland's 1776 Declaration of Rights said "that monopolies are odious, contrary to the spirit of a free government, and ought not to be suffered." (They are "odious" because they prevent people from entering markets where the well-to-do are already operating.) Maryland also provided that "no title of nobility, or hereditary honors, ought to be granted in this state." The Massachusetts Declaration of Rights of 1780 said, "No man, nor corporation, or association of men, have any title to obtain [from the government] *advantages,* or *particular and exclusive privileges,* distinct from those of the community, than what arises from the consideration of services rendered to the public; and this title [is] in nature neither hereditary, nor transmissible to children."[38]

It may seem paradoxical that the right to acquire property requires that certain kinds of property (a hereditary honor, a government-granted monopoly license) *not* be protected. But even communist governments, such as those of China and the former Soviet Union, protect private property. By definition, private property consists of goods held by some individuals to the exclusion of others. Communist governments own everything. They are the universal landlord. They have a right to do whatever they wish with their property: to build country estates or missiles, to manufacture, to farm, to let land lie waste. Those who are not part of the governing elite may use property only with the permission of the owner, the government. Yet no one regards communism as a system that protects property rights. That is because we implicitly, but usually not explicitly, understand property rights to include the right of *any* citizen to acquire property through his productive efforts and to use and keep what he earns.[39]

Later Reforms

It took Americans several decades to grasp the full practical application of the principle that all must be guaranteed the right to acquire property. The tradition of law favoring established wealth and privilege did not disappear right away. Corporations, for example, continued to be chartered through individual acts of state legislatures. That meant that people with political connections were more likely to be able to form such companies. However, beginning with New York in 1811, states developed general incorporation laws, which opened to every citizen, however poor, the legal right to incorporate under conditions applying equally to all.[40]

The law of nuisance was also changed to protect the rights of the less well-to-do. Under colonial law, writes legal historian William Nelson, "The older claimant's usage [of his land] would be elevated to the level of a property right and a more recent claimant would have to use his land so as not to interfere with the older right." In those days, says Morton Horwitz, the law "conferred on an owner the power to prevent any use of his neighbor's property that conflicted with his own quiet enjoyment." This right of established property tended to freeze in place the existing social order. The poor or middling entrepreneur had to overcome the law's bias in favor of the already wealthy. (Today property owners sometimes use zoning laws and environmental regulation for the same purpose. "Not in my back yard!" is the selfish principle at work.)[41]

By the early nineteenth century, judges in state courts came to believe, as Horwitz explains, that "because this [older] conception of ownership necessarily circumscribed the right of others to develop their land," it was inappropriate to American society because it violated the property rights of the poor. The older law of property came down from medieval times, when government protected the English gentry against competition from upstart artisans and manufacturers. Feudal law treated existing property relations as rightful and permanent. The rich were supposed to stay rich, and the poor to stay poor. Therefore "the anti-developmental doctrines of the [old] common law ... clashed with the spirit of economic improvement." In the years following the Revolution, "the idea of property underwent a fundamental transformation—from a static agrarian conception entitling an owner to undisturbed enjoyment, to a dynamic, instrumental, and more abstract view of property that emphasized the newly paramount virtues of productive use and development." Historian James Willard Hurst puts it this way: "Dynamic rather than static property, property in motion or at risk rather than property secure and at rest, engaged our principal interest."[42]

Under the old common law, for example, it was difficult to build a new dam or mill on any public river. The poor miller who had just opened a mill could be sued for damages by the established miller down the river if he obstructed the flow of water, even temporarily, in the operation of his mill. That rule soon changed. In an 1805 New York case, the judge ruled that the right to sue for interfering with the flow of water "must be restrained within reasonable bounds so as not to deprive a man of the enjoyment of his property." Otherwise, "he who could first build a dam or mill on any public or navigable river would acquire an exclusive right." That would conflict with the right of others along the river who might also want to use the water to mill grain. In a similar case in 1818, writes Horwitz, "the court held in favor of an upstream mill owner whose dam occasionally detained the flow of water for a number of days." The old common law maxim was *sic utere tuo ut alienum non laedas*—"use your own (property) in such a way that you do not injure another's." The judge in this case wrote that the sacred maxim *sic utere* "must be taken and construed with an eye to *the natural rights of all*." He meant the natural right, as stated in the Virginia Declaration of Rights, of "*acquiring . . .* property."[43]

This understanding prevailed in American law until recent times. Legal scholar Jeff Lewin writes, "In the early years of the twentieth century, legal positivism superseded natural rights as the dominant philosophy in American jurisprudence, particularly with respect to property rights." The legal community's Restatement of Torts in 1939 cut off nuisance law "from its natural rights origins, substituting a positivist right determined according to utilitarian criteria of cost and benefit." The positivist approach treats government limitations on the right to use one's own property "as a pure question of policy," no longer as a violation of individual rights. The problem then becomes, as Robert Bone notes, "how to justify limits on legislative power." If the right to acquire no longer has a foundation in nature, it is the gift of government. What government gives, government may take away. This is the world of Cass Sunstein, quoted above, who denies the existence of a natural right to property. But if there is no right to keep the fruits of one's honest labor, is there any longer a recognizable right to liberty?[44]

After the founding, nuisance law and other rules governing property rights were gradually brought into conformity with the primacy of the right to acquire. Established wealth that had been passed on from one generation of the same family to another mostly disappeared in America. Money and positions circulated rapidly, as the efforts of succeeding generations determined anew their place in society. Children of the poor usually did better than their parents, while children of the wealthy often fell back into the class of those who had to work for a living. Most Irish, Italian, Jewish, and Asian immigrants arrived without money or status. They were often disliked and mistreated by Americans already living here. They began with the lowest-paid and hardest work—the kind of work dismissed today as "dead-end jobs." Yet each of these groups produced children and grandchildren whose average wealth eventually surpassed that of white Anglo-Saxon Protestants.[45]

In accordance with the new understanding of property rights, the relations between rich and poor were transformed in early America. When economic relations are determined by at-will contracts, paternalistic attitudes give way to republican assertiveness and pride on the workers' part and to conciliation rather than harshness on the employers'. In a contract freely entered, both parties reach an agreement in which each offers something that the other wants. The laborer offers his labor, the employer his money. As contractors, both are equal. Gordon Wood points out that after the Revolution those who offered jobs for wages were no longer called "master" but "boss," as an indication of the more equal employer-employee relation. Hired hands in hotels insisted on being called "help" or "waiters," to distance themselves from the condition of permanent inferiority implied in the hateful name of "servant." The American rich and poor never developed the kind of class consciousness that has poisoned European politics. The poor and middle class have looked on the rich, not with destructive envy, but with the same confidence that Lincoln expressed in the passage quoted above, that one day they themselves or their children might also become wealthy. In contrast to Europe, as Madison saw, "the universal hope of acquiring property" pervaded America. (Madison failed to appreciate how reasonable this hope would prove to be. See chapter 5, on the property requirement for voting.)[46]

The Twentieth-Century Rejection of Property Rights

What we have displayed so far is the Founders' argument for property rights at the most fundamental level—at the level of the natural right to liberty with which all human beings are born. We have seen some of the things that government must do to secure the natural right of property owners, while at the same time securing the natural right of workers and other would-be owners, so that all could enjoy the fruits of their labor.

During the first century and a half of its existence, American property law was largely devoted to solving this problem.

Before the twentieth century, most Americans believed that a leading source of injustice was improper government intervention in the economy through high taxes, excessive bureaucracy, and artificial rules like entail and primogeniture that concentrated wealth in the hands of a privileged few. The Declaration of Independence complained that the British had "erected a multitude of new offices, and sent hither swarms of officers to harass our people, and eat out their substance."

In the twentieth century, a massive and successful critique of property rights has transformed government policy in this area. Government hostility to private property grew steadily until about 1980, when Ronald Reagan was elected president and a modest reaction set in. There were three "waves" in which government dramatically increased its authority over property. First was the Progressive Era, culminating in Woodrow Wilson's presidency. Second was President Franklin D. Roosevelt's New Deal of the 1930s. Third came the "regulatory revolution" of 1965–75, led by President Lyndon Johnson and the Democratic Congress. By 1975, even ordinary citizens had become used to high taxes and pervasive government controls over the use of their property.

In the 1990s, government was permitted to declare any piece of private property in America a wetland or an endangered-species habitat that its owner was no longer permitted to farm or build on. His land became in effect a government-mandated park. He retained nominal title, but the land had to be used as government wished, not as he wished. The surprising thing is that farmers and builders generally complained about these regulations only when they were administered dishonestly or incompetently, as when government declared a mostly dry piece of land a wetland (as it frequently did). Owners did not challenge the government's right to tell them not to farm or build on real wetlands (swamps, bogs, and marshes). For example, a farmer complained bitterly in a 1996 letter to the *Wall Street Journal* about regulators' mistakes in classifying part of his farm as a wetland, but he accepted without question the government's right to forbid him to cultivate his own land as long as the prohibition was based on "sound science."[47]

In the Founders' understanding, this kind of regulation would have been regarded as an unjust (because uncompensated) seizure of private property.

As Dennis Coyle and others have shown, twentieth-century American law has in important respects returned to the feudal approach. Both share the principles that no private person really owns property outright (what Jefferson called "in fee simple") and that owners of property cannot be trusted to use it well unless they are given detailed and ongoing direction by the government. "Arguments for feudallike encumbrance of private property have been heard throughout this century," writes Coyle:

> Francis S. Philbrick waxed nostalgic for feudalism in 1938, writing that "in the case of feudalism it is regrettable that there could not have been preserved the idea that all property was held subject to the performance of duties—not a few of them public." These sentiments were echoed nearly thirty years later by John Cribbet, who asserted that "the concept behind [feudal duties] was sound. . . . [T]he use of land is of more than private concern."[48]

In America today, as in most countries, all manner of legal obstacles stand in the way of the poor. Licenses and permits are needed before a person is permitted to go into most kinds of business. These are often granted only after a long struggle with a variety of government agencies—federal, state, and local. Sometimes the permit is denied or delayed indefinitely without explanation, often without a clear legal standard that applies equally to all. Government connections enable some businesses—but almost never new businesses—to get tax abatements or subsidies. Zoning often makes it difficult for the poor to develop their property in a productive way (much productive work in the home is forbidden). Zoning regulations are notorious for being applied on an ad hoc basis to aid or harm particular businesses, depending on the ideology and friendships of local officials. Legal monopolies granted by government (to cable and television broadcasters, for example) keep poorer would-be competitors out of the market. Complex regulations often favor existing businesses because their lawyers know the system. They have connections with government officials to arrange for exceptions, while their competitors do not.[49]

I do not want to exaggerate the extent of these obstacles. Hernando de Soto has shown that in Peru in the 1980s, constraints on acquisition were so pervasive that no one except well-connected elites could prosper. As a consequence, a massive underground economy grew up to evade the official system. One example: It was so difficult and expensive to get government permission to build a house that half of the population of Lima lived in houses illegally constructed on the black market. Peru, argues de Soto, has never had a true market economy. The same can be said of many so-called Third World countries.[50]

America today is still far from that point. Constraints on acquisition are real. They are pervasive in comparison with pre-1960s America. But people with drive and talent can still overcome them more easily in America than in almost any other place.

Reasons for the Rejection of Property Rights

How did America get to the point where the feudal approach to property came to seem, at least in some ways, more just than the Founders'?

Three leading arguments against property rights have been advanced in the twentieth century.

First, it is denied that there is a fundamental right to acquire and possess property. On the contrary, property is often conceived as the *enemy* of liberty. Property owners are said to be a "special interest" seeking to exploit, defraud, and oppress the people. The only way that property and liberty can be made compatible, in the new view, is to hem in property and redistribute money from rich to poor by means of pervasive government regulation and high taxes.

Second, private ownership of property was no longer regarded as an adequate way to promote economic growth. Government controls and planning were thought to be the best directors of an efficient and flourishing economy. For example, government took over the management of the farm economy in the 1930s because it became convinced that market failure is a necessary feature of capitalism.

Third, private property is said to be corrupting. This belief can be found on both the left and the right. Liberal historian Richard Hofstadter argues that the Founders' scheme promoted rapacious self-interest: "While they thought self-interest the most dangerous and unbrookable quality of man, they necessarily underwrote it in trying to control it. . . . [U]nder the competitive capitalism of the nineteenth century America continued to be an arena for various grasping and contending interests." Similarly, some conservative scholars argue that according to Locke (and presumably also the American Founders), "the individual's uninhibited pursuit of economic self-interest is both morally legitimate and conducive to the common good—a view directly contrary to that of both classical and biblical morality." In other words, a government that protects acquisition of private property is the enemy of religion and moral virtue.[51]

These are serious charges. We will confront them in the pages that follow.

Are Property Rights Unfair to the Poor? Early Arguments

An early blast against the Founders' understanding was J. Allen Smith's polemic, *The Spirit of American Government* (1907). The Constitution, Smith wrote, "aimed rather to protect the property and privileges of the few than to guarantee personal liberty to the masses. . . . Liberty, as the framers of the Constitution understood the term, had to do primarily with property and property rights," not with personal liberty. The Constitution was "planned and set up to perpetuate the ascendancy of the property-holding class" at the expense of "individual liberty as guaranteed by majority rule." Personal liberty and democracy, Smith implied, are incompatible with property rights.[52]

Smith's book was written in an angry, partisan tone. Historian Charles Beard made Smith's argument respectable in his enormously influential 1913 book, *An Economic Interpretation of the Constitution*. In a seemingly neutral tone, Beard presented what he called a "long and arid survey" of the property holdings of the members of the Constitutional Convention of 1787. He concluded that most members of the Convention were "immediately, directly, and personally interested in, and derived economic advantages from, the establishment of the new system." Beard left his readers with the strong impression that a narrow-minded, arrogant, and wealthy ruling class had written the Constitution to advance their private interests at the expense of the public good and the common people.[53]

President Franklin D. Roosevelt, a child of the Progressive Era, adopted a similar view of property rights. However, he knew better than to attack the Founders head-on. In his 1936 renomination acceptance speech, he praised the Founders for their successful war against "political tyranny" in 1776. But property rights, he argued, eventually resulted in "economic tyranny": "A small group has concentrated into their own hands an almost complete control over other people's property, other people's money, other people's labor—other people's lives." Against the rights of private property Roosevelt proposed to use "the organized power of government." A vivid sign of this was Roosevelt's proposal for a 99.5 percent income tax on all earnings over $100,000 per year. This was a complete reversal of the Founders' view that all people, even those who are successful, should be allowed to keep the honest fruits of their own industry.[54]

During the emergency atmosphere of the Great Depression, this new approach made sense even to many traditionally minded Americans. However, it gradually became clear that Roosevelt had initiated a revolution both in constitutional government and in the American conception of individual rights. After the much more radical reforms of the 1960s and 1970s, gov-

ernment controls over property became so thorough that nominal ownership of property often became meaningless. Businessmen complained that
"every single aspect of business activity requires seeking the approval of one
or more government agencies." This trend affected not only big businesses
but also small proprietors, farmers, and individual homeowners.

There is in fact a consistent argument behind today's liberalism, which
I call the New Liberalism, following John Dewey's distinction between new
and old liberals.[55] According to Dewey, who was probably the most influential theorist of the New Liberalism, the Founders' conception of human
rights is grossly inadequate. They were wrong in thinking that human rights
are absolute, based on an unchanging human nature: "Natural rights and
natural liberties exist only in the kingdom of mythological social zoology."
For Dewey, there are no absolutes. There is only progress or reaction.

Dewey also thought the Old Liberals were wrong in their belief that
"there are two different 'spheres' of action and of rightful claims; that of
political society and that of the individual," and that government should
stay out of the private sphere as much as possible. Instead, Dewey said that
government must overcome the Old Liberal public-private distinction. In
particular, Dewey wanted government to take control of private property,
because "private control of the new forces of production . . . would operate in the same way as private unchecked control of political power." That
is, it would be tyranny. The Founders thought that within the limits just
mentioned, life should be permitted to go on spontaneously in families,
neighborhoods, and local communities. Dewey thought that a just social
order "cannot be established by an unplanned and external convergence of
the actions of separate individuals." Only "organized social planning, put
into effect for the creation of an order in which industry and finance are
socially directed" will allow liberalism to "realize its professed aims." "In
short, liberalism must now become radical." The method of "intelligence
and experimental control" must become "the rule in social relations and
social direction."[56]

At the heart of Dewey's liberalism was his belief in "historic relativi-
ty," his conviction that there is no permanent human nature. "The real difficulty [with the Founders' perspective] is that the individual is regarded as
something *given*, something already there." For Dewey, the individual is
always made by some historical context but is nothing in himself. "[S]ocial
arrangements, laws, institutions . . . are means of *creating* individuals. . . . Individuality in a social and moral sense is something to be wrought out." Man
is capable of being socially constructed in many ways.

Dewey's notion, and his revolt against the liberalism of the founding,
goes back through Hegel to Rousseau, who was the first to suggest that

man has no definite nature but only the quality of malleability.[57]

If man on his own is nothing, two things follow, according to Dewey. First, man does hardly anything on his own; self-reliance and individuality are largely illusory. Qualities like "initiative, inventiveness, varied resourcefulness . . . are not gifts, but achievements." Even intelligence is not "a ready-made possession of individuals." That is because the social order, not nature, produces these qualities. "[T]he state has the responsibility for creating institutions under which individuals can effectively realize the potentialities that are theirs." That means there must be something like a cradle-to-grave welfare state, financed by government supervision of production and distribution of wealth. Second, there are no natural or divine standards defining the right way of life for man. Ideals and religions are fictions. There are no permanent, objective standards of right and wrong.[58]

To say with Dewey that man in himself is nothing is another way of saying that he is essentially a victim or essentially disabled. Here is the source of the New Liberal preoccupation with victimized groups. If we have no inherent inner resources, we must have been socially constructed to dominate or submit. Without intending to, says Dewey, the Founders made a world of "coercions and repressions that prevent multitudes from participation in the vast cultural resources that are at hand."[59] Without the help of government, some people will be exploited, wither, and die. Others, through no merits of their own, will end up on top.

It is not enough for government to protect people against obvious attacks by others. It is not enough for government to support strong families but otherwise leave people alone and require others to leave them alone. For Dewey, it is precisely when people are left alone that they are most vulnerable. Dewey and early liberals like Franklin Roosevelt worried most about the power of big business over the working man. Today liberals focus on women, racial minorities, and the disabled. The analysis in both cases is the same.

Lincoln and the Founders believed that all human beings are "disabled" and "victims" in the sense that nature and circumstances keep us from doing everything we might wish. But the Old Liberals also saw in human nature qualities like reason, self-control, ambition, pride, and spirited self-assertion. They thought that if government protects lives and properties from being taken away by others, most people will be able to take care of themselves and their families.[60] Lincoln's remedy for slavery was not affirmative action or public welfare but opportunity for all people, white and black, to keep the bread they earn with their own hands.

The story "The Little Engine That Could" illustrates the Founders' view perfectly. The weak train engine convinces herself ("I think I can") that she can carry the toys over the mountain to the children on the other side. The moral: virtues like perseverance and self-restraint in the face of the temptations of pain or pleasure enable us to perform the jobs of life, even when it looks like our disabilities might prevent us.[60]

Are Property Rights Unfair to the Poor? Recent Arguments

Jennifer Nedelsky, a scholar who is an explicit critic of the Founders, would replace the natural rights of Madison and the Founders with an ideal of "human autonomy." She argues, correctly, that the view of rights preferred by today's liberals requires the abandonment of the natural rights theory of the Founders: "The egalitarian vision [of today] is practically a reversal of this founding conception: whether the inequality of property is the result of liberty or not, it stands in the way of liberty and justice for all."[61]

What Nedelsky means is brought out in a case that she discusses, *Harris v. McRae.* In that decision the Supreme Court ruled that the Constitution does not give women a right to government-funded abortions. The dissenters from the decision asked, What good is the right to abortion for a poor woman who cannot afford to pay for it? Justice Brennan wrote:

> The Hyde Amendment's denial of public funds for medically necessary abortions plainly intrudes upon this constitutionally protected decision, for both by design and in effect it serves to coerce indigent pregnant women to bear children that they would otherwise elect not to have.

Thurgood Marshall's dissent agreed:

> If . . . a funded abortion is unavailable, [poor women] must resort to back-alley butchers, attempt to induce an abortion themselves by crude and dangerous methods, or suffer the serious medical consequences of attempting to carry the fetus to term. . . . [L]egal abortion is not a significant option for such women.[62]

In other words, if government fails to fund a right, one cannot be said to have the right.

Extending the argument beyond abortion, one must ask: How can a person be said to have a right to life if she is too poor to afford a doctor? Is one's right to pursue happiness secured without government-funded education from kindergarten to postgraduate work? How can a person living in poverty "pursue happiness"? This way of thinking about rights culminates, as Nedelsky frankly admits, in the demand for a redistribution of wealth so that all possess sufficient property to secure their "autonomy." Had this Brennan-Marshall view prevailed on the Court, it would have become "unconstitutional" in principle to cut back on any aspect of the welfare state. In fact, it would have given the Supreme Court the "constitutional" authority to mandate indefinite expansion of government programs redistributing the entire wealth of the nation. It would have become "unconstitutional" for government to allow those who have acquired property through their own efforts to keep the property they earned.

The Supreme Court majority in the *Harris* decision, says Nedelsky, "saw that once we acknowledge that some basic rights can only be enjoyed with state economic support, we have left the boundary of negative liberty behind (and, of course, further redistributive incursions on property are likely to follow)."[63] She regrets that the Court failed to repudiate the "negative liberty" of the Founders. The Court came within one vote of doing so in this case.

In the new conception of rights, liberty requires not just protection against being injured by others but "affirmative action," positive aid from those who have wealth to those who do not. At the extreme, one scholar claims a global human right to subsistence and basic material needs, for which wealthy nations ought to pay.[64] In the 1970s John Rawls gave a sophisticated argument in support of the position that those in need have a moral right to some of the possessions of those who are well off. Rawls argues that society must "regard the distribution of natural talents as a common asset." Contrary to Madison's claim that "the first object of government [is] the protection of different and unequal faculties of acquiring property," Rawls argues that unequal abilities should be socialized and redistributed by law. "There is no more reason to permit the distribution of income and wealth to be settled by the distribution of natural assets than by historical and social fortunes. . . . No one deserves his greater natural capacity nor merits a more favorable starting place in society."[65]

On the basis of Rawlsian ideology, today's laws and courts routinely force businesses and governments to pay injured individuals and make special provisions for the disabled even when the organization is not responsible for the injury or disability. In one typical lawsuit, a small business was held legally liable for the injury suffered by a car thief when he wrecked the car he had stolen from the business in an accident that admittedly resulted from his own negligence.[66]

In this New Liberal understanding, which has become increasingly influential in the course of the twentieth century, rights are no longer derived from human nature. Instead, a new ideal, which Nedelsky calls *autonomy*, in which man is liberated from the restraints and guidance of nature and reason, holds sway. This autonomy, far from being something that human beings possess by nature, can be secured only on the basis of a high degree of civilization. It requires the conquest of nature by human will. Rights are no longer conceived as a gift of God and nature. The ideal of human autonomy is created by the human will. The realization of that ideal requires that those who have intelligence, ambition, sobriety, wealth, and education be compelled to support those who do not have the same talents or fortunes. Rights derive, not from what one has in common with other human beings (the same human nature), but from what makes one inferior to others—victimization. Instead of all having the same rights to life, liberty, and property, rights now pertain to one's class. The poor have the right to be supported by those who work, and working people have the duty to support the poor.

Are Property Rights Unfair to the Poor? The Founders' Response

The rights of human nature, as the Founders saw it, are based on what man is and has by nature—his life, his liberty, and his ability to acquire property and pursue happiness. For the Founders, a right to decent housing—let alone a right to recreation—would be unintelligible. Yet those were among the new rights proclaimed by Franklin D. Roosevelt in his "second Bill of Rights."[67] A natural right is something one has by nature and deserves to keep. No one by nature possesses food, learning, and free access to medical care. No one by nature possesses the kinds of resources and autonomy demanded by Nedelsky. For the Founders, the fact that we lack these things does not give us a right to demand them of others. We are free to work for such things for ourselves and our families. But we *are* obliged by nature to leave other people alone in their reasonable pursuit of health, education, and property.

The presumption of the Founders is that normal human beings are capable of taking care of themselves, if only the artificial weight of legal privileges and restrictions—the legacy of medieval times—is removed. "The political philosophy behind limited government," writes Harvey Mansfield, "affirms that nature is more important than nurture: that humans have a fixed nature enabling them to overcome a background of poverty and deprivation."[68]

The Founders' doctrine of rights requires limited government: there is a realm of private life that government must respect and stay out of. This is

the distinction between state and society, public and private, that character-
izes American constitutionalism. The new view of rights obliterates that
distinction. As long as anyone is in want, government has the right and, if
it is feasible, the duty to intervene and supply the need. Trust in the capacity of individuals and private associations like families, businesses, and
churches to take care of everyday needs is replaced by distrust of the traditional family, business, and religion and trust in the expertise and good faith
of government bureaucrats.

These views and practices arise from a rejection of the Founders'
view that the origin of the rights of man lies in the rightful condition of
equal liberty. In the Founders' view, those who have more are not
required to give up their possessions to those who have less, except in the
case of the truly needy (see the chapter on welfare). Nor are they required
to give up their liberty to government experts. That was the European
system of aristocracy and kingship from which they were attempting to
free themselves.

Although the Declaration says we have a right to life and liberty, it
does not say we have a right to happiness. Unlike life and liberty, happiness
is not something we possess by nature. We cannot claim it as a right whenever we are miserable. Likewise, there is a right to acquire and possess property, but no right to be wealthy. Everyone has the capacity to *acquire* wealth
and *pursue* happiness, just as everyone has the capacity to live, be free, and
worship God. To possess a right, even to exercise it, does not guarantee that
it will lead to the end desired. Happiness is earned by talent and effort, or
enjoyed unbought through grace or good fortune.

All human beings by nature do possess life, liberty, the ability to pursue happiness, the ability to acquire property, and a mind that forms opinions by reason and conviction. These natural possessions, the "property" we
all own by nature, are the principal rights of man. Madison said:

> In its larger and juster meaning, it [property] embraces everything to
> which a man may attach a value and have a right; and which leaves to
> everyone else the like advantage. . . .
>
> In the latter sense, a man has a property in his opinions and the free
> communication of them.
>
> He has a property of peculiar value in his religious opinions, and
> in the profession and practice dictated by them.
>
> He has an equal property in the free use of his faculties and free
> choice of the objects on which to employ them.
>
> In a word, as a man is said to have a right to his property, he may
> be equally said to have a property in his rights.[69]

Is Private Property Inefficient?

Jefferson thought he had stated the undeniable common sense of the matter when he wrote, "Were we directed from Washington when to sow, and when to reap, we should soon want bread."[70] Yet it was widely believed during the twentieth century that government knows better than private individuals what should be produced, how, when, and in what quantity.

The farm policy introduced in the 1930s is a classic example. Farmers lobbied government, arguing that they could not flourish on their own. Government set up offices in farm communities all over the country to help them farm. It forbade them to plant certain crops at certain times. It subsidized production of some commodities, on the understanding that the market was inherently destructive of certain farm interests. It set the prices of oranges, peanuts, milk, and many other products.

Many other areas of the economy, such as banking, broadcasting, production of electricity, airlines, and railroads, have also been subjected to extensive government control.

In recent years, many have called for an American "industrial policy" to enable government officials to direct the investments of major industries into more prudent courses than the industries would choose on their own.

The Founders had responded to all these claims in advance. In general, the right to private property, wrote Madison, "encourage[s] industry by securing the enjoyment of its fruits." Founder James Wilson, author of *Lectures on Law*, the fullest account of property among the Founders, explains: "By exclusive property, the productions of the earth and the means of subsistence are secured and preserved, as well as multiplied. What belongs to no one is wasted by every one. What belongs to one man in particular is the object of his economy and care." Wilson cited the disastrous experiment with socialism in the early American colonies of Jamestown and Plymouth:

> During seven years, all commerce [in Plymouth] was carried on in one joint stock. All things were common to all; and the necessaries of life were daily distributed from the public store. . . . The colonists were sometimes in danger of starving; and severe whipping, which was often administered to promote labor, was only productive of constant and general discontent. . . . [T]he introduction of exclusive property immediately produced the most comfortable change in the colony, by engaging the affections and invigorating the pursuits of its inhabitants.[71]

In a famous passage of *The Federalist*, Hamilton makes the same point more crassly, perhaps even with a comic touch. Praising commerce, he writes:

> By multiplying the means of gratification, by promoting the introduc-
> tion and circulation of the precious metals, those darling objects of
> human avarice and enterprise, it serves to vivify and invigorate all the
> channels of industry and to make them flow with greater activity and
> copiousness. . . . [A]ll orders of men look forward with eager expecta-
> tion and growing alacrity to the pleasing reward of their toils.[72]

Defenders of property rights today often appeal to this argument for
efficiency and economic growth. In contrast, this was always a secondary
argument for the Founders. They defended the right above all because it is
just, because it is part of liberty, and because it is an indispensable condition
of free government.

Is Private Property Corrupting?

Earlier we quoted liberal historian Richard Hofstadter, who complained
that by protecting property rights America's Founders unleashed on their
own country degraded and degrading self-interest. Conservatives with aristocratic taste complain that nobler sensibilities are ignored and contemned
in a regime dominated by democratic commercialism. Certainly each of
these views has something to be said for it. But what, our Founders would
ask, is the alternative?

John Adams had a sensible appreciation of what was gained and what
lost in the choice for democracy and commerce. Speaking of the effect of
democracy on the people, he wrote, "That ambition which is inspired by
it makes them sober, industrious, and frugal. You will find among them
some elegance, perhaps, but more solidity; a little pleasure, but a great deal
of business." In *Democracy in America* Tocqueville presents an extended
contrast of the habits, attitudes, and manners of life produced by aristocracy and democracy, and the tone of his picture expresses a lingering
regret for the loss of aristocratic refinement, beauty, and greatness. Adams
also understood the vast difference between these ways of life, but he
spoke of the aristocratic way without Tocqueville's old-world taste for its
amenities:

> A monarchy . . . would produce so much taste and politeness, so much
> elegance in dress, furniture, equipage, so much music and dancing, so
> much fencing and skating, so much cards and backgammon; so much
> horse racing and cockfighting, so many balls and assemblies, so many
> plays and concerts that the very imagination of them makes me feel
> vain, light, frivolous, and insignificant.[73]

The point is that every regime has its particular manner of life, its particular virtues and vices. Commerce is potentially corrupting, but it can also contribute to the virtues of republican citizenship.

A few pages back I quoted a scholar who argues that Locke's theory of politics allows "the individual's uninhibited pursuit of economic self-interest." Whatever Locke may have thought, this was not the theory of Jefferson, Adams, and the other Founders. They believed that a system that guaranteed property rights would promote genuine morality, including, as we will see, the virtues taught by the classics and the Bible. And they would have denied that the American system allows an uninhibited pursuit of economic interest. Franklin stated the common sense of the matter in this way: "those vices that arise usually from idleness are in a great measure prevented. Industry and constant employment are great preservatives of the morals and virtue of a nation."[74]

The necessity to provide for oneself and one's family, together with wide-open opportunity to earn money, encouraged habits of sobriety, thrift, and industry.

Legally, the pursuit of money was moderated through most of American history by the requirement to pay debts, keep contracts, support one's family, and stay out of economic activities like prostitution and pornography that undermine the morals of society. Informally, business owners upheld the public morals by refusing (up to the 1960s!) to rent hotel rooms to unmarried couples; by giving preference to heads of households in their hiring decisions; by being loyal to longtime employees even after their usefulness had declined.

The Founders were wise enough to know that property is not an unambiguous good. Jefferson worried that "From the conclusion of this [Revolutionary] war we will be going down hill." The people "will forget themselves, but in the sole faculty of making money." Adams (and most of the other Founders) shared this concern. He wrote to Jefferson in 1819:

> Without virtue, there can be no political liberty. . . . Will you tell me how to prevent riches from being the effects of temperance and industry? Will you tell me how to prevent riches from producing luxury? Will you tell me how to prevent luxury from producing effeminacy, intoxication, extravagance, vice, and folly?[75]

Hamilton was also aware of the problems created by freedom:

> True liberty by protecting the exertions and talents of industry, and securing to them their justly acquired fruits, tends more powerfully than

any other cause to augment the mass of national wealth and to produce the mischiefs of opulence.

Hamilton acknowledged the difficulty, but then posed this sensible question: "Shall we therefore on this account proscribe liberty also? . . . Tis the portion of man assigned to him by the eternal allotment of Providence that every good he enjoys shall be alloyed with ills, that every source of his bliss shall be a source of his affliction—except virtue alone."[76]

This concern over the ills of a commercial society was hardly the Founders' last word.

For James Wilson, property ownership fosters the qualities needed for republican citizenship as well as other "virtues of civilized life":

> On property some of the virtues depend for their more free and enlarged exercise. Would the same room be left for the benign influence of generosity and beneficence—would the same room be left for the becoming returns of esteem and gratitude—would the same room be left for the endearing interchange of good offices, in the various institutions and relations of social life, if the goods of fortune lay in a mass, confused and unappropriated?

Aristotle had made a similar observation in his criticism of Socrates' proposed communism in Plato's *Republic*.[77]

In his *Notes on Virginia* Jefferson spoke of the virtues, fostered by farming, that are necessary for republican liberty:

> Those who labor in the earth are the chosen people of God, if ever he had a chosen people, whose breasts he has made his peculiar deposit for substantial and genuine virtue. . . . Corruption of morals in the mass of cultivators is a phenomenon of which no age nor nation has furnished an example. It is the mark set on those who, not looking up to heaven, to their own soil and industry, as does the husbandman, for their subsistence, depend for it on the casualties and caprice of customers.

Dependence on customers "suffocates the germ of virtue, and prepares fit tools for the designs of ambition." In a letter, Jefferson listed additional virtues of the farming life: "The moderate and sure income of husbandry begets permanent improvement, quiet life, and orderly conduct both public and private."[78]

Jefferson's praise of farmers was no doubt exaggerated, but he had a point. A profession that is self-subsistent surely promotes the virtues he names, although even in early America farmers were much more dependent on customers than Jefferson admitted. Virginia farmers could not eat their tobacco, the state's leading crop. Besides, he was wrong to think that other kinds of productive labor would not foster many of the same qualities of character that he praised in farmers.

We may add to these lists other virtues appropriate to a free people that are also nourished by protection of the right to acquire: honesty (because credit is indispensable in commercial transactions), sobriety (or the job will not be done well), frugality (to save in order to buy property or invest), civility (to please the boss and customers), self-restraint (to prevent one's capital from being squandered), and justice (to enable lawful satisfaction of one's needs through labor).

Property rights promote public as well as private virtues. A commercial economy built on the right to acquire will produce substantial wealth, a major component of national strength. Hamilton anticipates in *Federalist* No. 11 the growth of America, in part through its commercial spirit, to a "dangerous greatness" (as Europe would view it) from which it will one day "vindicate the honor of the human race, and teach that assuming brother [i.e., Europe] moderation." National wealth is a condition of national greatness as well as independence. As much as Jefferson longed for America to remain a simple republic of virtuous but poor farmers, even he could not help but admit that if America were to be free and civilized, it had to be commercial. After the War of 1812 he wrote:

> He, therefore, who is now against domestic manufacture, must be for reducing us either to dependence on that foreign nation, or to be clothed in skins, and live like wild beasts in dens and caverns. I am not one of these: experience has taught me that manufactures are now as necessary to our independence as to our comfort.[79]

Property ownership also calls forth nascent public spirit, as Tocqueville recognized:

> It is difficult to force a man out of himself and get him to take an interest in the affairs of the whole state. . . . But if it is a question of taking a road past his property, he sees at once that this small public matter has a bearing on his greatest private interests, and there is no need to point out to him the close connection between his private profit and the general interest.[80]

Today, Americans are often taught that money comes not from work and enterprise but from government programs and special privileges to which only the wealthy have access. That belief causes the virtues called forth by private property to give way to an ethic of dependency, characterized by sloth, envy, quarrelsomeness, lawlessness, resentment, and self-indulgence. The destructive effects of public housing on neighborhoods clearly illustrates this tendency. When homes and apartments are privately owned, tenants who vandalize them will be quickly evicted. Landlords who want the highest rent they can get have an incentive to keep their properties clean and neat. When good housing comes only through private ownership, citizens have a strong incentive to work, to obey the law, and to behave decently in order to acquire the money to buy. Pride in ownership and desire for comforts elicit the qualities of individual responsibility that make good citizens. Public housing undermines these traits, and the result is decay and slums.[81]

We should not fail to note Hamilton's celebration, in his 1791 *Report on Manufactures*, of productive effort for its own sake. A robust economy, he wrote enthusiastically, offers "greater scope for the diversity of talents and dispositions which discriminate men from each other." For Hamilton, human life was enriched not just monetarily but in regard to its proper end when its capacities were led into their proper work.

> To cherish and stimulate the activity of the human mind, by multiply-
> ing the objects of enterprise, is not among the least considerable of the
> expedients, by which the wealth of a nation may be promoted. Even
> things in themselves not positively advantageous, sometimes become so,
> by their tendency to provoke exertion. Every new scene, which is
> opened to the busy nature of man to rouse and exert itself, is the addi-
> tion of a new energy to the general stock of effort.[82]

Hamilton also praised "the spirit of enterprise," the daring self-asser-tion of great commercial leaders, as an admirable virtue that allows the martial qualities of soul, formerly associated only with war, to display them-selves before the world and receive their due honor. The world war that defeated Hitler and the cold war victory over communism are testimony to the accuracy of Hamilton's farsighted vision. America's capacity for great deeds that will be long remembered rests in considerable measure on her enormous wealth, the fruit of a long history of commerce and enterprise. The nation also profited from the entrepreneurial and independent spirit that won the day in the Normandy invasion, when many officers were killed in the early going and lowly lieutenants and sergeants took the ini-tiative and sustained the fight.[83]

A regime of property rights may lack the noble aspirations of a regime of self-denial. But in practice, it may promote public and private virtue more successfully than any alternative.

3

Women and the Right to Vote

*S*cholars today often lump together the Founders' treatment of women, slaves, and other supposedly oppressed groups. One feminist historian writes that "the American Revolution produced no significant benefits for American women. This same generalization can be made for other power-less groups in the colonies—native Americans, blacks, probably most prop-ertyless white males, and indentured servants."[1]

From this we would expect to learn that the Founders showed no concern for any of these "powerless groups." But their denunciations of slavery were frequent and eloquent, and, as we saw in chapter 1, dramatic antislavery actions followed. In a later chapter we will see that "property-less white males" also benefited from the Revolution. Over 90 percent of free males were eligible to vote soon after the ratification of the Constitution. By the 1820s most states had instituted near-universal suffrage for male citizens. Yet when we look for similar expressions of concern by the Founders about women, we find silence. Even more surprising from today's standpoint is that the women of that era had few complaints.

It is not only radical feminists who deplore the Founders' supposed indifference to women's rights. Mainstream textbooks also paint a gloomy picture. "When Jefferson spoke [in the Declaration of Independence] of 'the people,'" writes Lorna Mason in her eighth-grade history textbook, "he meant only free white men." Cummings and Wise's *Democracy under Pressure*, a college political science text, says, "And today, two centuries later, . . . women in America are still struggling for the full freedom and equality denied them by the framers." No effort is made in these books to understand how the Founders could have viewed women as equal without guaranteeing them the right to vote. Instead, it is assumed that the Founders were insincere or confused when they professed that all human beings have the same rights. Or else it is denied that they believed in equality at all.[2]

Historian Linda Kerber provides a twist on this view:

When in 1848 Elizabeth Cady Stanton came to write the Declaration of Sentiments for the New York Women's Rights Convention in Seneca Falls, she shaped it as a direct echo in form and substance of the Declaration of Independence. . . . There had been a blind spot in the Revolutionary vision. The promises of the Revolution had not been explored for what they might mean to women. The obvious way to make this point was to write a parallel declaration; to ask what the Declaration of Independence might have been like had women's private and public demands been included.[3]

Richard Bushman writes similarly in the *Reader's Guide to American History:* "The great changes [in women's rights] came later, when the implications of revolutionary principles were more fully recognized."[4]

On the surface, this latter approach appears to be generous toward the Founders: we cannot blame them for being born in a bigoted age. But actually it damns them. It says that they really did not understand the rights of humanity that they talked so much about. The Founders, in this view, were slaves to the ruling prejudices of their age, unable to recognize facts about equality that any schoolchild understands today. This way of thinking about the Founders rests on the premise of *historicism,* the claim that all human beings always have been, and always will be, imprisoned in a point of view peculiar to their time. But if the Declaration of Independence is true, historicism must be false, for the Declaration's argument rests on truths that claim to be eternal. As Lincoln said, "The principles of Jefferson are the definitions and axioms of free society . . . , applicable to all men and all times."[5]

Unlike Kerber's and Bushman's, our account of the Founders takes seriously their claim to have dedicated themselves to the rights of humanity. Although Kerber is correct in stating that the Seneca Falls Declaration echoed the Declaration of Independence, almost everything else she says is wrong. "The promises of the Revolution" were definitely "explored for what they might mean for women." This exploration led to important modifications of the patriarchal family as Americans had inherited it from England (see chapter 4). Nor were the Founders deaf to "women's private and public demands." There simply were no significant demands by women—not for voting rights, not for the right to preach in church, not for the abolition of different moral standards for men and women, and not for any of the other things demanded at Seneca Falls in 1848. In truth, the one thing that large numbers of women did demand at the time of the Declaration was the same thing that men demanded: the overthrow of the British attempt to govern the American colonies without their consent.

When we condemn the Founders for failing to live up to the principles of the Revolution, we assume that their idea of liberty is at heart the same as ours, even if they did not really understand it. That is why Gordon Wood writes that the ideas of the Revolution "made possible the anti-slavery and women's rights movements of the nineteenth century and in fact all our current egalitarian thinking."[6] With regard to slavery and voting rights, this view is more or less true. But the men and women of the founding era almost completely disagreed with today's feminist view—even the nineteenth-century feminist view—of women's rights and women's equality.

Many people today think women's liberty and well-being are better secured when the law allows for complete sexual freedom and treats men and women the same, and when women are encouraged to compete with men in the job market. The Founders thought laws allowing sexual license, ignoring the real differences between the sexes, and not just allowing but pushing women into the job market threatened women's liberty and well-being.

In the 1970s and 1980s, the Founders' view of women seemed indefensible. It was dismissed as obsolete and condemned as unjust. By the 1990s, the growing exploitation, abuse, neglect, and impoverishment of women could no longer be overlooked. Scholars and popular writers began to revive the case for the traditional family. It is now possible to reexamine the Founders' view of women without the blinding effect of the typical modern prejudice that we have all the answers.

Women and Men: Created Equal

Before we proceed, we must get past the most common misconception. Gordon Wood, a leading historian of the political theory of the founding, writes: "What was radical about the Declaration in 1776? We know it did not mean that blacks and women were created equal to white men (although it would in time be used to justify those equalities too). It was radical in 1776 because it meant that all white men were equal." James MacGregor Burns's college American government textbook is typical of many: "the Declaration . . . refers to 'men' or 'him,' not to women."[7]

It is easy to show that Wood and Burns are wrong.

The word "men" in the Declaration means mankind, human beings, male and female, of whatever color or race. That is obvious from parallel expressions commonly used during the founding era: "rights of men," "rights of man," "rights of mankind," "rights of humanity," "rights of human nature," "human rights," "rights of nature." Not one Founder denied that blacks were human beings. Still less did they, or could they, deny that women were human beings. Hamilton said what was generally believed: "Natural liberty is a gift of the beneficent Creator to the whole human race."[8] Women therefore have the same natural rights as men.

In his *Notes on Virginia*, Thomas Jefferson, the author of the Declaration, reproaches the Indians for failing to acknowledge this equality: "The [Indian] women are submitted to unjust drudgery. This I believe is the case with every barbarous people. With such, force is law. . . . It is civilization alone which replaces women in the enjoyment of their natural equality." Jefferson says "replaces" because barbarism deprives women of the equal rights with which they are born. Jefferson had in mind such things as historian Francis Parkman reports of the Indians: "Female life among the Hurons had no bright side. . . . On the march it was she who bore the burden; for, in the words of Champlain, 'their women were their mules.'" Civilized men, in Jefferson's view, do not abuse their superior natural strength. They treat women as free beings, not as slaves compelled to toil for their male masters. It is civilization that "first teaches us to subdue the selfish passions, and to respect those rights in others which we value in ourselves. Were we in equal barbarism, our females would be equal drudges."[9]

Today few would agree with Jefferson that women "enjoyed their natural equality" in the 1780s. Historian Kenneth Stampp states the conventional wisdom in his high-school history textbook: early American men "would not accept them as equals."[10] It is true that women did not have the same legal rights as men. In spite of this—as we will see in the next chapter, partly *because* of it—Jefferson's claim is defensible.

The U.S. Constitution: Hostile to Women's Rights?

A leading college government textbook states bluntly that the Framers of the Constitution of 1787 were indifferent to the rights of women. They "generally never even gave a thought to what we today call civil rights, the powers or privileges guaranteed to individuals and protected by law from arbitrary infringement."[11]

This claim is indefensible. In fact, whenever the Constitution speaks of "*privileges* guaranteed to individuals," women are always included by clear implication. Or are we to assume that the constitutional guarantee of "the *privilege* of the writ of habeas corpus" means that women (but not men) may be imprisoned without being charged with a specific crime? May ex post facto laws be passed as long as women but not men are their object? Are state laws "impairing the obligation of contracts" permitted when contracts are signed by women but not when they are signed by men? Obviously not.

Contrary to the impression we are often given, there is no mention of males anywhere in the U.S. Constitution. In this respect the Constitution differs from some other documents of the period. For example, the Constitution bases representation on "the whole number of free persons," not male persons, whereas the Northwest Ordinance, passed by Congress in 1787, says that "for every five hundred free *male* inhabitants there shall be one representative" to the assembly of a western territory. And in the 1780 Massachusetts Constitution "every *male* person" who satisfies certain requirements has the right to vote for the state house of representatives.[12]

It is true that the Constitution says of the president that "He shall hold his office during the term of four years." But this *he* is the generic, not the male, pronoun. For the Bill of Rights uses the same pronoun when it says, "No person . . . shall be compelled . . . to be a witness against *himself*." No one has ever maintained that this *himself* means that only males are protected by the Bill of Rights and that women may be compelled to be witnesses against themselves. The language of the Constitution includes women as well as men.

The Constitution of 1787 dealt with the right to vote by turning the matter over to the states. Whoever votes for the most numerous branch of the state legislature is also a voter for the House of Representatives (art. 1, sec. 2). As was the case with blacks, not one word of the Constitution had to be changed for women to obtain the vote. Indeed, also as with blacks, some women were already voting at the time the Constitution was adopted. Large numbers of women were voting in several states before the Nineteenth Amendment was finally approved in 1920.[13]

The Right to Vote: New Jersey

James MacGregor Burns's *Government by the People* has gone through fifteen editions, but it still mistakenly claims that "All states [in 1787] barred women from voting." Other textbooks mention that some women voted, only to dismiss the fact as irrelevant.[14] But it is of the highest importance for understanding the Founders' view of the matter.

The most remarkable case was that of New Jersey. It shows that, on this question at any rate, the Founders were hardly the bigots they have been made out to be. Women voted in large numbers in that state during the late 1790s and early 1800s.[15]

The New Jersey state constitution of 1776 stated that "all *inhabitants* of this colony, of full age, who are worth fifty pounds proclamation money, . . . and have resided within the county . . . for twelve months . . . shall be entitled to vote." Some historians speculate that this language was accidental, and that those who wrote it meant *males*. This is guesswork. There is little evidence on either side. We do know that New Jersey's 1790 revision of its voting law dutifully implemented the constitution's literal "all inhabitants" by referring to voters as "he or she." A 1796 law governing voting in federal elections, used the same language: "No person shall be entitled to vote in any other township or precinct, than that in which *he or she* doth actually reside. . . . Every voter shall openly, and in full view, deliver *his or her* ballot. . . ."[16] Neither of these laws aroused any particular opposition or controversy.

We must pause briefly and note the extraordinary character of this event. For the first time in history, the women of a political community shared with men the right, stated in public law, to select their rulers. There can be only one explanation of why it happened in the United States at this particular time, and in no other country at any previous time. Most Americans, including the members of the New Jersey legislature, believed in the fundamental principle of the Revolution, that all men are created equal. No other government had ever been grounded on this idea. This belief by itself was not enough to bring about female suffrage. But it made it thinkable as an option, while it had been unthinkable for most of human history. Historians have shown that partisan calculations led New Jersey politicians to take advantage of the gender-neutral wording of the state constitution and bring women to the polls in growing numbers.[17] But partisan motivations over the previous three thousand years of Western history had never led to such a result. Clearly, a new idea—the equality idea—changed the terms of what was politically possible. A further sign of this is that female voting generated little controversy in New Jersey for some years.

We know that at least some New Jersey women voted in the year of the Constitutional Convention. Historian Richard McCormick writes, "A Burlington poll list of 1787 contained the names of Iona Curtis and Selveria Lilvey, presumably women."[18] The first newspaper discussion of female voting in New Jersey did not occur until 1797, when the Federalist candidate in a hotly contested election to the state legislature was supported (unsuccessfully) by the women of Elizabethtown. In the Adams-Jefferson presidential election of 1800, and in other subsequent elections, women voted in large numbers throughout the state.

Strictly speaking, only women (and men) who owned property were eligible to vote under the New Jersey law. That meant single women or widows. Married women were not counted as property owners because property within a marriage was legally credited to the husband. In practice, however, the property qualification for voting was carelessly enforced. Married women and even female slaves were often admitted to vote.[19]

In 1800 the New Jersey Assembly considered a law that would have stated, "the inspectors of elections shall not refuse the vote of any widow or unmarried woman of full age." One representative wrote: "The House unanimously agreed that this section would be clearly within the meaning of the [New Jersey] Constitution, and as the Constitution is the guide of inspectors, it would be entirely useless to insert it into the law. The motion was negatived. Our Constitution gives this right to maids or widows, black or white." It was later said that the votes of two or three women of color swung the election of a state legislator in 1802.[20]

Female voting came to an end in 1807. A close electoral battle between Newark and Elizabeth over the location of a new courthouse inspired massive voting fraud on both sides. Women (and of course men) were in the thick of it. "Women and girls, black and white, married and single, with and without qualifications, voted again and again." This episode became the excuse for an 1807 law that restricted the franchise to free white males. This law directly violated New Jersey's constitution, which the courts thereafter dishonestly refused to acknowledge. The representative who promoted the new law most vigorously was the same Jeffersonian Republican who had nearly been defeated in 1797 by the Federalist women of Elizabeth.[21] One partisan pamphleteer had complained that "towns and populous villages [where Federalists had greater strength] gain an unfair advantage over the country by the greater facility they enjoy over the latter, in drawing out their women to the election."[22]

Women also voted elsewhere in America during the founding era. Robert Dinkin, a historian of early American voting, writes, "Records from a few Massachusetts towns show that a number of widows who owned substantial property did exercise the franchise on occasion" during the colonial period. A New York newspaper reported that "two old widows tendered, and were admitted to vote" in 1737.[23] Records are sparse, so it is likely that other incidents of female voting occurred in these and other states, both before and after the Revolution.

Men and Women: Common Interest?

Commenting on the New Jersey episode, historian Edward Turner noted, "There is no evidence that women ever sought to gain or retain the right to participate in elections, and subsequently they accepted their exclusion with indifference." What explains this indifference? It is a common feminist view today that the women of the past unconsciously participated in their own oppression because their outlook on the world had been socially constructed by male dominance. As Sandra Bartky writes, "The values of a system that oppresses us . . . take up residence inside our minds."[24] But this begs the key question: Were women oppressed during the founding era?

In 1807 most Americans of both sexes thought that women were well represented by their men whether they voted or not. Women were indifferent to voting rights because they did not think their husbands, fathers, and brothers had an interest opposed to their own. The women of New Jersey were quite willing to vote when they had the chance. But they did not protest when they were no longer permitted to vote after 1807.

The early American assumption that men and women have, or believe they have, a common interest seems to be confirmed by male-female voting patterns after women began voting in 1920. For many decades, the only divergence between men and women was a slight female preference for Republicans, which lasted until 1964. According to an early survey, 3 percent more women than men favored Harding for president in 1920. In presidential elections from 1948 to 1960, the Republican was favored by more women than men by an average margin of about 3.5 percent. (Contrary to a common belief, that includes the election of 1960; if women alone had voted, Nixon would have defeated Kennedy.) In 1964 there was virtually no gender gap. By 1968 women voted more Democratic than men by a 2 per cent margin. This gap widened to 6 percent in 1984, and it has remained close to that ever since (it was 6 percent in 1996).[25]

But even here the statistics are misleading. In 1996, a Wirthlin poll found that married women split their vote evenly (44 percent each) between presidential candidates Dole and Clinton. However, working women—a category that includes large numbers of single women, divorcees, and widows—supported Democrat Clinton over Republican Dole by a 21 percent margin, according to the Voter News Service exit poll; Clinton's lead among widows and divorced women was even higher, 33 percent. It is *unmarried* women who account for most of the much publicized "gender gap." In other words, this gap is really a "marriage gap," not a gender gap. It is a gap not so much between the sexes as between women who (for the most part) enjoy the support of a husband and women who (for the most part) are potentially or actually dependent instead on government. Pollster Kellyanne Fitzpatrick, commenting on the fact that some women voted heavily Democratic in 1996, said that "women see government as their insurance."[26]

Since the late 1960s the American tradition of lifelong marriage has been in decline. In 1970, only 3 percent of the population over age seventeen was divorced; by 1995, that figure had tripled to 9 percent. In the same twenty-five-year period, the percentage of adult Americans who had never married rose from 16 to 23 percent.[27] It was in this context of widespread marital breakdown that large numbers of women voters began to perceive their interest to be different from men's.

The Right to Vote: The Founders' Arguments

Modern historians bristle with indignation over the absence of female voting rights in earlier American history. But in New Jersey, no agitation led to women's voting rights, and no agitation followed their demise. It is fair to conclude that the men as well as women of the founding generation viewed female voting as an option that was permitted but by no means required by the principle that all men are created equal. Since women did not vote in most states, and eventually lost the vote in New Jersey, it is also fair to conclude that the Founders leaned against it.

What argument could have led them to this conclusion that we today find so surprising or dismaying?

In 1764, James Otis became the first American of the founding era to discuss women's rights in print. Musing upon the idea of equality, he wrote, "Are not women born as free as men? Would it not be infamous to assert that the ladies are all slaves by nature? . . . [In] a state of nature, . . . had not every one of them a natural and equitable right to be consulted in . . . the formation of a new original compact or government?"[28] In principle, Otis was saying, the answer had to be yes. This follows from the idea of equal natural liberty, which means that no one, male or female, has the right to rule another without that other's consent. There are no natural masters or natural slaves.

Feminist historian Linda Kerber comments, "Although Otis could raise embarrassing questions and imply their answers, on this as on so many points of theory, his developing mental illness prevented him from suggesting constitutional devices for implementing them."[29] Kerber assumes that Otis's questions obviously point to female voting rights. She assumes that he failed to reach this conclusion because of his deteriorating mental health. But almost all of the men and women of the founding generation believed that all men and women are created equal. And they all rejected the inference that equal natural rights requires equal voting rights. Surely they were not all mentally ill! Before condemning them, we must try to understand them.

As a practical matter, no Founder believed that every individual in society had to vote in order for government to be based on consent. No one today believes it either. Texas, for instance, denies the vote to those who are incapable of giving a rational vote (the mentally incompetent and children), those who are not full members of the community (resident aliens), and those who have turned against the community and are deprived of the vote as a punishment (convicted felons).

In addition to these easy cases, the Founders believed that the right to vote ought to be limited to those who are in a position to cast their vote freely and deliberately. That is why they often favored a requirement that voters own property or at least pay taxes, as we will see in the chapter on the property requirement for voting. Hamilton quotes Blackstone to explain:

> "If it were probable that every man would give his vote freely, and without influence of any kind, then, upon the true theory and genuine principles of liberty, every member of the community, however poor, should have a vote. . . . But since that can hardly be expected, in persons of indigent fortunes, *or such as are under the immediate dominion of others,* all popular states have been obliged to establish certain qualifications, whereby, some who are suspected to have no will of their own, are excluded from voting; in order to set other individuals, whose wills may be supposed independent, more thoroughly upon a level with each other."[30]

The italicized words refer to women and older children; the exclusion of married women from voting rests on the same basis as the exclusion of children and the propertyless poor. Women's votes are likely to follow those on whom they are financially dependent, their husbands. John Adams wrote:

> Such is the frailty of the human heart, that very few men who have no property, have any judgment of their own. They talk and vote as they are directed by some man of property, who has attached their minds to his interest. . . . [M]en who are wholly destitute of property . . . [are] to all intents and purposes as much dependent upon others, who will please to feed, clothe, and employ them, as women are upon their husbands, or children on their parents.[31]

Poor males soon successfully challenged this belief. It became evident that in a country like America, with wide-open opportunity for everyone to acquire money, there was little of the kind of dependency of the poor on the wealthy that Blackstone, Hamilton, and Adams feared. But because of the division of labor within the household, the dependency of women on men was great. Their judgments, for this and other reasons, were presumed to be similar to those of the men on whom they depended. Hamilton and Adams implied that to give wives the vote was in effect to double the vote of their husbands.

A few men of the founding generation believed that the principles of the Revolution might include voting rights for women. Daniel Dulany, in a widely read pre-Revolution pamphlet, wrote:

> But that the reader may perceive how strictly the principle of no person's being taxed without their consent hath been regarded [by Britain in the past], it is proper to take notice that upon the same occasion writs were likewise directed even to women who were proprietors of land in Ireland to send their deputies to consult and consent.[32]

Writing in 1803, St. George Tucker, a Virginia professor of law, had no difficulty with this reasoning:"With regard to the property of women, there is taxation without representation; for they pay taxes without having the liberty of voting for representatives; and indeed there seems at present no substantial reason why single women should be denied this privilege."[33]

Richard Henry Lee, a prominent Virginia Founder, agreed that "no taxation without representation" *could* mean that unmarried women should vote. He wrote to his sister:

> You complain that widows are not represented [in the Virginia legislature]. . . . The doctrine of representation is a large subject, and it is certain that it ought to be extended as far as wisdom and policy can allow; nor do I see that either of these forbid widows having property from voting, notwithstanding it has never been the practice either here or in England. . . . [I] would at any time give my consent to establish their right of voting.

But Lee argued that this right was in any event not necessary, "seeing that the representatives themselves, as their immediate constituents, must suffer the tax imposed in exact proportion as does all other property taxed. . . . This, then, is the widow's security as well as that of the never married woman, who have lands in their own right."

Lee admits, as Carol Berkin and Leonard Wood's high-school history textbook points out, that the American Revolution fought against this very thing, "virtual representation." A leading claim of Americans against the British in the decade leading up to independence was that taxation and other laws may rightfully be imposed on people only by themselves or by deputies of their choice. The British had replied that Americans were *virtually* represented in Parliament; the members of the House of Commons could be trusted to look out for the common good of the whole British Empire. To which the Americans answered: to rule someone without that person's consent is to make that person one's slave. Representation can only be by elections, in which the governed choose their rulers by periodic vote.

Lee therefore attempted to answer the objection that women cannot be "virtually represented" by their husbands, fathers, and brothers because they do not vote. He wrote:

> When we complained of British taxation we did so with much reason, and there is great difference between our case and that of the unrepresented in this country. The English Parliament nor their representatives would pay a farthing of the tax they imposed on us but quite otherwise. Their property would have been exonerated in exact proportion to the burdens they laid on ours.[34]

Lee's argument makes sense as long as the issue is taxation, which affects all property owners equally. But what about laws that affect women differently from men, for example, the very laws that denied women the right to vote? Can women be said to be "virtually represented" with respect to these kinds of laws? In this case, are not women in the same situation as the Americans who complained of being taxed by a British parliament in which they could not vote for representatives?

Lee does not answer these questions. But the implicit answer of the Founders generally, including Lee, was that marriage and children create a community of love and interest that protects women far more effectively than the right to vote. We will see in the next chapter that they had good reasons for holding this view of the family.

The Right to Vote: Changing Circumstances

In one sense, the family as most Americans know it today has not changed much in two hundred years. Three out of four American children still live in households headed by a married husband and wife. Women still perform the bulk of household duties. Many stay home with their children when the children are young. The hard-driving married career woman so conspicuous on television and in the movies is still the exception. True, only 32 percent of married women participated in the labor force in 1960, while 61 percent did in 1995. But this figure includes women who worked as little as one hour per week or "15 hours or more as unpaid workers in a family enterprise" during the week of the survey. Only one-third of married women work full time, and many of those are childless or have grown children.[35]

Yet in another sense, family life has been revolutionized. The domestic work of the family has been much reduced over time because of stunning advances in technology, wealth, medicine, and nutrition.

During the founding era running a household was a full-time job for most women. They had none of the machines that make domestic life today so much more convenient. Everything took longer. There were no cars or supermarkets. Food had to be prepared from scratch. There were no refrigerators. Clothes had to be washed by hand, and water carried in and heated on the stove. Nor could Americans in 1776 expect to live long. Children often died young. So did their parents. A woman might have to bear six or eight children to raise three or four to adulthood. Many years of a mother's life would be consumed in household tasks and the personal supervision of the very young.

In this sterner world, childrearing and the way of life that goes with it—called by Adams a "retired mode of life," and characterized in another founding era document as exclusion from "promiscuous intercourse with the world"—occupied for many women the whole of their adult life.[36] Most women of the late 1700s were confined by a necessary division of labor to a life that really did separate them from the world of politics.

As America grew wealthier, women bore fewer children, machines and gadgets eased the labor at home, and better health opened up many years of life after children. Women had more time to pursue interests beyond the confines of the home. Without neglecting their families, they got more involved in the affairs of their communities. With these changing circumstances, the original arguments against women's voting seemed less compelling. The right to vote was granted to women by Wyoming as early as 1869. It was secured for all women by the Nineteenth Amendment in 1920. For similar reasons, women eventually came to serve on juries and legally to own property on the same terms as men. In these respects, the modern movement for equal political rights for women is fully compatible with the founding principles. But the question remains: Are traditional sex roles in the family and in the job market compatible with the Founders' dedication to equal rights, or does the family stand in the way of genuine equality?

We will answer that question in the next chapter.

4

Women and the Family

$\mathscr{I}$n the last chapter, we saw that the Founders' principles are compatible with voting rights for women and that changes in circumstances since the late eighteenth century made female voting more practicable. But we also saw that the women as well as men of the founding period placed the family first, in the belief that family integrity was indispensable for the public safety and happiness. Underlying this was the view that there are natural differences between the sexes, differences that correspond to the traditional gender roles in the family. Today, few American universities would knowingly hire a professor who agreed with this. At least one has fired a professor who did.[1] In this chapter, we will try to understand the Founders' view of women and the family, not as it is so often caricatured and therefore easily dismissed today, but as they understood it themselves. And we will show that the findings of current social science research support the Founders' views.

The Differences between Men and Women: The Founders' View

Today it is often said that the Founders believed women "lacked . . . rationality" (philosophy professor Morton White). According to another scholar, they held that higher education for women was "beyond their intellectual capacity." An eighth-grade history textbook asserts bluntly, "Women were thought to be . . . less intelligent than men." Historian Marc Kruman writes that "Women were excluded [from the vote] because of a presumed incapacity for sound reasoning."[2] All these writers are incorrect.

Founder James Wilson wrote unequivocally that women are "neither less honest, nor less virtuous, *nor less wise*" than men. However, women's intelligence was thought to be of a different character than men's. Wilson quoted with approval the poet Milton's line on man (as opposed to woman): "For contemplation and for valor he was formed." And indeed, the superior male aptitude for mathematical and abstract reasoning has been established in numerous recent scientific studies. So also has the superior female aptitude in accurate assessment and manipulation of people's emotions and motives and in "everything requiring verbal fluency and articulation."[3]

But the reality of female intelligence does not mean that there are no politically relevant differences between the sexes. Richard Henry Lee's letter to his sister, part of which we quoted in the previous chapter, alluded to one of the chief traits traditionally identified as feminine: "Perhaps 'twas thought rather out of character for women to press into those tumultuous assemblages of men where the business of choosing representatives is conducted." Lee is referring to women's disinclination to engage in pushing, shoving, combat, and other forms of direct and open competition or explicit aggressiveness. John Adams expanded on this in a 1776 letter:

> But why exclude women [from voting]? You will say, because their delicacy renders them unfit for practice and experience in the great businesses of life, and the hardy enterprises of war, as well as the arduous cares of state. Besides, their attention is so much engaged with the necessary nurture of children, that nature has made them fittest for domestic cares.[4]

A more authoritative expression of the consensus in the founding era is the *Essex Result*. This was an official statement of Essex County, Massachusetts, on a proposed 1778 state constitution. As in the Adams letter, here too women's *equal* "mental powers" are distinguished from the *difference* between the feminine and masculine temperaments and the manner of life that follows from that difference:

> Women what age soever they are of, are also considered as not having a sufficient acquired discretion [to vote]; not from a deficiency in their mental powers, but from the natural tenderness and delicacy of their minds, their retired mode of life, and various domestic duties.[5]

Men, in contrast, were expected to display the more active and assertive virtues. James Madison wrote in *The Federalist* that American liberty rests on "the vigilant and manly spirit which actuates the people of America—a spirit which nourishes freedom, and in return is nourished by it." The opposite of this spirit was "effeminacy." Washington, for example, feared the "luxury, effeminacy, and corruptions" caused by foreign commerce. The Founders did not condemn effeminacy because they were antifemale. A predominance of feminine qualities *in men* meant weakness. It meant being dependent on others. In a nation, it meant possible enslavement by another nation. The Declaration of Independence says with pride that Americans opposed "with manly firmness his [the King's] invasions on the rights of the people." John Adams spoke of the American need to cultivate "all great, manly, and warlike virtues."[6] If women are naturally "fittest for domestic cares," as Adams claims, then men are fittest for nondomestic activities like politics and war.

Today, these supposed differences between men and women are dismissed as stereotypes.Some believe that such differences are merely imaginary and deny that they exist at all. Others admit that the differences are real, but they say that the differences are rooted not in nature but in what is called "the social construction of gender." We will see that the best of the latest research supports the opinion of the Founders.

Ideological Equality versus Natural Equality

Sociologist Edward Kain is typical of today's conventional wisdom. He believes that if girls prefer dolls over guns, it is because "parents reinforce sex-appropriate play behavior in their children, . . . and provide sex-stereotyped toys as early as their first year of life." If men outperform women in intensely competitive jobs, it is because children "develop into masculine and feminine human beings, based on the definitions of masculinity and femininity found in their particular culture." Kain believes in the social construction of gender, or cultural determinism—the idea that differences in human conduct have little or no relation to natural differences but are created by society.[7]

Carl Degler's *In Search of Human Nature* describes the rise of this idea in American social thought. Typical of its devotees was Margaret Mead, the most famous anthropologist of the century. She once wrote that "many, if not all, of the personality traits which we have called masculine or feminine are as lightly linked to sex as are the clothing, the manners, and the form of head-dress that a society at a given period assigns to either sex." This twentieth-century belief in cultural determinism—"decoupling behavior from nature," Degler calls it—was motivated, he argues, by ideology. There was a strong desire among social scientists to prove that the sexes are naturally similar in every respect, out of a belief that this was required by "equality."[8]

This ideological equality, which denies and tries to destroy natural differences, is totally opposed to the natural equality of the Declaration of

Independence, which recognizes and protects the equal rights, and therefore the natural differences, of all. The purpose of a government based on equal rights, as Madison said in *Federalist* No. 10, is "the protection of . . . the different and unequal faculties" or abilities of each citizen. This diversity, Madison believed, is "sown in the nature of man." A free society will therefore be built on a division of labor, not only among individuals of different talents, but also between the sexes, insofar as each sex has its typical talents and inclinations.

The view that sex differences are caused by environment and society is still widely accepted among journalists and intellectuals who are driven by the dominant ideological approach of the twentieth century. But Degler points out that there has been a growing reaction against that approach in the last thirty years, especially among neo-Darwinians looking into connections between biological differences and evolutionary survival strategies. These researchers have returned in some degree to the position of the American Founders.

The Differences between Men and Women: Recent Research

The feminist former chairman of Stanford University's Psychology Department has written:

> (1) Males are more aggressive than females in all human societies for which evidence is available. (2) The sex differences are found early in life, at a time when there is no evidence that differential socialization pressures have been brought to bear. . . . (3) Similar sex differences are found in man and subhuman primates. (4) Aggression is related to levels of sex hormones, and can be changed by experimental administrations of these hormones.

In other words, many of the old stereotypes about men and women are true. Solid evidence for this is found in hundreds of recent scientific studies, conveniently summarized in Ann Moir and David Jessel's *Brain Sex: The Real Difference between Men and Women.*[9]

One of the most dramatic of these studies comes from the psychohormonal research unit of the Johns Hopkins University Hospital and School of Medicine. A group of girls had been accidentally exposed to high levels of male hormones (androgens) before birth, as a result of an antimiscarriage drug taken by their mothers. The girls were brought up in typical family environments. Yet they proved to be "significantly different from their matched controls" (girls of the same race, intelligence, and socioeconomic background but with normal hormones). This 1972 study proves that the differences between men and women are based on nature, not only socialization.

1. Nature points most women toward, and most men away from, the care of small children. The androgen-exposed girls showed a "lack of interest in infants. . . . Some girls in this group distinctly disliked handling little babies and believed they would be awkward and clumsy. By contrast, many of the control girls rated high in enthusiasm for little children . . . and took every opportunity to get in close contact with them." In spite of being brought up as girls, the male hormones made them act like stereotypical boys in their lack of interest in babies and small children.

2. By nature, men are more likely than women to gravitate toward technical expertise and full-time careers. The androgenized girls "differed from their matched controls in the preferred toys of childhood. They were indifferent to dolls, or openly neglectful of them. They turned instead to cars, trucks, and guns, and other toys that traditionally belong to boys. . . . Lack of interest in dolls later became a lack of interest in infants." As they got older, the majority of them "subordinated marriage to career, or else wanted an occupational career other than housewife concurrent with being married." For most of the control girls, on the other hand, "marriage was the most important goal of their future."

3. Most women naturally shy away from the intense, overt competition that leads to success in the job market and war. Most of the Hopkins girls exhibited what researchers call "tomboyism." "The common denominator of many tomboyish activities in girls is a high level of physical energy expenditure, especially in the vigorous outdoor play, games, and sports commonly considered the prerogative of boys." The control girls had little interest in athletic play and "preferred to play with other girls."

4. By nature, women care far more than men about being attractive to others. The androgenized, tomboyish Hopkins girls "preferred the utilitarian and functional in clothing, rather than the chic, pretty, or fashionably feminine," the preference of the control girls to whom they were being compared.[10]

Unintentionally confirming the Hopkins study, Israeli kibbutzim in the 1950s and 1960s attempted perhaps the most serious effort ever made to eliminate gender roles in a society. Children and adults of both sexes wore the same clothes and were assigned the same tasks. The children lived and slept together in common areas and played with the same toys. But as the years went by, the traditional sexual differences began to assert themselves. Adolescent girls insisted on undressing in the dark and kept their living areas cleaner. They preferred indoor work, such as staffing the children's living quarters, and courses like psychology. Boys were more aggressive, gravitated toward studies like physics, and took on the harder farming jobs. The adult women opened a beauty parlor. Men began to dominate in the leadership roles in the commune. The sociologist who chronicled this transformation later wrote:

> As a cultural determinist, my aim in studying personality development in Kiryat Yedidim in 1951 was to observe the influence of culture on human nature or, more accurately, to discover how a new culture produces a new human nature. In 1975 I found (against my own intentions) that I was observing the influence of human nature on culture.[11]

We should not fail to mention the undeniable difference between women and men in physical strength, a difference far greater than is generally believed. This difference is particularly striking in the bodily skills required in war. In a Navy study, only one woman in one hundred was able to carry the P–250 pump used to put out fires on shipboard; 96 percent of men could. Not one woman was able to meet minimal standards for the MK–82 bomb lift used in naval aviation; 50 percent of men could. Only 3 percent of women meet the same military physical fitness standards as the average man. In Army basic training, women sustain five times as many limited days due to injury as men do. This is not even to mention the weakening effect of pregnancy.[12]

It is obvious, of course, that not all women share the typical characteristics of their sex. Nor do all men. The Hopkins girls had "male" brains in their female bodies because of a drug their mothers took; but some women are born that way. As girls they are aggressive tomboys. As adults they often become hard-driving career women. One study of twenty-five women in top management positions found that as children all twenty-five had been tomboys. The authors of this study try to explain away these girls' tomboyism as a product of their fathers' encouragement, but the *natural* inclination and talent of the girls for intense physical activity, vigorous outdoor play, and aggressive competitiveness shine through.[13]

The Founders were aware of such exceptions. Although some occupations, such as law, were closed to women at that time, all single and most married women were free to start their own businesses or work for whoever was willing to hire them. Many women remained single and did both. They were involved in most professions during the founding era.[14]

In spite of such occasional exceptions, recent research strongly supports the Founders' view that "nature has made [women] fittest for domestic cares" and that women are naturally suited for, and generally (not always) prefer, a "retired mode of life" centering in the household.

Is the Family Good?

Most people who are honest with themselves will remember many instances confirming the natural tendencies of male and female nature that we have described here, among both children and adults. Those who deny them are often surprised to find that these tendencies assert themselves in spite of every effort to bring up children in a gender-free environment. A comical instance: One New York feminist who refused to buy her daughter a doll returned home one day to find her giving her toy trucks a bath.[15]

These tendencies can easily be seen to be compatible with the traditional division of labor in the family. In pre-1960s America, wives primarily concerned themselves with bearing and tending children and managing the internal affairs, as well as the emotions, of the household. Husbands were expected to devote themselves to protecting the family and acquiring the money it needs, as well as serving as the moral guide for the children, especially the boys, as they got older. They were viewed as the essential and trusted link between the family and the outside world.

The question remains, however, whether the family, with its traditional division of labor, is good for women and children—and men. Many people today consider any affirmation of the "nurturing role of the mother"— a foundation of the family—"as a threat to the liberation of women."[16]

When the Founders used the word family, they meant above all a married couple and their children. The Founders rarely discussed the virtues of the family, because the subject was not controversial. Men and women alike agreed with Founder Benjamin Rush: "To be the mistress of a family is one of the great ends of a woman's being."[17] Likewise, to be the master of a family was considered good for a man, and to be brought up by one's married biological parents good for a child.

Today these views are highly controversial. Indeed, since the 1960s the family has often been portrayed as a breeding ground of pathology and oppression. "There are many reasons for the high rate of violence in families," writes sociologist Murray Straus. "One of the most fundamental is that families actually train people to be violent." According to Straus, "the marriage license is a hitting license" and spanking is "training in violence" that "lays the basis for child abuse and wife-beating."

For psychoanalyst Alice Miller, the structure of the traditional family "could well be characterized as the prototype of a totalitarian regime." The fact that Germans "had received what is considered a good, strict upbringing" contributed, she maintains, to the rise of Hitler and Nazism. Her 1983 book, *For Your Own Good,* was popularized by John Bradshaw's *The Family* (1988), which in turn inspired a multitude of self-help books in the 1990s.

Stephanie Koontz summed up the new consensus in *The Way We Never Were: American Families and the Nostalgia Trap* (1992). Speaking of families in pre-1960s America, she writes: "Beneath the polished facades of many 'ideal' families . . . was violence, terror, or simply grinding misery that only occasionally came to light."[18]

As we will see, recent research shows that the truth is almost the exact opposite of what these writers say.

Is the Family Good for Women?

Sociologist Murray Straus, whom we just quoted, writes that "a typical citizen walking down the most dangerous street in Lincoln, Omaha, or Chicago is safe compared to being in an average American home." Let us see.

The U.S. Department of Justice conducts a National Crime Survey, in which thousands of crime victims are interviewed every year. The survey demonstrates beyond any doubt that the "average American home" (a home whose core is a married man and woman) is by far the safest place for a woman to be. "Intimates" (defined in the survey as boyfriends, ex-boyfriends, husbands, and ex-husbands) indeed often are a threat, but primarily to unmarried, separated, or divorced women. "Intimates" victimize divorced women more than eight times as often as married women, and separated women thirty times as often. Further, if we look at all crimes of violence against women, not just those committed by "intimates," we find that the advantage again goes to married women living with their husbands. Never-married and separated women are victimized by violent crime almost four times as often as married women; divorced women are victimized over seven times as often.[19]

Surveys indicate that particularly high rates of violence between "intimates" occur among lesbians. One study reported, "In response to the question, 'Have you ever been abused by a female lover/partner?'; slightly more than half of all respondents replied in the affirmative." Another survey of

350 lesbians who had previous lesbian and heterosexual relationships reported substantially higher rates of victimization by their former female partners than by their former male partners. Sociologist Lettie Lockhart remarks on the "silence and denial surrounding lesbian violence," perhaps, as various social scientists speculate, because of "the well-meaning liberal position that lesbian couples are just like heterosexual couples" or because "the reality of lesbian battering" is threatening to the "dream of a lesbian utopia—a nonviolent, fairly androgynous, often separatist community struggling for social justice and freedom for themselves and other oppressed groups."[20]

The connection between intact marriage and nonviolence is not hard to understand. In today's America, sex has no necessary connection to lasting love, and marriage is optional. Women are encouraged to give themselves to their lovers and then, if they like, to trash them like yesterday's newspaper. While the lovers are together, both partners know that the relationship may end at any moment. With no formal commitment to the future, there is far less incentive to restrain oneself in dealings with one's partner or to make sacrifices for the common good.

Further, a woman who rejects a man to whom she has once given herself, often cutting off access to his child as well, almost always provokes his anger. As a glance at the once rare but now all too common newspaper stories of the murder of women shows, this kind of anger often leads to violence. When the laws and customs discouraged divorce and condemned sex and childbearing outside marriage, occasions for jealous rage were far less common than they are today. Men who assault women consistently report "feeling powerless in respect to their intimate partners"— and so they are, in a world where people treat these deep longings of the soul so lightly.[21]

The separation of sex from love, and love from marriage, is therefore a perfect recipe for violence against women.

Marriage is good for women, however, not primarily because it protects them from violence, but above all because it is closely connected with their happiness. Historian Jan Lewis has shown that the popular magazines of the founding era were full of articles, written by both men and women, celebrating "Matrimonial Felicity" (the title of one such piece). Jefferson, whose wife had died, frequently contrasted his situation, in the midst of the bitter party politics of the 1790s, with the happiness of marriage and family. Shortly after her marriage, he wrote to his daughter Mary:

> Without an object here which is not alien to me, and barren of every
> delight, I turn to your situation with pleasure in the midst of a good

family which loves you, and merits all your love. Go on, my dear, in cultivating the invaluable possession of their affections. The circle of our nearest connections is the only one in which a faithful and lasting affection can be found.

In a later letter he wrote, "it is in the love of one's family only that heartfelt happiness is known." Abigail Adams expressed her happiness in marriage in one of many loving letters to husband John: "Well ordered home is my chief delight, and the affectionate domestic wife with the relative duties which accompany that character my highest ambition."[22]

The pleasures and benefits of marriage, even when it is less than perfect, stand out in contrast with the pain of divorce and single motherhood. Single and divorced women with children also have much higher poverty rates than married women. Divorce as a solution for marital difficulties has proved to be much less emotionally satisfying for women (and men) than it is believed to be. A researcher who interviewed over one hundred divorced men and women reports that ten years after divorce, "life has been far more difficult than most imagined it would be." Many reported "second divorces, chronic loneliness, poor relationships with their children, or enduring feelings of betrayal and abandonment." Finally, marriage is good for women because it enables them to have their children provided for by a man who loves them as an extension of his own being, as opposed to a judge, bureaucrat, boyfriend, or ex-husband who scarcely cares.[23]

Is the Family Good for Children?

Recent studies back up the Founders' view that children are happiest, and best educated in heart and mind, when they are raised by their married biological parents.

Children do best when they have a mother and a father because men and women complement each other in the way they treat their children. Mothers tend to focus on physical and emotional needs; fathers on character traits such as self-discipline, self-reliance, and willingness to take risks. David Blankenhorn sums up the difference: "My mother loves me unconditionally because I am her child. My father loves me, but he tends to make me work for it. Lucky is the child who receives both varieties of parental love." And when parents practice what they preach, children acquire the moral qualities they will need to be citizens of a free country. For John Adams, the "foundation of national morality must be laid in private families. . . . How is it possible that children can have any just sense of the sacred obligations of morality or religion, if, from their earliest infancy, they learn that their mothers live in habitual infidelity to their fathers, and their fathers in as constant infidelity to their mothers?" Hardly anyone of the Founders' generation would have disagreed.[24]

The 1988 National Health Interview Survey of Child Health found that "young people from single-parent families or stepfamilies were 2 to 3 times more likely to have had emotional or behavioral problems than those who had both of their biological parents present in the home." Other studies show that illegitimacy and divorce are specifically associated with children's poor school performance, poor self-control, drug abuse, criminality, and incapacity to provide for themselves and form stable marriages when they become adults. Allan Bloom observed that bright college students who are emotionally scarred by their parents' divorces also often lack the intellectual daring needed for penetrating thought. Professor Leon Kass writes, "Countless students at the University of Chicago have told me and my wife that the divorce of their parents has been the most devastating and life-shaping event of their lives." Therapist Andre Derdeyn confirms this observation: "Those of us who conduct psychotherapy continue to hear the anger, pain, and longing associated with separation and divorce of parents. Our patients focus on the separation, long for parental contact and caring, and often consider the divorce as the major event of their childhoods."[25]

Immediately after a divorce, children typically suffer intense grief, fear, anger, and a shaken sense of identity. Even five years later, after escaping the supposedly unhappy household and settling into a new arrangement, only one-fourth of children approve of the divorce. After ten years, serious emotional and behavioral problems persist. Typical children of divorce first lose touch with their fathers, who become "treat dads" disconnected from their children's moral formation, or else disappear altogether from their lives, instead of providing their children with affirming love, moral guidance, and discipline. Later the children's bond with their mothers often deteriorates as well.[26]

The absence or breakdown of marriage appears to be the single leading cause of child abuse. We can see this whether we look at the past or the present. Historian John Demos has shown by a careful analysis of court records and other sources that child abuse in colonial New England was extremely rare. That, of course, is when families were governed according to principles that are widely rejected today.[27]

The U.S. Department of Health and Human Services' 1993 Incidence Study of Child Abuse reported that "children of single parents were at higher risk of physical abuse and of all types of neglect and were overrepresented among seriously injured, moderately injured, and endangered children."

Compared with children living with both parents, these single-parent children had a "77-percent greater risk of being harmed by physical abuse," an "87-percent greater risk of being harmed by physical neglect," and a "120-percent (or more than two times) greater risk of being endangered by some type of child abuse or neglect."[28]

Children who do not live with their married biological mothers and fathers are in greater danger not only in single-parent households but also in stepparent families. Psychologists Martin Daly and Margo Wilson found that "preschoolers in stepparent–natural parent homes" were "40 times as likely to become abuse statistics as like-aged children living with two natural parents." Abuse rates were 19 times as great for children five to ten years old, and 10 times for eleven- to seventeen-year-olds. (In this study, children living with adoptive parents were not found to be at greater risk of abuse.)[29]

Who is doing the abusing? As the fairy tales used to say, stepparents are more frequent abusers than married biological parents. The study just quoted reports that in households where both stepchildren and natural children of the perpetrator were present, the stepchild, not the natural child, was almost always the victim. Other studies have found very high rates of abuse by mothers' boyfriends against the mother's children. Birth parents are also more abusive when there is no spouse present. In the 1986 Second National Family Violence Survey, single mothers reported "a 71 percent greater rate of very severe violence toward their children than did mothers in two-parent homes"; and "the rate of severe and very severe violence toward children was higher among single fathers than among single mothers."[30]

If we look at sexual abuse in particular, the patterns are the same. A 1985 national survey found that boys were "primarily at risk in two family constellations: when they lived with their mothers alone or with two non-natural parents." Girls "showed markedly higher risk under all family circumstances except that of living with two natural parents." University of Iowa researchers found that the risk of sexual abuse was about six times greater for children living with stepfathers than for those living with their biological fathers, and about four times greater for children living with stepmothers than for those living with biological mothers.[31]

Day care and babysitters, often used in single-parent and dual-career households, have been found by many studies to have the same negative effect on young children as divorce and single-parenthood, although to a lesser degree. Social scientists have found that day-care children are "more anxious, aggressive, and hyperactive" than those cared for at home by their mothers. They are less willing to trust and obey their parents and other adults. They tend to withdraw emotionally from others and to have trouble making friends. They are also "less persistent in dealing with a difficult problem." In a study of third-graders, extensive infant care outside the home "was the single best predictor (in a negative direction) of children's peer relationships, compliance, work habits, emotional health, sociometric status, and report card grades." These problems occur with children of all social classes, in both high-quality and low-quality day care as well as with in-home sitters.[32]

Finally, when children are raised by divorced, separated, or unmarried women, they lack their father's moral guidance and discipline. They are less likely to develop habits of self-restraint and a conscience to back up such habits. Boys raised without fathers are statistically far more likely to become violent criminals—and therefore to become abusers of women and children. Unmarried mothers today often live in communities where many other mothers are also unmarried, and that means they live among a substantial population of predatory men. Thus abused single mothers unleash the next generation of abusers upon each other's daughters and daughters' children—and upon each other.[33]

Is the Family Good for Men?

John Adams wrote to Abigail Smith, just before their marriage, "You shall polish and refine my sentiments of life and manners, banish all the unsocial and ill natured particles in my composition." Modern research confirms that single and divorced men are far more likely than married men to live in an irresponsible, aimless, and destructive manner. Married men work harder and are more future-oriented than single men. Bachelors have much higher rates of almost every social ill on which statistics are kept: criminal behavior, victimization by crimes, unemployment, disease, mental disorders, drunkenness and drug addiction, suicide, and even rates of accidents.[34]

I regret that I must recite the data in this and the previous two sections in such a cumbersome way. But what else can one do when facts that the Founders felt little need to discuss are so widely denied in our time? Future scholars looking back at us will wonder how the nature of family life could have become so widely misunderstood, especially by those with the most extensive educations. These observers of the future will see easily what seems so hard for us: much of today's research either proves the obvious in some laborious manner or, as we saw in the case of Murray Straus, distorts the facts in order to make the case against the traditional family. The common sense of the Founders—and, for that matter, of Aristotle—is vindicated by much of this research.[35]

Legal Supports for the Family in the Founding Era

From the time of the founding until relatively recently, laws were written to support stable family life. The marriage contract was not treated like an employment contract, where the employer may terminate or the employee may quit without cause. It involved promises binding the will of the contracting persons long into the future. It said, in effect, that if you want sexual intimacy, it must be with a person of the opposite sex, and you must agree to stand by your partner for life.

There were many reasons for this requirement, but the most important is that the family was viewed as a basic element of a good society. Although individuals were free to choose not to marry, it was thought that marriage was the best institution for the vast majority. Further, sex often leads to the birth of a person—a child—whose interest is not identical to the sometimes selfish interests of one or both of its parents. This is particularly true of the father, whose attachment to children is by nature less strong than that of the mother, as the Hopkins study showed. The child cannot be consulted when the marriage contract is made; but once he is born, he needs love, protection, and support, and no one (including trained social workers) is as motivated to provide these things as his married biological parents. James Kent, a prominent early American legal writer, explained:

> The wants and weaknesses of children render it necessary that some person maintain them, and the voice of nature has pointed out the parent as the most fit and proper person. The laws and customs of all nations have enforced this plain precept of universal law. . . . The obligation of parental duty is so well secured by the strength of natural affection, that it seldom requires to be enforced by human laws.[36]

Today we must add that this "natural affection" declines when a parent's (usually a father's) connection to his children is weakened by divorce or failure to marry.

For these reasons, the Founders were mostly libertarian in the area of property and the economy. They expected that consenting adults could be generally trusted to look out for their own interests when it came to labor, employment, and other money dealings. And once a marriage was contracted, they were also quite libertarian in the regulation of family members in their dealings with each other, as we will see, except for serious injury proved in court. They did not want government officials second-guessing parents and spouses in the internal affairs of the family. But the Founders were quite moralistic (as we would say) when it came to sex and marriage. The law placed strict limits on anything that might prevent appropriate marriages from taking place or that might lead to family breakup. They thought that individuals could be trusted with considerable freedom in private life to take care of themselves and their children, but only in a society where strong families are the norm

People get married and stay married for four main reasons:

- the *happiness* that comes from love, sex, security, familiarity, children, and governing a household within an institution that embodies mankind's aspiration toward enduring and permanent love

- the *usefulness* of the partners to each other and to their children in bearing and raising children, in cooking, cleaning, and other domestic cares, in making money and providing protection, and taking care of each other in old age

- the *moral teaching* of religion and reason, both of which affirm the connection between lasting marriage, respect of parents by children, and care of children by parents

- the *social and legal supports* for marriage, including social disapproval (dishonor, shame, and exclusion from polite society) for sex and childbearing outside marriage, and, in earlier times, the constraints of the law, which forbade no-fault divorce, abandonment of a spouse, and sex outside marriage

Clearly, the law cannot by itself produce the passions and convictions that make for enduring marriages. But it can weigh in on the side of these four considerations by supporting healthy desires and opinions. As John Adams wrote, "Reason holds the helm, but passions are the gales. . . . [T]he passions . . . should be gratified, encouraged, and arranged on the side of virtue [by the law]." The following are some of the ways in which the Founders put the law to work on behalf of family integrity.[37]

Definition of marriage. The law allowed marriage of a man and a woman only. Same-sex "marriages" were excluded because it went without saying that the purpose of marriage is not primarily love or companionship or mutual support but producing and raising children. Bigamy and polygamy were also forbidden. America was not to be a despotism in which the powerful males have multiple wives while the poor males go without. (In 1879, the Supreme Court pointed out that polygamy was practiced elsewhere in the world only under despotic governments in Asia and Africa.)[38]

Sex outside marriage. The law discouraged any indulgence in or public portrayal of sex outside marriage. Most forms of nonmarital sex, including incest, adultery, sex with children, fornication, homosexuality, bestiality, and prostitution, were illegal and generally punishable. Public nudity was forbidden. Pornography and obscenity were outlawed. Illegitimate children had no legal standing as part of a family. They had no claim to inheritance or other benefits of legitimate birth.

Divorce. The law treated marriage as permanent, "for better or for worse," with few exceptions. In the South divorce was simply forbidden in the early republic. In the North it was permitted but granted on very few grounds. So confined, women and men were more likely to cultivate the friendship and mutual concessions that sustain marriage when romantic and erotic ties weaken. James Kent remarked that "facility of separation" tends to "destroy all mutual confidence, and to inflame every trifling dispute." In his 1791 law lectures, James Wilson agreed: "When divorces can be summoned to the aid of levity, of vanity, or of avarice, a state of marriage frequently becomes a state of war or stratagem."[39]

Legal authority of parents. The law imposed few restrictions on parental control over their children's education and well being, thereby encouraging the natural affection and pleasure that parents take in raising their offspring. James Wilson wrote:

> It is the duty of parents to maintain their children decently, and according to their circumstances; to protect them according to the dictates of prudence; and to educate them according to the suggestions of a judicious and zealous regard for their usefulness, their respectability, and their happiness.

However, Wilson defended the fact that the law did not interfere with parental authority except in cases of extreme abuse: "The decent reserve which the common law has shown, with regard to the relation between parent and child, should be admired." In Wilson's view, the law is likely to do more harm than good when it intrudes "in the nice feelings and tender transactions" of parents and children "with a rude and indelicate management." In America today, a mere suspicion of child abuse by a child protective services social worker is sufficient for compulsory removal of a child from his home.[40]

Property and children. In the eyes of the law, a married woman became one person with her husband, in the legal phrase *feme covert.* A single woman or widow *(feme sole)* had property rights similar to those of men. She could own property, sue and be sued, and make wills and contracts. Under "coverture," as it was called, these rights were exercised by a husband on behalf of the couple. Normally, all property, including his wife's wages, legally belonged to the husband. For her part, the wife was legally obliged to care for the children.

Those who discuss this topic today are sure that women were sorely oppressed by these practices and laws. However, the *rights* of husbands were granted on the understanding that they would perform corresponding *duties*. Above all, a husband was legally bound to provide for his wife and children. A Virginia bill drafted by Jefferson said, "All able bodied persons . . . who shall desert wives or children, without . . . providing for them . . . shall be deemed vagabonds, and shall be sent, by order of an Alderman, to the poor house, there to be kept to labor . . . not exceeding thirty days." If his wife owed any debts before the marriage, her husband became liable for them. A husband alone was held responsible for crimes committed by himself and his wife together. He had to pay any debts she might assume for ordinary purchases and necessities. If a marriage was dissolved, the husband, as head of the family, received custody of the children along with the legal responsibility to maintain them.[41]

Founder James Wilson explained the reason for these policies in his law lectures: "the general presumption and the universal wish ought to be, that between husband and wife, there subsist or may subsist no difference of will or of interest. . . . [T]he husband and wife are considered as one person by our law." The only exception is in cases of serious abuse or injury: "whenever any outrage is threatened or committed against the peace or safety of society, as well as against the refined rules of the conjugal union, the law will interpose its authority." Coverture was intended to secure the common interest of husband and wife by granting the husband sole authority in the external relations of the household, while requiring him in turn to fulfill his duties to his family. Coverture was called "the great bond of family union."[42]

Here is the occasion to refute a common misconception about the legal status of women during the founding era. Many believe that in early American law women were men's property, that men could do with women as they pleased. It is also thought that the Founders opposed education for women. These views are untrue. In Wilson's "Lectures on Law," just quoted, he indignantly denounces these very things, male tyranny over women and denial of education to women. In ancient Greece, he wrote:

> Education was either entirely withheld from them; or it was directed to such objects as were fitted to contract and debase, instead of elevating and enlarging the mind. When they were grown up, they were thrown away in marriage, without being consulted in the choice; and by entering the new state, they found the severe guardianship of a father succeeded by the absolute dominion of a husband. . . .
>
> Let us now turn our attention to Rome. You recollect that, by a law of Romulus, "the wife fell into the power of the husband." . . . [By this law,] colored with the unnatural fiction that, on a solemn marriage,

the wife was adopted by the husband, he acquired over her all the tremendous plenitude of Roman paternal power. . . .

By the precepts of Christianity, and the practice of Christians, the dignity of marriage was, however, restored.[43]

We should also add a brief word about the Founders' approval of male authority in the family and community. In her famous "remember the ladies" letter to her husband, Abigail Adams wrote, in a bantering tone: "If particular care and attention is not paid to the ladies [in the laws of the new nation], we are determined to foment a rebellion, and will not hold ourselves bound by any laws in which we have no voice, or representation." John responded with a serious jest:

> Depend upon it, we know better than to repeal our masculine systems. Although they are in full force, you know they are little more than theory. We dare not exert our power in its full latitude. We are obliged to go fair, and softly, and in practice you know we are the subjects. We have only the name of masters, and rather than give up this, which would completely subject us to the despotism of the petticoat, I hope General Washington and all our brave heroes would fight.

That is, as Camille Paglia has explained in her typical blunt manner: "We *have* what they want. I think woman is the dominant sex. Men have to do all sorts of stuff to prove that they are worthy of a woman's attention." Women dominate men in the whole realm of emotion and love, family and children, the realm celebrated by music and viewed by both sexes as somehow far more important than money and prestige. As George Gilder argues, supporting Adams's point, there is a sense in which men only become women's equals with the aid of social and legal supports for male authority. And there is both historical and current scientific reason to think that the destruction of these supports in recent decades is related to women's growing contempt for men, and men's declining interest in women and marriage. In the short run, Adams was right: women's power grows when male authority declines. But in the long run, when men lose their place of honor in the family and the society, women will suffer.[44]

Republicanizing the Family

So far we have described the Founders' conception of the family as though it were the same as that of their European forebears. In fact, the Founders' understanding of the family had a dramatic "republicanizing" effect.

John Locke's *Two Treatises of Government* (1689) had attacked patriarchalism in the name of equality and liberty. Americans applied these principles not only to political despotism but also to the patriarchal family of their ancestors. The American family after 1776 was based on a new view of women as equal partners with their men, although men and women were still to occupy separate spheres in life. Historian Jan Lewis notes that "Revolutionary-era writers held up the loving partnership of man and wife in opposition to patriarchal dominion as the republican model for social and political relationships." Whereas a century earlier couples "were supposed to be guided by their parents," in the late 1700s they "expected to choose their own spouses and married primarily for love." Abigail Adams expressed the new view when she wrote: "I will never consent to have our sex considered in an inferior point of light. Let each planet shine in their own orbit. God and nature designed it so—if man is Lord, woman is *Lordess*—that is what I contend for."[45]

In this more egalitarian view of the family, women's role was seen as different from, but equal in rank to, men's. Women's importance in forming the character of citizens—their children's and their husbands'— was frequently discussed and praised. A 1789 issue of *Christian's Magazine* said that "it is . . . to the virtues of the fair . . . that society must be indebted for its moral, as well as its natural preservation." Historian Linda Kerber has called this new idea of women's role "republican motherhood."[46]

Tocqueville's chapter on the equality of the sexes in *Democracy in America* catches well the older American paradox: women voluntarily submitted to male authority in marriage, yet they conceived of themselves as men's equals. Their men acknowledged that equality. Tocqueville explicitly drew the contrast with Europe's patriarchalism:

> In Europe, . . . women are regarded as seductive but incomplete beings. . . . American legislators . . . punish rape by death. . . . In France, where the same crime is subject to much milder penalties, it is difficult to find a jury that will convict. Is the reason scorn of chastity or scorn of women? I cannot rid myself of the feeling that it is both. [T]he Americans . . . think of men and women as beings of equal worth, though their fates are different. . . . [A]lthough the American woman never leaves her domestic sphere, . . . nowhere does she enjoy a higher station.

The American elevation of women is also illustrated by a striking fact reported by historian Jay Fliegelman: "Whereas before 1775 virtually all extant family portraits present the father standing above his seated family, after that date the vertical or hierarchical composition gives way to a horizontal or equalitarian composition in which all family members are shown on the same plane."[47]

Legal changes followed. Several states "applied and developed a body of law allowing *femes coverts* [married women] to own separate property." All states abolished primogeniture, which had given eldest sons priority in inheritances, so that daughters now inherited more nearly equally with their brothers. Divorce law was reformed in most Northern and some Southern states. In Pennsylvania, for example, permissible grounds were widened to include adultery, cruelty, abandonment, and impotence. Divorced women were given feme sole status, enabling them to get credit and go into business. They could obtain alimony from their ex-husbands for their support when the husband was at fault.[48]

Allowing cruelty as a ground for divorce was one response to Abigail Adams's concern over men's abuse of their wives under the old order:

> In the new code of laws which I suppose it will be necessary for you to make, I desire you would remember the ladies, and be more generous and favorable to them than your ancestors. Do not put such unlimited power into the hands of the husbands. Remember all men would be tyrants if they could. . . . Why then not put it out of the power of the vicious and the lawless to use us with cruelty and indignity with impunity? . . . Regard us then as beings placed by providence under your protection and in imitation of the Supreme Being, make use of that power only for our happiness.[49]

This is not an early statement of feminism, as it has sometimes been taken to be. As is clear from the last sentence quoted—which echoes the Bible (Ephesians 5)—she is proposing not the abolition of male authority but curbs on its abuse.

Revisions of divorce law in the early republic were not meant to weaken the bonds of the family or to condone moral laxity. In Pennsylvania, for instance, when a divorce was granted for adultery, the adulterer was forbidden to marry his lover. Nor could women leave their husbands because of a "growing sense of dissatisfaction and emptiness." (According to a recent study, women initiate 75 percent of divorces today, and this is the reason they give most often.)[50] Unless her husband's misbehavior was serious, a woman had to put up with him when she found herself unhappy. (Similarly, a man had to put up with his wife.) If she got a divorce, she would lose custody of the children. Mothers are usually more attached to their children than fathers are, and fathers are rarely eager to raise children on their own. Thus the older custody law gave each party a strong incentive to find a way to preserve harmony in the home.

In today's perspective, the Founders' family laws seem severe. But the Founders might ask us: "Which society shows more concern for women and children? Which does a better job protecting their rights to life, liberty, and the pursuit of happiness? Your society," they might argue, "shows infinite tenderness toward spouses who want divorces on the basis of fleeting passions or petty resentments. But is it not more compassionate for the law to encourage parents to marry and, once they are married, require them to provide their children with a stable home? How can it be good to allow men to walk out on their wives and children and to allow women to kick out their husbands and ban them from daily contact with their children? Does it really make sense for government to take money out of the pockets of married men and women and transfer it to women who intentionally bear children without husbands? A society dominated by intact families does a better job protecting women and children against crime, poverty, and sadness. It also gives men powerful incentives to behave responsibly: love, interest, shame, and honor. Above all, it gives most children their own mother and father to raise, support, and love them.

"Your society," the Founders might say to us, "is plagued by high rates of child abuse by 'boyfriends' and stepfathers, the exploitation and brutalization of women and their children by predatory sons raised by unmarried mothers, and poverty and loneliness for millions of men, women, and children. You seem to think that government programs—such as affirmative action for women, rape hot lines, campaigns against 'deadbeat dads,' bureaucratic supervision of child-rearing, and battered women's shelters—are the answer. But these policies do not confront the root cause of the growing victimization, irresponsibility, and heartbreak all around you. That root cause is the breakdown of morality, especially the morality that supports marriage and the family."

I do not mean to say—and the Founders would not have said—that everything was rosy in earlier America. Obviously, the old system had its costs. Exceptional women of superior talent in areas reserved for men were unlikely to bring that talent to fruition. Men and women who chose their mate foolishly usually had to live with that choice for the rest of their lives. For those, marriage could be dreary and stifling. But the laws and customs that limited male and female choices were believed to be on balance good for everyone, especially children. We of course are free to disagree. But the question remains: Have we found a better way? Or are we, in the name of liberty, endangering the lives and liberties of growing numbers of Americans?

The Decline of the Family and the Degradation of Women

American elites, soon followed by the rest of the country, rejected traditional morality in the 1960s and 1970s. One consequence was the sexual
revolution, which broke down the old stigma against divorce, illegitimacy,
and nonmarital sex. Families rapidly began to fall apart, or failed to form at
all. Before 1965, men and women knew they would be regarded as dis-
honored, and perhaps shunned altogether by their families, friends, employers, and communities, if they broke away from the customary structure of
family life. They knew that their children would suffer as well. Now they
know that whatever they do will be socially acceptable, and there are plenty of therapists and counselors to assure them that divorce and nonmarital
sex are solutions, not problems. From 1970 to 1995 the number of divorced
American adults tripled from 3 to 9 percent, and the proportion of children
living in single-parent households grew from 12 to 27 percent.[50] From
1970 to 1993, illegitimate births tripled from less than 11 percent to over
31 percent of the total.[51]

The government now subsidizes single motherhood by giving women
who have children without husbands medical care, housing, food, cash, and
other benefits. (See chapter 6, on welfare.) Meanwhile the mass media cel-
ebrate the "de-moralization" of sex. In *Time* magazine, for instance, Barbara
Ehrenreich writes: "Sex can finally, after all these centuries, be separated
from the all-too-serious business of reproduction. . . . [Sex] belongs
squarely in the realm of play."[52] Movies and television promote the same
message. When sex is cut off in this way from marriage and children, there
is no longer any reasonable ground on which to criticize unfaithfulness to
a wife or husband, sex between unmarried people, homosexual acts or
homosexual "marriages," prostitution, or pornography. Even incest and sex
between adults and children now have their defenders.

Many public schools—usurping what has traditionally been a family
prerogative—instruct children in the techniques of sex, both heterosexual
and homosexual, including the mechanics of condom use, thus in effect
promoting this de-moralized view of sex. In addition, government distrib-
utes contraceptives to children in many states without parental knowledge
or consent. And as long as a judge and doctor can be found to approve,
twelve-year-old girls have a federal right to an abortion without parental
consent.[53]

In addition to children, older women suffer disproportionately from
the breakdown of the family. Since there are few social customs and no laws
to discourage adultery and divorce, monogamy, especially for successful
men, is being replaced by de facto polygamy with younger women. Their

wives are often forced to choose between tolerating infidelity and being left in the cold.[54] At the same time, the degradation of women is on the rise. These phenomena are related. The new sexual morality denies that men and women have any duties toward each other beyond whatever feels good or makes for a "meaningful relationship." Pornography and vulgarity in the popular culture make the implication explicit: sex, and therefore women, are "no big deal."

Welfare generates its own antifemale moral (or immoral) stance. It enables women to have children without a husband to support them and her. This means, as social critics Norman Dennis and George Erdos write, that the men in their lives are liberated from

> the expectation that adulthood involves lifelong responsibility for the well-being of their wife, and fifteen or twenty years of responsibility for the well-being of their children. . . . [Y]oung men who are invited to remain in a state of permanent puerility will predictably behave in an anti-social fashion.

They become indifferent to women except as objects of pleasure or sources of money. In England, boyfriends of single mothers on welfare call their women "bitches" and their homes "kennels," as in "the bitch is in her kennel."[55]

American rap music betrays the new dehumanization of women in the crudest and most explicit possible terms. The lyrics of Ice-T's 1992 *Body Count* album gloat over images of women's sexual degradation, murder, and dismemberment. In a world without marriage, the abuse of women and teenage girls is glorified as an expression of manliness and nobility.[56]

The new sexual ethic has been defended as necessary to women's liberation from male domination. Yet from the Founders' viewpoint, we seem to have combined the two extremes condemned by James Wilson: "the cruel tyranny of savages, which condemns the fair sex to servitude, and the sordid selfishness of luxury, which considers them solely as instruments of pleasure." Many Americans pride themselves on their rejection of the older customs, praised by Wilson, that required "the rights of beauty and feminine weakness [to be] highly respected and tenderly observed."[57] In communities where marriage has almost completely broken down, women are expected to be the principal providers, through jobs or welfare checks, while men join gangs and engage in sports and male camaraderie in the streets. In the middle class, women who expect to stay home with their children when they get married are viewed by their prospective mates as freeloaders unwilling to pull their weight.

The new roles of men and women parallel in surprising ways the early American Indians' way of life as described by Jefferson and Thomas Paine. For Jefferson, it was "a barbarous perversion of the natural destination of the two sexes" for Indian women to be forced to do the hardest work, while the men exerted themselves only in sport or fighting. As Paine described them, Indian marriages "have no other ceremony than mutual affection, and last no longer than they bestow mutual pleasure." "The women among the Indians are what the Helots were among the Spartans, a vanquished people, obliged to toil for their conquerors." Paine's assertions are confirmed by historian Francis Parkman, who wrote that Huron females enjoyed "a youth of license," in which they slept with anyone they pleased, followed by "an age of drudgery." (Paine alone among the Founders praised Indian-style free love; he failed to see the link between Indian sexual license and Indian oppression of females. In both cases, the strongest passion of the strongest person is permitted to rule.)[58]

The modern state has also seen a breakdown of the family on generational lines. Traditionally, parents and children both benefited from the family as a mutual aid society. It was the welfare agency of first resort. The old, feeble, and sick received care from the children they had raised and nurtured years before. In our time Social Security, Medicare, and welfare programs have created a bureaucratic substitute for this mutual-support role of the family. The result has been increasingly bitter relations between generations. A popular bumper sticker of the 1990s often appeared on recreational vehicles: "I'm spending my children's inheritance." Behind the joke is the reality of retired parents physically and emotionally isolated from their children and grandchildren, who no longer care and provide for them.

These well-known patterns of contemporary American life—patterns deplored by large numbers of Americans—suggest that the Founders may have been more correct than we might wish in their view of women and the family.

Conclusion

Why were the Founders not feminists? Let us be clear. It is not because they were ignorant of the implications of their conviction that "all men are created equal," as is so often said today. It was because they believed that the rights and interests of women and children would be secured only if most adults in society got married and stayed married. That meant, in their view, different legal rights and responsibilities for men and women. They rejected feminism because, in their view, life, liberty, and the pursuit of happiness were at stake. Without clear legal rights and responsibilities in the realm of love and sex, children will be uncared for and adults will be abandoned and mistreated. The brutalized characters that such a society will produce will not be capable of the self-restraint and courage necessary for liberty.

For marriage to endure and succeed, the Founders thought, men and women must make mutual concessions. The typical man must accept the fact that he will spend most of his adult life working not only for himself but also for a woman and children who would find it hard to make it on their own. The typical woman must accept the fact that she will spend most of her adult life managing a household, including cooking and cleaning for her husband and children. If this kind of mutual dependency sounds bleak today, perhaps it is because many Americans no longer understand that the good things in life require effort, love, and postponement of immediate gratification. A world in which courtship and marriage are replaced by transitory "relationships" is not a world of happiness and joy. For far too many men, women, and children, it is a world of pain and degradation.

5

Was the Founding Undemocratic?
The Property Requirement for Voting

*F*or the past century, liberals and progressives have frequently argued that the American founding was undemocratic. Their arguments have been consistently false or misleading.

Historian Gordon Wood has called Charles Beard's *Economic Interpretation of the Constitution,* published in 1913, "the most influential history book ever written in America." In Beard's view, the U.S. Constitution was an antidemocratic document written by a "small and active group of men immediately interested through their personal possessions in the outcome of their labors." This happened in part because "A large propertyless mass was, under the prevailing suffrage qualifications, excluded at the outset from participation (through representatives) in the work of framing the Constitution."

Beard's book had the appearance of scholarly objectivity. It was, as Beard described it, "a long and arid survey" of the interplay of economic interests and the framing and ratifying of the Constitution. However, its apparent neutrality masked a highly partisan conclusion. Richard Hofstadter, a liberal historian, gave this assessment: "Like so many of his contentions, it proceeds from several undeniable facts to a misleading conclusion."

Beard was in fact building on a late nineteenth-century consensus: the Constitution is undemocratic. Conservative historians of that day praised it for that reason, while liberals denounced it. J. Allen Smith was a typical and influential Progressive Era critic of the Constitution. His *Spirit of American Government* bluntly stated:

> We forget that when our government was established the principle of majority rule was nowhere recognized—that until well along in the nineteenth century the majority of our forefathers did not even have the right to vote. . . . Then a great popular movement swept over the country, and in the political upheaval which followed, the masses secured the right of suffrage.[1]

As we will see, this is simply incorrect.

Today, openly leftist historians like Michael Parenti continue to echo the Beard-Smith line: "As of 1787, property qualifications left perhaps more than a third of the white male population disfranchised." The authors of most history and government textbooks know better. They avoid outright confrontation with the founding on this point. Instead, they denounce by insinuation. But they send students the same message: if America is a democracy today, it only became so after a long, hard struggle against the legacy of the founding.

"Since democracy is rule by the governed," write Larry Berman and Bruce Murphy in their college text, *Approaching Democracy,* "all citizens must have an opportunity to influence the activities of the government. That opportunity is best expressed by the institution of universal suffrage, the requirement that everyone must have the right to vote." However, say Berman and Murphy, "Only a minority of people—white, landowning males over the age of 21—could exercise full citizenship rights in 1787." Karen O'Connor and Larry Sabato's widely used *American Government* says that "most states had numerous requirements that had to be met before a man could vote. . . . In general, the idea of voting rights or any other kind of rights was not something that particularly troubled the Framers." The unstated conclusion in both texts is that America's founding was undemocratic and that an important reason was the property requirement for voting.

History texts used in secondary schools, such as Robert Divine's *America: The People and the Dream,* teach the same lesson. Divine says that "the writers of the state constitutions . . . urged the states to 'go slow' with universal manhood suffrage—voting rights for all male citizens. These leaders had a number of concerns. They doubted that all Americans—especially those without property, wealth, or formal education—were capable of choosing trustworthy officials. . . . As a result of these concerns, the state constitutions established restrictions on voting rights. Most of these constitutions required voters to be men who were at least 21 years of age. In addition, voters had to own a specific amount of property or pay a certain amount of taxes."[2]

The textbooks are in effect continuing to propagate the doctrines of Beard and Smith, without actually embracing their extreme views. From the quotations given here—and most other texts have their equivalents—one gets the impression that democracy existed in name only in early America, that the states excluded large numbers of free men from the suffrage, and that no one among the Founders gave much thought to the question of voting rights. On all three points, the truth is the exact opposite.

First, we will show in this chapter that America was already highly democratic during the founding era. Shortly after the adoption of the Constitution, most free men (about 85 to 90 percent) could vote. By the 1820s, almost all property qualifications for voting had been abolished.

Second, we will see that the Founders gave considerable thought to the question of voting rights. Their opinions were divided, but not, as we have been told, because some Founders believed in equality and others did not. A few Founders thought property requirements for voting were simply wrong, like slavery. Most of them defended limitations on voting rights, not only as compatible with the equality principle, but as required by it. Both sides agreed that all men are created equal. They disagreed on the application of that principle.

Finally, we will show that those who supported near-universal male suffrage ultimately had the better of the argument, from the point of view of the equality principle. But those Founders who favored a property qualification for voting would have been right, if their view of the American economy had been correct. The circumstances of the poor in America today resemble, in disturbing ways, the conditions that the Founders thought would justify limits on voting rights. Their reflections may therefore help us understand a serious problem in current politics.

Who Had the Right to Vote?

In my introductory course in American politics, I sometimes ask students who, in the U.S. Constitution of 1787, had the right to vote for members of the House of Representatives. These choices are offered: (a) males over twenty-one who pay taxes; (b) white males over twenty-one; (c) white males over twenty-one who own at least $200 worth of property; (d) those in each state who are eligible to vote for the largest branch of the state legislature. Many students choose (a), (b), or (c) instead of the correct answer, (d). The prevailing prejudice that they have absorbed in high school and in other courses is so strong that some students still get it wrong even after we have covered the topic in class.

The Constitution excludes no one from voting or holding office on the basis of race, sex, wealth, or any other criterion. Suffrage requirements are left in the hands of the states. Because state laws varied, some women (see chapter 3) and a large number of blacks and the poor were already voting in the 1780s and 1790s.

The Constitution directs that whoever in each state is permitted to vote for the most numerous branch of the state legislature shall also be a voter for the federal House of Representatives. Senators were chosen by popularly elected state legislatures. As for presidential elections, state legislatures were permitted to determine how each state's presidential electors would be chosen. In the election of 1792, the people chose some or all of their presidential electors in six states, while the state legislatures chose them in the other nine. By the 1820s the people elected presidential electors in almost every state. Not a single word of the Constitution had to be changed for all Americans to have the right to vote in House and presidential elections.

On the eve of the Revolution, voters in every colony had to meet certain property qualifications. (For state-by-state qualifications during the founding era, see table 5.1.) The requirement was typically fifty acres of land or forty pounds' worth of property. The colonial electorate varied from a low of about 50 percent to a high of about 80 percent of free males, depending on the colony. Using these numbers, we may estimate that 65 percent of adult males could vote. By our standards that number seems low. At the time, however, it may have been the most inclusive electorate in the world. Colonial Americans had to read Thucydides and Plutarch, historians of Greek and Italian cities two thousand years old, to find examples of democratic liberty that could rival their own, with a few minor exceptions.[3]

During the revolutionary years the American electorate became even more democratic. Of the fifteen states in existence in 1792, at the end of Washington's first presidential term, all but four had reduced or abolished their formal property qualifications. One of these, Massachusetts, did not enforce its qualification in the 1790s. That leaves only three states out of fifteen—Rhode Island, Connecticut, and Virginia—that fully retained their colonial restrictions on voting.

By 1792 ten states had eliminated, or nearly eliminated, any property qualification for voting. In these states (the first ten in table 5.1), at least 90 percent of free adult males were probably eligible to vote. In the other five states the electorate was typically 70 to 75 percent of free males, except for New York, whose voting eligibility of less than 70 percent was the lowest of any state.

The federal government also set a property requirement for voters in the Northwest Territory (the mostly unsettled area west of Pennsylvania and north of the Ohio River). Land was easily available there, but it is unknown how many of the tiny number of early settlers had clear title to fifty acres by 1792.

In sum, the American electorate grew from about 65 percent in colonial days to about 85 to 90 percent in the 1790s. The states were well on their way to the universal adult male citizen suffrage that was nearly accomplished by the 1820s.

Ten of the fifteen states in 1792 also limited the right to be a candidate for public office. The requirement ranged from a "freehold"—that is, any real estate (New York, Virginia)—to standards that called for more wealth than was expected of voters. Thus the government officers in these states would always be property owners.

Further, nine states made property the basis of a distinction between eligibility to vote for and/or serve in the state house of representatives and senate. That was done in two ways. In all these states, senators had to own more property than representatives, sometimes two or three times as much. (This was also a provision of the federal Northwest Ordinance of 1787.) In addition, New York and North Carolina required senate voters to own more property than voters for the lower house. Maryland's senate was elected indirectly; ordinary voters selected well-to-do electors, who in turn elected the senate. In six of these states, governors had to own even more property than senators. The amounts required for senators and governors were sometimes substantial, clearly limiting the offices to men of superior wealth.

It seems odd that there were few complaints about the office-holding restrictions during these years when many were complaining about the limits on the right to vote. Even today, research is lavished on voting rights, but there is very little on property limits for holders of public office. One study found that, in spite of these limits, the average wealth of men who served in state legislatures declined considerably from the colonial period through the founding era. As the wealthy were elected less frequently, some even complained that "men of sense and property have lost much of their influence."[4]

In sum, the founding era saw a considerable expansion of the number of voters from what was already a quite democratic electorate during the colonial era to an electorate that included almost all adult male citizens by the 1790s.

Why Were Voting Rights Expanded?

We are inclined to ask why the Founders were such hypocrites as to affirm government by consent of the governed while keeping a substantial number of people from voting. We ask this question for the same reason that we ask why some of them said they believed in equality but held slaves. That question deserves an answer, and we will provide it.

But we should first ask a different question: Why, in a world that had been ruled for centuries by unelected elites, did Americans extend the right to vote to most adult males? The Europe from which the Americans came was governed by aristocrats, monarchs, and priests. England was one of very few places where commoners had some share in elections. Yet the number who voted there was considerably smaller than the number who voted in America even during colonial times.

Table 5.1
Property Qualifications for Voting and Holding Office in 1792

State or government[a]	Property requirement for voters[b]	Property requirement for office holders	Men eligible to vote (%)[c]
The colonies before 1776	Most required £40 of property or 50 acres. All had some property requirement.	Member of house of reps.: Same as for voters in Conn., R.I., Pa., S.C.; £40 freehold[d] in N.Y.; 1,000 acres or £500 in N.J.; 100 acres in N.C.; 500 acres in Ga. Other offices: none.	65
New Hampshire (1792)	None.	Representative: £100 estate. Senator: £200 freehold. Governor: £500 estate.	100
Vermont (1786)	None.	None.	100
Kentucky (1792)	None.	None.	100
New Jersey (1776)	Property worth £50 "proclamation money" (i.e., currency, which declined considerably in value during the founding era). Ignored in practice in 1790s.	Representative: property worth £500 proclamation money. Senator: property worth £1,000.	95
Georgia (1789)	Taxpayer.	Representative: 200 acres or £150 property. Senator: 250 acres or £250 property. Governor: £1,000 property, including 500 acres.	95
Delaware (1792)	State or county taxpayer.	Representative: freehold (any value). Senator: 200-acre freehold, or £1,000 property.	95
Massachusetts (1780)	£60 property (in paper curency), or freehold with annual income of £3. Ignored in practice in 1790s.	Representative: £100 freehold or £200 other property. Senator: £300 freehold or £600 other property. Governor: £1,000 freehold.	95
Pennsylvania (1790)	State or county taxpayer, or son of freeholder.	None.	95
South Carolina (1790)	50-acre freehold or town lot; or payment of 3-shilling tax.	Representative: 500 acres with 10 Negroes. Senator: £300 freehold. Governor: £1,500 freehold.	90
North Carolina (1776)	Taxpayer for house of representatives; 50-acre freehold for senate.	Representative: 100 acres. Senator: 300 acres. Governor: £1,000 freehold.	House: 95; Senate: 80.
Maryland (1776)	50 acres or property worth £30 "current money." These voters also chose electors (owning £500 property), who would elect the senate.	Representative: property worth £500 current money. Senator: £1000 property. Governor: £5,000 property, (including £1,000 freehold).	70–75
Virginia (1776)	50 acres, or 25 acres cultivated with house; or town lot with house.	Representative and senator: freeholder.	70–75

Table 5.1—*Continued*

State or government[a]	Property requirement for voters[b]	Property requirement for office holders	Men eligible to vote (%)[c]
Rhode Island (1663)	Real estate worth £40, or yielding 40 shillings annual income.	None.	74
Connecticut (1662)	Real estate yielding 40 shillings annual income, or other property worth £40.	None.	75
New York (1777)	For elections of town and city officials: Freeholder (any value) or 40-shilling leaseholder. For assembly: owner of £20 freehold or payment of 40 shillings annual rent. For senate and governor: £100 freehold.	Representative: None. Senator: Freeholder. Governor: Freeholder.	Assembly: 58–75. senate, governor: 29–40.
Northwest Ordinance of 1787	50-acre freehold. (This federal law governed the territories that later became Ohio, Indiana, Michigan, Illinois, and Wisconsin.)	Representative: 200 acres. Senator: 500 acres.	Unknown
U.S. Constitution of 1787	"The electors [for the House of Representatives] in each state shall have the qualifications requisite for the electors of the most numerous branch of the state legislature." Presidential elections: state legislatures determine the method of appointing electors. In 1792 some or all electors chosen by popular vote in 6 states, by state legislatures in 9. In 1832, by popular vote in 23 states, by legislature in 1.		85–90

Sources: Various; for details, see note 5.

[a]Dates refer to year of state constitution. Rhode Island and Connecticut did not adopt new constitutions after 1776 but kept their old colonial charters in force.

[b]All states except Rhode Island, Connecticut, and Virginia had reduced their property requirements by 1792. In Massachusetts, the formal qualification was higher than before 1776, but nonenforcement made it a de facto reduction.

[c]Does not count those disqualified for other reasons, such as residency, mental illness, slavery, criminal record, or loyalty to Britain during the Revolution.

The surprise, historically speaking, is that property qualifications for voting, which were accepted without complaint before 1760, diminished so rapidly after 1776. (There was a similar rapid growth of opposition to slavery, after a long colonial period of unquestioning acceptance.) The explanation is obvious. The principles of the Revolution—the logic of government by consent—pointed toward the broadest possible electorate, in the same way that those principles made manifest the injustice of slavery.

Americans revolted against Britain on the ground that they were taxed and governed without their consent. This is the nub of most of the complaints listed in the Declaration of Independence. Americans had argued that consent was a right of *Englishmen*. But they also argued—and this was their fundamental position—that consent was a right of *human beings,* "founded in the law of God and nature, and [one of] the common rights of mankind."[6] The Declaration says that governments derive "their just powers from the consent of the governed." Why? Because if all are created equal, then all are born free, and no one may rule another without that other's consent. If a country is too large to be ruled by the people in person, consent must be expressed through elected representatives. In the civil state, voting for public officials is the way we continue to exercise our inalienable right to liberty.

In debates on voting rights during the founding era, those who favored the most inclusive franchise appealed directly to these arguments of the Revolution. In 1778 and 1780 the citizens of Massachusetts deliberated over two proposed state constitutions that set a property qualification for voting. One town insisted that "excluding persons from a share in representation for want of pecuniary qualifications is an infringement on the *natural rights* of the subject." Another town made explicit the connection between equality, liberty, and voting rights:

> All men were born equally free and independent, having certain natural and inherent and unalienable rights, among which are the enjoying and defending life and liberty, and acquiring, possessing, and protecting property [quoted from the 1776 Pennsylvania Declaration of Rights]; of which rights they cannot be deprived but by injustice, except they first forfeit them by committing crimes against the public. . . . [H]ow can a man be said to be free and independent, enjoying and defending life and liberty and protecting property, when he has not a voice allowed him in the choice of the most important officers in the legislature, which can make laws to bind him and appoint judges to try him in all cases as well of life and liberty as of property?

A third town admitted that some people fail to acquire property because of laziness or other defects. But, they asked,

> shall it from thence be argued that thousands of honest, good members of society shall be subjected to laws framed by legislators, the election of whom they could have no voice in? Shall a subject of a free commonwealth be obliged to contribute his share to public expenses, . . . and be excluded from voting for a representative? This appears to us in some degree slavery.[7]

New Jersey critics exposed and denounced the implication that property owners somehow have superior rights to nonowners:

> We cannot conceive the wise author of our existence ever designed that a certain quantity of the earth on which we tread should be annexed to

man to complete his dignity and fit him for society. Was the sole design
of government either the security of land or money, the possession of
either or both of these would be the only necessary qualification for its
members. But we apprehend the benign intentions of a well regulated
government extend to the security of much more valuable possession—
the rights and privileges of freemen, for the defense of which every kind
of property and even life itself have been liberally expended.

Besides, as another Massachusetts town said, property owners are not
necessarily more responsible than nonowners. For when the members of
government "are all men of considerable property," they may increase taxes
on the poor, "and by that means ease their own estates, and bring a heavy
burden on those who have no power to remove it."[8]

Arguments for the Property Qualification I: Consent

These are powerful arguments. Nevertheless, most of the leading Founders
held that some property qualifications were appropriate. For the Progressive Era historians whom we quoted earlier, that was easy to understand:
the Founders were antidemocratic. Our current textbooks and scholars follow this view or something close to it. Historian Marc Kruman writes,
"Colonial and revolutionary Americans believed that a man's economic
independence earned him membership in the political community."[9] He
implies that the Founders' rhetoric of equality was insincere. Kruman is
appealing to the correct proposition that if all are born equal, then in principle communities should be formed by consent of all the governed, not
only by those who are economically independent.

Kruman is right to this extent: a man's right to vote was, at least in
some states, earned by economic independence. But the Founders did not
equate voting rights with community membership. Otherwise neither
children nor women could have been members, which they certainly were.
More important, all the Founders embraced the equality principle, explicitly and emphatically. Therefore they must have believed that a limitation of
the right to vote was perfectly compatible with the equality of human
beings. Their belief is defensible, as we will now see.

According to the Declaration of Independence, all men are created
equal. All are born free and deserve to remain free. It follows that no one
may take away another's liberty; in other words, no one may rule another
without that other's consent. Rule without consent is slavery. That means,
first, that government derives its just powers from the consent of the governed; and second, that governments are instituted to secure the rights to

life, liberty, and the pursuit of happiness. Consent and security of rights: these are the only two considerations consistent with the Declaration that could justify the property qualification for voting. And they are exactly what did justify it.

The "Stake in Society" Argument

But exactly who are "the people" or "the governed" that must consent? How do we know who are members of the community and who are outsiders or transients? The Virginia Declaration of Rights states that "all men, having sufficient evidence of permanent common interest with, and attachment to, the community, have the right of suffrage." In Virginia, "sufficient evidence" included residency and land ownership. In a letter to Thomas Jefferson, Edmund Pendleton, a leader of revolutionary Virginia, explained that voting

> should be confined to those of fixed permanent property, who cannot suddenly remove without injury to that property or substituting another proprietor, and whom alone I consider as having political attachment. The persons who when they have produced burdens on the state, may move away and leave them to be borne by others, I can by no means think should have the framing of the laws, but may stay, enjoying their benefits and submitting to their obligations as a kind of sojourners, so long as they like them, and then remove.

Even today, most would agree that foreigners and transients are not truly part of a community and therefore should have no right to vote. For Pendleton, the propertyless are not really any different from such "sojourners" or visitors, because nothing attaches them to the community.

In his reply, Jefferson exposed the weakness of Pendleton's "stake in society" argument:

> I was for extending the rights of suffrage (or in other words the rights of a citizen) to all who had a permanent intention of living in the country. Take what circumstances you please as evidence for this, either the having resided a certain time, or having a family, or having property, any or all of them. Whoever intends to live in a country must wish the country well, and has a natural right of assisting in the preservation of it.[10]

Jefferson's dispute with Pendleton concerned adult male citizens who vote and perform military service. Jefferson was willing to take residence *or* family (a wife and children) *or* property ("any or all of them") as evidence of attachment to the community. Pendleton wanted to treat nonowners of landed property as if they were resident aliens, which of course they were not. Jefferson saw that Pendleton's rule would exclude many adult males who really were proper members of the community.

Four other states adopted a version of the Virginia Declaration of Rights language, namely, that only those "having sufficient evidence" of "interest with, and attachment to, the community" should be voters. Yet three of these states, in agreement with Jefferson, rejected Virginia's conclusion that landed property was a necessary part of that evidence. Pennsylvania required only that voters be taxpayers and residents. Delaware adopted Pennsylvania's rule in 1792. In Vermont residency alone was enough to qualify for voting. To avoid all doubt, Maryland, which did have a property requirement, changed Virginia's wording to: "every man, *having property in,* a common interest with, and an attachment to the community" (Maryland's addition is italicized). We conclude that the "stake in society" argument alone could not and did not support the property qualification.[11]

The history books usually mention "stake in society" as the sole reason for property restrictions on suffrage during the founding era. Daniel Boorstin's *History of the United States,* for example, says: "It was believed that only by owning property would you have a 'stake' in good government." Historian Stanley Katz writes of "the prevailing view [in 1788] that only men of property had the kind of stake in government that entitled them to participate in it."[12] Yet Virginia may be the only state that justified its property qualification in this way. Those who reflected on the question of voting rights and supported a property qualification usually had other, stronger reasons for their view.

The "Will and Judgment of One's Own" Argument

For consent to be real, voters who give it ought to have a will and a judgment of their own. That is why Texas, like other states, denies the vote to children and the mentally incompetent. Children's opinions mirror those of their parents, on whom they depend. The *Weekly Reader* poll of school children has correctly predicted every presidential election since it started in 1956, with only one exception.[13] People with mental disorders are also excluded from voting because they are presumed to have no will or judgment of their own. Even today, immigrants seeking citizenship must show an elementary knowledge of how America is governed. A person who is unaware of such rudiments cannot give a meaningful vote.

Many Founders defended the property qualification on the ground that a person without property could not have a free will and judgment of his own. In the chapter on voting rights for women (chapter 3), we quoted this passage from Alexander Hamilton's 1775 *Farmer Refuted*:

> "If it were probable that every man would give his vote freely, and without influence of any kind, then, upon the true theory and genuine principles of liberty, every member of the community, however poor, should have a vote. . . . But since that can hardly be expected, in persons of indigent fortunes, . . . all popular states have been obliged to establish certain qualifications, whereby, some who are suspected to have no will of their own, are excluded from voting; in order to set other individuals, whose wills may be supposed independent, more thoroughly upon a level with each other."[14]

Hamilton's point of departure was "the true theory and genuine principles of liberty," which require the consent of *all* the governed, just as the Declaration says. A remark of James Madison clarifies Hamilton's view:

> It would be happy if a state of society could be found or framed, in which an equal voice in making the laws might be allowed to every individual bound to obey them. But this is a theory, which like most theories, confessedly requires limitations and modifications; and the only question to be decided in this as in other cases, turns on the particular degree of departure, in practice, *required by the essence and object of the theory itself.*[15]

If some are not permitted to vote, it must either be because their votes would somehow distort the real "consent of the governed," or because the "object of the theory," security of individual rights, will not be attained. Hamilton's concern was consent. (Madison's, we will see later, was with the object of the theory.) Hamilton did not fear the opinions of the poor. He feared that the poor would not really have opinions of their own and that they would magnify the votes of some voters at the expense of others.

Whose opinions would the poor magnify? John Adams, discussing the same topic in a 1776 letter, stressed the connection between the lack of informed judgment of the poor and their lack of a will of their own, making them easy targets of manipulation by the powerful:

> Men in general, in every society, who are wholly destitute of property, are also too little acquainted with public affairs to form a right judgment, and too dependent on other men to have a will of their own. . . . Such is the frailty of the human heart, that very few men who have no property, have any judgment of their own. They talk and vote as they are directed by some man of property, who has attached their minds to his interest. . . . [M]en who are wholly destitute of property . . . [are] to all intents and purposes as much dependent upon others, who will please to

feed, clothe, and employ them, as women are upon their husbands, or children on their parents.[16]

Other leading Founders had the same reservation about universal suffrage. At the Constitutional Convention of 1787, Madison worried that propertyless voters would "become the tools of opulence and ambition." In the same Convention debate, Gouverneur Morris argued universal suffrage would increase the influence of the wealthy: "Give the votes to the people who have no property, and they will sell them to the rich. . . . The time is not distant when this country will abound with mechanics and manufacturers who will receive their bread from their employers. . . . The man who does not give his vote freely is not represented. It is the man who dictates the vote."[17]

A Virginia writer likewise observed that the purpose of his state's property requirement was "to prevent the undue and overwhelming influence of great landholders in elections" by excluding from the vote the landless "tenants and retainers" who depend "on the breath and varying will" of the wealthy.[18]

Even Thomas Paine, in many ways the most radical democrat among the Founders, would have denied the vote to "servants," including government employees, because "their interest is in their master, and depending upon him in sickness and in health . . . they stand detached by choice from the common floor."[19]

We are likely to react to these arguments with cynicism. Is it really plausible that the poor would be denied a vote because it was thought that they would magnify the power of the wealthy? Actually, such things did happen in early American history. After 1800 the middle classes tended to support Jeffersonian Republicanism, while the "meaner sort" and the wealthy tended to vote Federalist. William Cooper of New York, the wealthy father of novelist James Fenimore Cooper, effectively organized the poor of his town to vote for his hand-picked Federalist candidates. He preferred to get votes by doing favors for them. But if he had to, writes David Fischer, "Cooper bullied recalcitrant citizens who insisted upon voting as they pleased, threatening to foreclose a mortgage or withhold a coveted favor." Just as Hamilton, Adams, Madison, and Morris predicted, the poor voted in accord with the town's leading man of property.[20]

Edmund Randolph, a member of the Federal Convention of 1787, combined the "stake in society" and the "free will and judgment" arguments in this way: "The elementary idea of a right of suffrage in the election of a legislative deputy is that the elector possess as nearly as may be free will and a common interest with the persons to be represented. Were we to suppose a society small enough to be managed by a pure democracy, every member of it having free will would have an equal vote."[21]

Later we will explain why property ownership came to be seen as unnecessary for the "free will and judgment" of poor voters.

Arguments for the Property Qualification II: Securing Rights

Another line of argument used to justify the limitation on voting—an argument more disturbing to us—was that the consent principle, if applied without reservation, was dangerous to property rights. The Address of the Massachusetts Convention, justifying to the people of that state the property qualification in the proposed 1780 state constitution, explained:

> Your delegates considered that persons who are twenty-one years of age, and have no property, are either those who live upon a part of a paternal estate, expecting the fee thereof, who are but just entering into business, or those whose idleness of life and profligacy of manners will forever bar them from acquiring and possessing property. And we will submit it to the former class, whether they would not think it safer for them to have their right of voting for a representative suspended for a small space of time, than forever hereafter to have their privileges liable to the control of men, who will pay less regard to the rights of property because they have nothing to lose.[22]

John Dickinson, speaking at the Constitutional Convention of 1787, put it more bluntly: property qualifications for voters are "a necessary defense against the dangerous influence of those multitudes without property and without principle, with which our country will in time abound."[23] In other words, the poor do not respect property rights because they hope to profit by taking property from owners. Therefore they should be denied the vote.

Did this mean that Dickinson, the Massachusetts Convention, and many others who held this view rejected the equality idea when it came to putting it into practice? Let us approach this question by recalling the basic problem of democracy as the Founders diagnosed it in the 1780s. At the beginning of the Revolution, Americans believed that their rights would be well protected if only they could get free of Britain, with its parliament, lords, and king, and govern themselves by laws of their own making. They least expected any danger to their rights from the people themselves. In John Adams's words in 1774, "A democratical despotism is a contradiction in terms."[24]

The experience of democracy during the late 1770s and 1780s did not confirm the Founders' early optimism. A number of instances of "democratical despotism"—for example, state laws that in effect canceled debts by allowing them to be paid in inflated paper currency—alarmed sensible men and was a leading impulse toward the Constitutional Convention of 1787. Some began to fear, in Hamilton's words, that "republican government" might be inconsistent with "the order of society." George Washington reported with alarm in 1786 that "even respectable characters speak of a monarchical form of government without horror."[25]

The problem was inherent in the terms of the Declaration of Independence. On the basis of the equality of men, that document draws two conclusions: the object of government is to secure the rights of mankind; and government should be based on consent. The problem arises when the people consent to laws that deny some people their rights. Madison provides an example: "Where slavery exists, the republican theory becomes . . . fallacious."[26] The majority that consents to make slavery lawful deprives the minority of their rights to life, liberty, and property.

When consent endangers the very purpose of government, one of two things must be done if individual rights are to be secured. One is to qualify the consent principle so that the will of some or all of the people is excluded from government, allowing government to protect rights. The other solution is to arrange the political institutions and form the character and minds of the people in such a way that they will have less opportunity, and less desire, to oppress others.

The Framers of the Constitution of 1787 chose the second of these solutions. The purpose of that document was to employ what Madison called "inventions of prudence" that would prevent "democratical despotism" by reconciling majority rule with minority rights. Madison tried to show, in the famous *Federalist* No. 10, how representative government over a large territory would discourage the formation of oppressive majorities. First, the process of election would "refine and enlarge the public views" if, as Madison hoped, the people chose men who were superior to the people themselves in intelligence and decency. Second, a large republic would embrace a great variety of different interests, so that it would be hard for any one interest to be adopted by a majority of the society against a minority. These two things would make it less probable that a majority would execute any "improper or wicked project," such as "an abolition of debts" or "an equal division of property."[27]

These and other devices, such as the separation of powers, legislative checks and balances, and federalism, were the structural means by which the people's will might be prevented from abusing the rights of the minority. But would they be enough? With regard to the argument of *Federalist*

No. 10, Hamilton had already predicted in 1787 that Madison's theory would be insufficient because even in a large country, "The assembly when chosen will meet in one room if they are drawn from half the globe, and will be liable to all the passions of popular assemblies." They would quickly find common interests to invade the rights of the minority.[28] Besides, each state government was drawn from a narrower society than the whole nation, with much greater likelihood of sinister combinations against some minority. The "large republic" argument would not help there. Evidently something more was needed. Perhaps a property qualification for voting would help.

Madison's Views on Voting Rights

Madison reflected on the suffrage question in the 1780s, during the era of constitution making, and again at the end of his life in the 1820s. His opinions on this topic were more fully developed than those of any other leading Founder.

In his thoughts on suffrage, Madison never forgot what he called "the theory of free government," namely, "the fundamental principle that men cannot be justly bound by laws in making of which they have no part." Nevertheless, he was aware that the large-republic argument of *Federalist* No. 10 would not by itself produce responsible government. Madison turned to an additional device: a limitation of the electorate, or part of the electorate, by a property qualification.

He was aware of the dangers of limiting the franchise. At the Constitutional Convention of 1787, Madison acknowledged that "A gradual abridgment of this right has been the mode in which aristocracies have been built on the ruins of popular forms." Nevertheless,

> Viewing the subject in its merits alone, the freeholders [that is, landowners] of the country would be the safest depositories of republican liberty. In future times the great majority of the people will not only be without landed, but any other sort of property. These will either combine under the influence of their common situation, in which case the rights of property and the public liberty will not be secure in their hands; or, which is more probable, they will become the tools of opulence and ambition, in which case there will be equal danger on another side.[29]

Toward the end of his life, Madison corrected what he regarded as his error when he recommended a property requirement for voters in federal elections (a recommendation rejected by the Convention). Those without property, he now said, should have the right to vote for at least one house of the legislature. Their exclusion would violate "the vital principle of free government that those who are to be bound by the laws, ought to have a voice in making them. And the violation would be more strikingly unjust as the lawmakers become the minority."

Already in 1788 he had recommended that Kentucky follow the example of New York and North Carolina, where a "freehold or equivalent of a certain value" was "annexed to the right of voting for senators, and the right [was] left more at large in the election of the other house." (As we mentioned earlier, other states aimed at the same object by requiring that state senators own a sizable estate.) This mode of election, said Madison,

> secures the two cardinal objects of government, the rights of persons, and the rights of property. The former will be sufficiently guarded by one branch, the latter more particularly by the other. Give all power to property, and the indigent will be oppressed. Give it to the latter and the effect may be transposed. Give a defensive share to each and each will be secure.

By the 1820s Madison was seriously worried about the prospect of a growing class struggle between "wealthy capitalists and indigent laborers." At present, he wrote, "The United States have a precious advantage also in the actual distribution of property, particularly the landed property; and in the universal hope of acquiring property." But this happy state, he feared, would not last. As America grows, "a populousness not greater than that of England or France, will reduce the holders to a minority." In Madison's dreary view, "it is a lot of humanity" that "a large proportion" of those without property will be "necessarily reduced by a competition for employment to wages which afford them the bare necessities of life." America will then have "reached the stage of society in which conflicting feelings of the class with, and the class without property, have the operation natural to them in countries fully peopled": full-scale class struggle. It "might lead to contests and antipathies not dissimilar to those between the Patricians and Plebeians at Rome." At that point, when "the majority shall be without landed or other equivalent property and without the means or hope of acquiring it, what is to secure the rights of property against the danger from an equality and universality of suffrage, vesting complete power of property in hands without a share in it?"

Madison's gloomy predictions did not come true. Instead of declining, workers' wages have risen dramatically over the course of American history. True, only a small proportion of Americans are substantial landowners.

But many own their own homes, and a large majority have possessions and income that keep them far from the dire poverty that Madison feared would be their lot. Party divisions in today's America are far more complex than a class struggle of rich against poor. Democrats find their principal support among those who have inherited their wealth, intellectuals, single women, the nonworking poor, and others supported by government, some of them very well-to-do. Republicans are more likely to be middle-class and lower-middle-class workers, entrepreneurs, small businessmen, and those who have just acquired or are still acquiring their wealth.

Madison's worries remind one of Karl Marx's equally false prediction about the class struggle that he believed would grow from the declining wage rate and impoverishment of the workers under capitalism. Marx hoped and expected that this struggle would lead to the overthrow of liberal democracy and property rights. Madison agreed with Marx in his analysis of future trends within capitalism. But the proletarian revolution that Marx anticipated as the beginning of heaven on earth would have been condemned by Madison as a nightmarish repetition of the same old class struggle that had poisoned the politics of ancient Greece and Rome.

By the 1820s, property qualifications had all but vanished. After New York and North Carolina, no state adopted a property-based senate electorate. Instead, in 1821 New York opened the franchise for both senate and house elections to all taxpayers. Somewhat lamely (given his predictions), Madison resigned himself to future political control by those without property. He hoped that democracy would be saved by devices such as larger districts and longer terms of office for one branch of the legislature; "the difficulty of combining and effectuating unjust purposes throughout an extensive country"; "republican laws of descent and distribution [requiring equal shares for each child in inheritance], in equalizing the property of the citizens"; and "the popular sense of justice, enlightened and enlarged from a diffusive education."[30]

In spite of his bleak vision of the future, Madison's faith in democracy outweighed his anxieties.

Merits of the Arguments for Limiting Voting Rights

Madison and John Adams defended property qualifications for voters at their states' constitutional conventions in the 1820s (although Madison proposed admitting "house keepers and heads of families").[31] In Massachusetts the qualification was dropped; long after most other states, Virginia eventually followed in 1850. Madison and Adams did not welcome the arrival of universal suffrage. They feared the propertyless poor. They were not wrong, given their principles, to propose limits on the suffrage to protect the rights of individuals. But they judged the facts of their time incorrectly. No such limits were necessary.

Madison was aware that property rights would be supported not only by actual owners but also by those who have the "hope of acquiring property."[32] However, he thought the American economy would snuff out that hope as the population grew and all the land was bought up. James Wilson, a leading figure at the Federal Convention of 1787, judged the situation more accurately.

Like Madison, Wilson had at first supported the property qualification, praising it in 1774: "All those are [rightly] excluded from voting whose poverty is such, that they cannot live independent, and must therefore be subject to the undue influence of their superiors. Such are supposed to have no will of their own: and it is judged improper that they should vote in the representation of a free state." By the 1790s Wilson could endorse the provisions of those states without a property qualification, saying: "this right is extended to every freeman, . . . who, by having property, *or by being in a situation to acquire property,* possesses a common interest with his fellow citizens; and who is not in such uncomfortable circumstances as to render him necessarily dependent, for his subsistence, on the will of others."[33] Wilson now saw that almost every American, however poor, is "in a situation to acquire property."

Far from being lackeys of the rich, the poor were developing the same sturdy habits of self-reliance as the farmers that Madison and Jefferson liked to praise. Workers were no longer servants dependent on their masters; they were free employees who could, and often did, quit and move on to another job. Artisans who were once closely tied to patrons now "produced for impersonal markets," writes historian Gordon Wood. "No longer were apprentices dependents within a family; they became trainees within a business." Far from wanting to seize and redistribute the property of the wealthy, the poor saw America as a land where they, or their children, could prosper if they worked hard, postponed gratification, and obeyed the law.[34]

As we saw in the chapter on property rights, America's lack of class conflict was primarily due, not to the easy availability of land, but to the political regime itself, in the way that it defined and protected the right to acquire property. It was after the land was peopled from coast to coast that American wealth grew most dramatically. Madison feared for the future because he did not grasp the full meaning of Locke's account of how wealth grows through laws encouraging industry, investment, and production. Under the laws guaranteeing the right to use and acquire property, labor counted far more than land. Farms had value, but so did factories, shops, and offices peopled by businessmen and employees. In a country that protects the fruits of honest industry, the real sources of wealth and income were talents like intelligence, strength of character, inventiveness, entrepreneurial daring, tenacity, self-control, and ambition. More than fertile soil or any other physical thing, including money, these personal qualities led to success in America.[35]

Certainly the institutional devices defended by Madison in *Federalist* Nos. 10 and 51 helped defuse the possibility of class struggle. No doubt, as Madison hoped, the widespread public education of the poor, especially in the North, helped to spread sensible opinions about the rights of mankind, including the right to acquire and keep property. But most effective of all was the education provided by the regime itself, with its wide-open opportunities for the hardworking to have a house and livelihood of their own, by virtue of their own talents and efforts, without the leave of a master or patron. In this way, what Madison called the "most common and durable source of faction,"[36] the division between the rich and the poor, was kept under control in America. The poor were persuaded that protection of the rights of property holders would also secure their own rights—and their children's—to acquire property of their own. And so they did. Eventually, America became the wealthiest country in the world, and poverty was conquered to a greater degree than ever before in human history. It was safe, and therefore just, to allow almost all adult men—later, adult men and women—to vote.

6

Poverty and Welfare

$\mathcal{D}$id Americans before the twentieth century lack compassion for the poor? Did they treat the poor with indifference, or even cruelty? That is the impression given by most high school and college textbooks. Few students ever learn that government-funded welfare, not to mention generous private charity, has existed throughout American history.

James MacGregor Burns's *Government by the People,* a college text, says: "Contemporary American liberalism has its roots in Franklin Roosevelt's New Deal programs, designed to aid the poor and to protect people against unemployment and bank failures." He implies that the poor received no government aid or protection before the 1930s. Reinforcing this impression, Burns goes on to say, "American conservatism has its roots in the political thinking of John Adams, Alexander Hamilton, and many of their contemporaries. . . . Most conservatives opposed New Deal programs and the War on Poverty in the 1960s. . . . Human needs, they say, can and should be taken care of by charities."

Larry Berman and Bruce Murphy's *Approaching Democracy* gives a similar slant: "While poverty has existed in the United States since the early colonial days, it first reached the public agenda in the early 1900s as a result of the writings of muckraking journalists." If poverty "first reached the public agenda" only then, readers are likely to conclude that government did nothing about it before that time. Nothing in Berman and Murphy contradicts that conclusion.[1] Most history textbooks present accounts that are the same as, or similar to, the accounts given by these political scientists.

These claims about the American past are untrue or misleading. America has always had laws providing for the poor. The real difference between the Founders' and today's welfare policies is over *how,* not *whether,* government should help those in need. Neither approach has a monopoly on compassion. The question is, what policies help the poor and what policies harm them?

Conservatives today sometimes make the same mistake as liberals about America's past. Reacting to what they regard as the excesses of the modern welfare state, they tend to assume that poor relief in early America was entirely private. They continue to echo Barry Goldwater's statement in *Conscience of a Conservative,* written before he ran for president in 1964: "Let welfare be a private concern. Let it be promoted by individuals and families, by churches, private hospitals, religious service organizations, community charities and other institutions that have been established for this purpose."[2] Goldwater apparently did not realize that the Founders would have rejected such a policy as heartless.

Scholarly historians of welfare in America present a more accurate picture. But they too tend to dismiss the approach of earlier Americans, including the founding generation. The historians are generally dismayed by the earlier distinction between the deserving and undeserving poor. They tend to present the earlier welfare system as either a well-intentioned—or a mean-spirited—failure.

Michael Katz, for example, commenting on poorhouses, strongly endorsed by Thomas Jefferson, writes, "Miserable, poorly managed, underfunded institutions, trapped by their own contradictions, poorhouses failed to meet any of the goals so confidently predicted by their sponsors."

In the standard history of welfare in America, Walter Trattner writes that early American observers "concluded that no one ought to be poor, and there was little tolerance for the able-bodied pauper. The only cause of such poverty, it was assumed, was individual weakness. . . . [B]y the late eighteenth and early nineteenth century, Americans began to believe that poverty could, and should, be obliterated—in part, by allowing the poor to perish. . . . Stereotypes rather than individuals in need dominated the public mind." Trattner does not hide the ideology behind his judgments; at the end of the book he enthusiastically endorses President Clinton's national health care and welfare proposals.[3]

We will see that the Founders would have something to say in response to Katz's and Trattner's harsh and misleading words.

Jefferson and Franklin on Welfare

From the earliest colonial days, local governments took responsibility for their poor. However, able-bodied men and women generally were not supported by the taxpayers unless they worked. They would sometimes be placed in group homes that provided them food and shelter in exchange for labor. Only those too young, old, weak, or sick, and who had no friends or family to help, were taken care of in idleness.

The Founders had little to say about the topic of poor relief. Like the family, welfare was not a controversial topic. Two of their rare statements on the subject occur in writings provoked by foreigners: Jefferson's *Notes on Virginia,* written in answer to questions posed by a Frenchman, and an article criticizing the British welfare system written by Franklin for the British press.

Jefferson explained the Virginia poor laws at the time of the Revolution:

> The poor, unable to support themselves, are maintained by an assessment on the tithable persons in their parish. This assessment is levied and administered by twelve persons in each parish, called vestrymen, originally chosen by the housekeepers of the parish. . . . These are usually the most discreet farmers, so distributed through their parish, that every part of it may be under the immediate eye of some one of them. They are well acquainted with the details and economy of private life, and they find sufficient inducements to execute their charge well, in their philanthropy, in the approbation of their neighbors, and the distinction which that gives them. The poor who have neither property, friends, nor strength to labor, are boarded in the houses of good farmers, to whom a stipulated sum is annually paid. To those who are able to help themselves a little, or have friends from whom they derive some succors, inadequate however to their full maintenance, supplementary aids are given, which enable them to live comfortably in their own houses, or in the houses of their friends. Vagabonds, without visible property or vocation, are placed in workhouses, where they are well clothed, fed, lodged, and made to labor. Nearly the same method of providing for the poor prevails through all our states; and from Savannah to Portsmouth you will seldom meet a beggar.

In his proposed Virginia "Bill for Support of the Poor," Jefferson explained that "vagabonds" are "able-bodied persons not having wherewithal to maintain themselves, who shall waste their time in idle and dissolute courses, or shall loiter or wander abroad, refusing to work for reasonable wages, or to betake themselves to some honest and lawful calling, or who shall desert wives or children, without so providing for them as that they shall not become chargeable to a county." In the poorhouse to which vagabonds are sent, there would be an overseer, a "discreet man . . . for the government, employment, and correction of the persons subject to him." The bill restrained the overseer "from correcting any of them with more stripes than ten, at one time, for any one offence."

In the *Notes on Virginia* passage just quoted, Jefferson referred to "those without strength to labor." In his proposed bill, they were more precisely described as the "poor, lame, impotent [i.e., weak], blind and other inhabitants of the county as are not able to maintain themselves."

The terms "tithable," "parish," and "vestrymen" in the passage above refer to the pre-Revolutionary Southern practice of assigning care of the poor to the local Anglican church. In keeping with the spirit of the Revolution, which separated church from state, Virginia transferred this task from church to county government in 1785, as Jefferson had proposed.

Poor children whose families could not provide for them, including orphans, were put out to suitable persons as apprentices, so that they would learn "some art, trade, or business" while being of use to those training them. However, this was not to be done, in Jefferson's plan, until they had attended public school for three years, if necessary at public expense.[4]

All the typical features of early American welfare policy can be seen in Jefferson's descriptions and proposals:

1. The government of the community, not just private charity, assumes responsibility for its poor. This is far from the "throw them in the snow" attitude that is so often attributed to pre-1900 America.

2. Welfare is kept local, so that the administrators of the program will know the actual situations of the persons who ask for help. This will prevent abuses and freeloading. The normal human ties of friendship and neighborliness will partly animate the relationship of givers and recipients.

3. A distinction between the deserving and undeserving poor is carefully observed. Able-bodied vagabonds get help, but they are required to work in institutions where they will be strictly disciplined. Children and the disabled, on the other hand, are provided for, not lavishly, but without public shame. The homeless and beggars will not be abandoned, but neither will they disgrace the streets. They will be treated with toughness or mercy according to their circumstances.

4. Jefferson's idea of self-reliance was in fact family reliance, based on the traditional division of labor between husband and wife. Husbands were legally required to be their families' providers; wives were not. Nonsupporting husbands were shamed and punished by being sent to the poorhouse.

5. The poor laws were not intended to go beyond a minimal safety net. Benefit levels were low. The main remedy for poverty, in a land of opportunity, was marriage and work.

Jefferson regarded the poor laws as less important antipoverty measures than laws to promote the economic self-sufficiency of the common man, such as the abolition of primogeniture and entail. As Jefferson boasted to John Adams, "These laws, drawn by myself, laid the axe to the root of the pseudo-aristocracy." As we saw in the chapter on property rights, such laws restricting the use and ownership of private property were remnants of feudalism, where the common people were kept in their place by discouraging property owners from making the most economical use of the property they had or by making it hard for the poor to acquire property of their own. In America, said Jefferson, "everyone may have land to labor for himself if he chooses; or, preferring the exercise of any other industry, may exact for it such compensation as not only to afford a comfortable subsistence, but wherewith to provide for a cessation of labor in old age."[5]

When Benjamin Franklin lived in England in the 1760s, he observed that the poverty problem in that country was much worse than in America. Britain did not limit its support of the poor to a safety net provided under conditions that prevented abuse. There, the poor were given enough that they could live in idleness. The result was to increase poverty by giving the poor a powerful incentive not to become self-supporting. Franklin wrote:

> I am for doing good to the poor, but I differ in opinion of the means. I think the best way of doing good to the poor, is not making them easy in poverty, but leading or driving them out of it. In my youth I travelled much, and I observed in different countries, that the more public provisions were made for the poor, the less they provided for themselves, and of course became poorer. And, on the contrary, the less was done for them, the more they did for themselves, and became richer. There is no country in the world where so many provisions are established for them [as in England], . . . with a solemn general law made by the rich to subject their estates to a heavy tax for the support of the poor. . . . [Yet] there is no country in the world in which the poor are more idle, dissolute, drunken, and insolent. The day you [Englishmen] passed that act, you took away from before their eyes the greatest of all inducements to industry, frugality, and sobriety, by giving them a dependence on somewhat else than a careful accumulation during youth and health, for support in age and sickness. In short, you offered a premium for the encouragement of idleness, and you should not now wonder that it has had its effect in the increase of poverty.[6]

We see in Franklin's diagnosis a striking anticipation of today's welfare state, in which, as we will see later, poverty has increased as benefits have grown since the 1960s.

Franklin's understanding of the welfare paradox—that aid to the poor

must be managed carefully lest it promote indolence and therefore poverty—was shared by most Americans who wrote about and administered
poverty programs until the end of the nineteenth century.

The Declaration and the Obligation to Help the Poor

These were the Founders' practical proposals and views on poor relief.
Their policies were intended to help the poor in ways that did not violate
the rights of taxpayers or promote irresponsible behavior. From Jefferson's
standpoint, poverty programs that help people who choose not to work are
unjust. Far from being compassionate, compelling workers to support
shirkers makes some men masters and other men slaves: workers are
enslaved to nonworkers. That violates a fundamental principle of the Declaration of Independence.

Jefferson's whole career was devoted to the establishment of a government that would secure the rights of ordinary people against "pseudo-aris-
tocrats" who would oppress them. To say that all men are born with a right
to liberty means that no man has the right to rob another of the fruits of
his labor. That principle goes for any person or group in society, whether it
be European aristocrats, slaveholders, or those today who despise "dead-end
jobs" and "chump change." (In a 1989 survey, almost 75 percent of unemployed inner-city young people said they could find a job without difficulty.) As Abraham Lincoln explained in his debates with Douglas: "It is the
same tyrannical principle. It is the same principle in whatever shape it
develops itself. It is the same spirit that says, 'You work and toil and earn
bread, and I'll eat it.'"[7]

Jefferson affirmed his principled opposition to government redistribution of income from the rich to the poor in this statement:

> To take from one, because it is thought his own industry and that of his
> fathers has acquired too much, in order to spare to others, who, or
> whose fathers, have not exercised equal industry and skill, is to violate
> arbitrarily the first principle of association, the guarantee to everyone
> the free exercise of his industry and the fruits acquired by it.[8]

The "first principle of association" is the right to liberty, including the right
to the free exercise of one's industry and its fruits.

According to the Declaration of Independence, we have an unalienable or natural right only to those things that we possess by nature. We are
born alive and free, so life and liberty are natural rights. But no one has a

natural right to a decent income or free medical care.

Jefferson's opposition to transfer payments from taxpayers to the poor might be taken to mean, as libertarian law professor Richard Epstein argues, that "the basic rules of private property are inconsistent with any form of welfare benefits." Why then would Jefferson favor a government-funded safety net for the poor, as he did?

In John Locke's language, the law of nature teaches not only self-preservation but also the preservation of others, when one's "own preservation comes not in competition." Political society, which is organized for the security of its members' lives as well as their liberty and property, is obliged to respond to those in need. Those who refuse to work may be compelled; those who cannot work deserve the community's support. One might compare the Founders' conception of welfare to a social insurance policy. Even taxpayers benefit from the policy because there may come a time when they too need help. Epstein admits that welfare can be justified in such a view. But, he says, "benefits must be set low, perhaps uncomfortably low, in order to discourage perverse behavior undertaken solely to become eligible for benefits," and Epstein despairs that government could do so. He seems unaware of early American welfare policy. For that is exactly what Jefferson's plan, and Virginia's practice, achieved. Support of the poor was therefore part of the Founders' liberalism, but only on Jefferson's terms, that is, on the terms of the working man's right to liberty.[9]

Welfare Policy in the Founding Era and After

Jefferson's and Franklin's views were shared by most Americans during and after the founding era. James MacGregor Burns suggested, in the quotation on the first page of this chapter, that "conservatives" like Adams and Hamilton opposed government support of the poor. He cites no evidence to support that insinuation, because there is none.

Walter Trattner's *From Poor Law to Welfare State: A History of Social Welfare in America* criticizes early American welfare policy, as I mentioned before. Yet his book presents a mostly accurate picture of what was done. Trattner shows that the earlier policies have much to recommend them. Trattner says, "Most communities [in colonial America] attacked the problem of poverty with a high degree of civic responsibility." The same is true, in his telling, of the founding era and after. A historian of welfare in New York State during the founding era agrees: "Local communities attempted as best they could to assist their destitute neighbors, balancing compassion with economy, benevolence with discipline."

In colonial times, some communities supported the poor in their own homes or in the homes of others. As the poor population grew, many concluded that "outdoor relief" was leading people to look on welfare as an entitlement and creating a class of permanent dependents. Consequently, at the beginning of the nineteenth century, emphasis shifted to "indoor relief"—almshouses and workhouses. Now, writes Trattner:

> Public assistance would be confined to institutional care, mainly for the "worthy" or hard-core poor, the permanently disabled, and others who clearly could not care for themselves. Also, the able-bodied or "unworthy" poor who sought public aid would be institutionalized in workhouses where their behavior not only could be controlled but where, removed from society and its tempting vices, they presumably would acquire habits of industry and labor.

The nineteenth century was "the great era of institution building."

> For most people such institutions were not places of permanent, or even long-term, residence. . . . They were . . . temporary shelters for the jobless during times of depression and widespread unemployment; maternity homes for young, unmarried pregnant women; and places of last resort for orphans and sick, helpless, and childless elderly persons. . . . [A]lthough they generally were dreaded, poorhouses often served as key life supports amidst the harshness and uncertainty of existence in early industrial America.

Because public aid was so limited, there was wide scope for individual acts of generosity and liberality. Today's conservatives are right to point to private charities as an important source of poor relief in the old days. Even before the Revolution, writes Trattner, "Private philanthropy complemented public aid; both were part of the American response to poverty. While, from the outset, the public was responsible for providing aid to the needy, . . . as soon as they could afford to, private citizens and a host of voluntary associations also gave generously to those in distress."

After the Revolution and throughout the nineteenth century, hospitals for the poor, educational institutions, YMCAs, and Salvation Army branches were established in growing numbers all over America by public-spirited citizens. Like the public workhouses, these private charities distinguished between deserving and undeserving poor. Good character, it was thought, would enable most people to become self-sufficient. These agencies tried to build the character of their recipients through education, moral suasion, religious instruction, and work.

Marvin Olasky has shown in detail in *The Tragedy of American Compassion* how eighteenth- and nineteenth-century Americans combined Franklin's hardheaded realism about the ill effects of indiscriminate generosity with a warmhearted sympathy for those who fell into need through no fault of their own. Private welfare was often given by religious groups, and recipients were expected to pray, worship, and repent of the lazy habits and self-indulgence (such as excessive drinking) that often led them to seek assistance in the first place. Americans of that day believed that God himself set the proper example: his mercy is infinite—but only to the repentant who strive to mend their ways.[10]

From the Founding to 1965

Let us step back for a moment and look at poverty in a wider perspective. If we rank poverty and welfare policies in terms of quantity of money and material goods given to people who are poor, then today's policies are far more effective than the Founders'. Benefit levels are much higher, and far more people are eligible for support. That is what leads historians like Michael Katz to condemn the earlier approach as a failure.

However, if poverty and welfare policies are judged by their effectiveness in providing for the minimal needs of the poor while dramatically reducing poverty in a society over time, then America before 1965 could be said to have had the most successful welfare policy in world history. By the same benchmark, post-1965 poverty programs have failed.

Two centuries ago most Americans—at least 90 percent—were desperately poor by today's standards. Most houses were small, ill-constructed, and poorly heated and insulated. Based on federal family income estimates, 59 percent of Americans lived in poverty as late as 1929, before the Great Depression. In 1947, the government reported that 32 percent of Americans were poor. By 1969 that figure had declined to 12 percent, where it remained for ten years. Since then, the percentage of poor Americans has increased to about 15 percent. In other words, before the huge growth in government spending on poverty programs, poverty was declining rapidly in America. After the new programs were fully implemented, poverty stopped declining and began to rise.[11]

The recipe for America's enormously successful pre-1960s antipoverty program was:

1. Establish free markets and protect property rights. Keep taxes and regulation at a minimum to encourage the poor to provide for

themselves through their own work and entrepreneurship. (See chapter 2, "Property Rights.")

2. Provide strong government support for lifelong marriage and for a morality of self-controlled self-assertion (a morality combining industriousness, self-restraint, and basic decency with the vigilant spirit that says "Don't tread on me"). The self-reliant family was to be the nation's main poverty program. (See chapter 4, "Women and the Family," and chapter 7, "Immigration and the Moral Conditions of Citizenship.")

3. As the poverty program of last resort, provide minimal, safety-net public and private support in local communities for the poor whose families were unable or unwilling to provide for them.

In the older America, most poor people were free to work or go into business without asking permission from government. Low taxes and minimal regulation allowed them to keep almost all of the fruits of their labor. The stability of marriage encouraged men to meet their family obligations. Government officials, teachers, and writers praised the dignity of responsible self-support and condemned irresponsible dependency on government handouts. In the middle ages a serf might have worked hard all his life, but much of what he produced went into the hands of a wealthy landowner. In most countries of the world, including America today, government regulation and licensing requirements often prevent the poor from entering and competing freely in the market. Besides, much of what the working poor earn through their own efforts is taxed away to support those who do not work.

In the nineteenth century, a few American intellectuals, typically influenced by European thinkers opposed to the Founders' idea of property rights, questioned the idea of individual responsibility. By 1900, many intellectuals were turning away from the traditional American view that in a free country destitution usually comes to the able-bodied from a defect in character, while frugal and industrious conduct usually leads to an adequate living.

Amos Warner, author of the influential *American Charities* (1894), wrote that unemployment, not shiftlessness and drunkenness, was the most frequent cause of poverty. Robert Hunter's *Poverty* (1904), another important book of the Progressive Era, blamed unemployment almost entirely on "miserable and unjust social conditions." Around the same time, Edward Devine, the editor of *Charities,* a leading periodical of the welfare reformers, said: "We may safely throw overboard, once and for all, the idea that

. . . there is any necessary connection between wealth and virtue, or between poverty and guilt." The new solution: increase benefit levels and eligibility and remove the moral stigma from poverty, whatever its cause.

Of course, the Founders had never claimed that all poverty was caused by bad character. Jefferson's poor law had made a clear distinction between those who were able to work but preferred not to and those whose age or disability prevented them from working. The new approach tended to blame indiscriminately what later came to be called "the system" for poverty of every kind.[12]

In spite of this intellectual assault on traditional welfare policy, the Founders' approach persisted—in modified form, to be sure—until the 1960s. Contrary to common opinion, for example, Franklin Roosevelt's New Deal modified but did not greatly change the older pattern. Social Security was originally sold as an insurance scheme in which workers funded their own retirement. Christopher Jencks explains how different was the original congressional conception of AFDC (Aid to Families with Dependent Children) from today's welfare:

> When Congress established ADC in 1935, it thought it was subsidizing a set of state programs known as "mothers' pensions." These programs had been established to ensure that indigent widows of good character did not have to place their children in orphanages. Not all states explicitly restricted benefits to widows, but most states did limit benefits to mothers who could provide their children with a "suitable" home. Local officials usually interpreted this requirement as excluding unwed, separated, and divorced mothers, on the grounds that such women set a poor moral example for their children.

However, the 1935 law had been based on a report written by bureaucrats in the Children's Bureau who made sure that the language of the law would permit (although not require) states to give aid to divorced women and single mothers. Looking back on the episode, Frances Perkins, FDR's liberal secretary of labor, said that she

> felt that the Children's Bureau had let her down on the provision of aid to mothers with dependent children. . . . She said it never occurred to her, in view of the fact that she'd been active in drives for homes that took care of mothers with illegitimate children, that these mothers would be [eligible for aid]. She blamed the huge illegitimacy rates among blacks on aid to mothers with dependent children.

Perkins, like most Americans at that time, accepted the older distinction between the deserving and undeserving poor, a distinction based on moral conduct.[13]

State governments gradually loosened welfare eligibility standards and increased benefit levels during the 1940s and 1950s. But it was not until the mid-1960s that welfare was officially conceived as a right to be demanded of society by anyone in need, regardless of conduct or circumstances.

Poverty and Welfare Policy after 1965

Before 1965, most Americans believed that property rights and the marriage-based family were the most effective means to get people out of poverty. After 1965, government policy and elite opinion turned against the older view. We described the new conception of property rights in chapter 2. In order to help the poor, government raised taxes on the working poor. In the name of safety and environmentalism, it set up licensing requirements and regulations that make it harder for the poor to go into business building houses, repairing air conditioners, exterminating insects, fixing cars, or running a store or restaurant. Local governments set up building codes that were meant to guarantee safe dwellings and businesses, but which deprive the poor of inexpensive housing. Code requirements drive up the costs of new houses by tens of thousands of dollars. Moreover, government routinely tears down poor people's houses that are not "up to code" for defects as minor as peeling paint. The city of Dallas demolished over a thousand private homes between 1992 and 1995, most of them in low-income and minority areas, sending previous residents onto the welfare rolls or into the streets as homeless.[14]

The most destructive feature of the post-1965 approach has been its unintentional promotion of family breakdown, which is a recipe for the neglect and abuse of children, the widespread crime that such abuse fosters, the impoverishment of women and children, and the loneliness and anguish of everyone involved.

We discussed the reasons that people get married and stay married (or used to) in chapter 4, "Women and the Family": happiness, usefulness, moral obligation, and the penalty of shame and the law for those who misbehave. Post-1965 policies and ideas have ravaged all four of these supports of marriage. Recent welfare policies have particularly undermined the usefulness of marriage for many women, at least in the short-term horizon in which people sometimes make such decisions. Marriage makes possible an efficient division of labor for raising children and providing for the care and livelihood of people of all ages. In the usual arrangement, the husband is the principal provider and protector, and the wife bears and tends the children when they are young.

George Gilder has explained better than anyone else the role of welfare in family breakdown. Most women have a natural superiority to men in affairs of love and the heart, including especially bearing and nurturing children. Every known society regards sex and love as a gift of a woman to a man. What, then, can a man offer a woman? To put it bluntly, money and honor. Women rarely marry men who make less money than they do or whose social rank is below their own (unless the men have a good career in prospect), and women frequently divorce men who make less. Men and women quickly lose romantic interest in each other when one of the partners cannot offer an equalizing contribution.

When increasingly generous government support became widely available to women in the 1960s, illegitimacy and divorce grew dramatically. As Gilder writes, "Female jobs and welfare payments usurped the man's role as provider, leaving fatherless families." Welfare destroys the incipient families of the poor by making the struggling male breadwinner superfluous and thereby emasculating him emotionally. His response is predictable. He turns to the supermasculine world of the street: drinking, drugs, male companionship, and crime. "This is the source of the tangle of pathology in the ghetto: the dissolution of the ties that bind men to their children."[15]

The incentive structure of the modern welfare state is similar to the one that Franklin condemned in old England, except that ours is more generous and more tolerant of single motherhood. Since 1965, when President Lyndon Johnson inaugurated the modern War on Poverty, total annual government welfare spending has grown from less than $9 billion (1.3 percent of gross domestic product) to $324 billion (5 percent of GDP) in 1993. Between 1965 and 1994, the government spent $5.4 trillion on poverty programs, enough money to buy every factory, office building, hotel, motel, airline, trucking company, and all manufacturing equipment in the United States.

Although much of this money goes to administrators and overhead, welfare almost always pays unskilled single mothers more than they could get by working or marrying. In 1995 there were seventy-seven different federal welfare programs, and many more were run by states and local communities. Just counting the top six federal programs (Aid to Families with Dependent Children, food stamps, Medicaid, housing, nutrition assistance, and energy assistance), a single mother of two was eligible in 1995 for benefits that were the equivalent of a job paying $11.59 per hour in California, $13.13 in New York, and $14.66 in Massachusetts ($24,100, $27,300, and $30,500 annually). In California and New York, the value of this package of welfare benefits was only 15 percent below the average salary in the state; in Massachusetts, the value was 4 percent higher. Minimum wage jobs do not even come close to competing with welfare in most states. These figures do not take into account state and local benefits. In New York City, the total value of all benefits available to the average single mother of two in 1995 was $40,000 per year, or $19.24 per hour.

From the point of view of the usefulness of marriage, the choice of the poor to forgo work is, as Charles Murray writes, "the behavior of people responding to the reality of the world around them and making the decisions—the legal, approved, and even encouraged decisions—that maximize their quality of life." Robert Rector explains:

> The current welfare system may be conceptualized best as a system which offers each single mother . . . a "paycheck." . . . She will continue to receive her "paycheck" as long as she fulfills two conditions: (1) she must not work; and (2) she must not marry an employed male . . . [Welfare] has converted the low-income working husband from a necessary breadwinner into a net financial handicap. It has transformed marriage from a legal institution designed to protect and nurture children into an institution that financially penalizes nearly all low-income parents who enter into it.[16]

This kind of conduct will decrease but will remain massive under the welfare reforms promoted by conservatives in the 1990s. Forcing single mothers to work in exchange for welfare makes welfare more burdensome, but it does not remove its attractiveness altogether. The government-guaranteed jobs and day care that such schemes often require simply make the money less convenient. The basic problem—that government makes it affordable for women to bear and raise children without husbands, while living independently in households of their own—is still there. Large numbers of women will continue to live in this way until Americans once again distinguish between the deserving and undeserving poor, and provide the undeserving only with the basic necessities in strictly governed group homes that show society's disapproval of women bearing children outside of marriage and of able-bodied men refusing to work. Or, to put it positively, if a society really believes that marriage is the best arrangement for the well-being of men, women, and children, then its laws and customs must reflect that belief seriously, consistently, and effectively.

High benefit levels and irresponsible attitudes toward sex and marriage create a world in which many children have few ties to their fathers and often do not even know who they are; in which women, mostly unmarried, are frequently beaten, raped, and exploited by the predatory men so often produced by these fatherless families; and in which many men join gangs and take up crime as a way of life. This is a world not only of poverty but also of barbaric brutalization, emotional chaos, and ever present danger. It increasingly resembles Hobbes's state of nature, where life is "solitary, poor, nasty, brutish, and short."

One cannot help being reminded of Benjamin Franklin's final verdict on the British welfare system—a system, he argued, that promoted poverty by supporting people who chose not to work:

> Repeal that [welfare] law, and you will soon see a change in their manners. St. *Monday*, and St. *Tuesday*, will soon cease to be holidays. *Six days shalt thou labor*, though one of the old commandments long treated as out of date, will again be looked upon as a respectable precept; industry will increase, and with it plenty among the lower people; their circumstances will mend, and more will be done for their happiness by inuring them to provide for themselves, than could be done by dividing all your estates among them.[17]

7

Immigration and the Moral Conditions of Citizenship

$\mathcal{A}$merica has a long and generous tradition of welcoming as equal citizens a larger number of immigrants, from a greater variety of national and religious origins, than any other nation in history. Shortly before the Civil War, Abraham Lincoln gave a beautiful speech in Chicago on the tie that binds American citizens together and makes them one people. There are many Americans, he said, who are not blood descendants of the American Founders:

> If they look back through this history to trace their connection with those days by blood, they find they have none, they cannot carry themselves back into that glorious epoch and make themselves feel that they are part of us, but when they look through that old Declaration of Independence, they find that those old men say that "We hold these truths to be self-evident, that all men are created equal," and then they feel that that moral sentiment taught in that day evidences their relation to those men, that it is the father of all moral principle in them, and that they have a right to claim it as though they were blood of the blood, and flesh of the flesh, of the men who wrote that Declaration—and so they are. That is the electric cord in that Declaration that links the hearts of patriotic and liberty-loving men together, that will link those patriotic hearts as long as the love of freedom exists in the minds of men throughout the world.

Although Lincoln was speaking to European-Americans, there is nothing in his account of citizenship that is limited to Europeans. Any human being is capable of becoming an American, because the equality principle that defines America, as Lincoln wrote on another occasion, is "an abstract truth, applicable to all men and all times."[1]

Despite this understanding of American citizenship, the United States has always set limits on immigration or naturalization. Until 1870, only whites were eligible for citizenship, and almost all immigration came from northern and western Europe. After the huge 1880–1914 immigration

wave, of which southern and eastern Europeans made up a large proportion, numbers were kept relatively low by the restrictive immigration legislation of the 1920s. The 1965 Immigration Act tremendously increased
the numbers and changed the sources of immigrants. This law in effect
made it harder for Europeans and easier for non-Europeans to come to
America. Between 1990 and 1994, over 1.2 million people per year—80
percent of them non-Europeans—immigrated into the United States. This
does not include the 275,000 or more who enter and remain illegally each
year. In 1997 the government estimated that there were 5 million immigrants residing in the United States in violation of the law.[2]

Most Americans think these levels are too high. A 1989-90 survey
found that 74 percent of non-Hispanic white citizens and 75 percent of
Mexican-American citizens agreed with the statement, "There are too
many immigrants." In 1994, California voters approved Proposition 187,
which bars illegal aliens from receiving welfare benefits or free public education. In 1995 the U.S. Commission on Immigration Reform recommended that immigration be reduced by one-third, and that immigration
policy be changed to bring in more skilled and fewer unskilled workers.[3]

This raises the question: Are Americans' historical and current attitudes
on immigration somehow un-American? Or are immigration limits in
accord with American principles?

The prevailing view among mainstream scholars and in the popular
media is that if we believe in human equality, it is unfair to deny entry to
anyone. Especially objectionable, in their view, was the earlier American
practice of considering the potential immigrants' national origin in deter-
mining immigration policy. Yale political scientist Rogers Smith, for example, believes that this practice was "quite obviously . . . inconsistent with
the ideals of liberty and equality professed in . . . the nation's 'Creed.'" Anything less than large-scale immigration is "undemocratic," *Time* magazine
writes.[4]

Opponents of today's high levels of immigration generally accept the
view that the equality principle requires open borders or something close
to them. Therefore, to make the case for limits, they tend to talk about economics or culture or ethnicity rather than liberty and equality. When they
do address principle, they often embrace what may be called an ethnocultural conception of America that rejects or severely qualifies Lincoln's the-
sis, quoted above, that what defines America is the idea of equality in the
Declaration of Independence. For example, M. E. Bradford, a conservative
traditionalist, wrote that when immigration policy is founded on "natural
rights imperatives," it is "certain to boil over into a demand for less and less
restriction" on immigration. John O'Sullivan, editor of the conservative

journal *National Review*, agrees. He rejects the view that "Americans are defined by their allegiances to a set of liberal political principles, notably liberty and equality, outlined in the Declaration of Independence and embodied in the Constitution."[5]

The American Founders would reject both of today's dominant views. They would agree with those who say that America is based on the principle that all human beings are born free and equal. But they would reject the conclusion that this requires minimal or no restraints on immigration. The Founders supported the view that a nation may, and sometimes must, set limits on immigration, even to the point of considering national origin. But they based this view on the equality principle, not on its rejection.

Washington on Immigration

George Washington frequently commented on immigration and citizenship. His approach, shared by most of the founding generation, had two main features. First, America should generously welcome as equal citizens people from many nations and religions. Second, the numbers and kinds of immigrants may need to be limited with a view to the qualities of character required for democratic citizenship.

Washington wrote, "The bosom of America is open to receive not only the opulent and respectable stranger, but the oppressed and persecuted of all nations and religions." His openness to non–Protestant citizenship is evident in his letter to the Hebrew congregation in Newport, written just after he had been elected America's first president:

> The citizens of the United States of America have the right to applaud themselves for having given to mankind examples of an enlarged and liberal policy worthy of imitation. All possess alike liberty of conscience and immunities of citizenship. It is now no more that toleration is spoken of as if it were by the indulgence of one class of citizens that another enjoyed the exercise of their inherent natural rights, for happily the Government of the United States, which gives to bigotry no sanction, to persecution no assistance, requires only that they who live under its protection should demean themselves as good citizens in giving it on all occasions their effectual support.[6]

In Washington's account, America is different from, and superior to, countries based on a common ethnic or racial background, or a common religion, because its government protects the "inherent natural rights" of all human beings. As a result, for the first time since ancient Israel, Jews could become full citizens of a political community.

Washington's generous (the older meaning of *liberal*) conception of citizenship was widely held in America. In spite of a strong aversion to Catholicism among a fervently Protestant American people, the Continental Congress of 1774 invited the French-speaking Catholics of Quebec to "unite with us in one social compact, formed on the generous principles of equal liberty." On the potentially explosive religious question, Congress wrote,

> We are too well acquainted with the liberality of sentiment distinguishing your nation to imagine that difference of religion will prejudice you against a hearty amity with us. You know that the transcendent nature of freedom elevates those who unite in her cause above all such low-minded infirmities.

The common ground of "natural and civil rights," taught in the writings of "your immortal countryman, Montesquieu," would be the basis of the union.

Some are inclined to dismiss this episode as a cynical move born of desperation, considering the strong anti-Catholic sentiments voiced against the earlier Quebec Act. But the view stated in the letter to Quebec proved to be the authentic expression of the American mind in the founding era. Its principles became the basis for extending religious liberty to all Americans in the early state constitutions and laws.[7]

Washington's openness to common citizenship with those who were neither Protestants nor descended from Englishmen did not, however, lead him to favor unlimited immigration. He believed that immigrants of the wrong sort and in the wrong quantity would endanger American liberty. The purpose of government is to secure the rights to life, liberty, and the pursuit of happiness. Immigration policy, like all public policy, must be tailored to that end. When Washington affirmed American openness to immigrants "of all nations and religions," as quoted above, he continued by saying, "we shall welcome [them] to a participation of all our rights and privileges, if by decency and propriety of conduct they appear to merit the enjoyment."[8] Likewise, he did not say to the Newport Jews that people of all religions were welcome in America regardless of their conduct. He said that the government requires "that they who live under its protection should demean themselves as good citizens in giving it on all occasions their effectual support."

Whenever he discussed immigration, Washington linked his "liberal" vision of a multinational and multireligious America with a "conservative" concern about the character of those who would become Americans. To Jefferson in 1788 he wrote that the new U.S. Constitution "would render this country the asylum of *pacific and industrious characters* from all parts of Europe . . . by giving security to property, and liberty to its holders." Washington's hope that America might become an "asylum to the *virtuous* and persecuted part of mankind, to whatever nation they may belong," led him to go out of his way to encourage immigration from the Netherlands. To a Dutch preacher recently arrived in New York, Washington wrote: "This country certainly promises greater advantages, than almost any other, to persons of moderate property, who are determined to be sober, industrious, and virtuous members of society." The Dutch, he said, had these qualities, and they were also known to be "friends to the rights of mankind." They would be "a valuable acquisition to our infant settlements."[9]

Besides being concerned about immigrants' character, Washington also noted the problem created when too many foreigners settle at one time in one location. In a letter to Vice President John Adams, he wrote:

> the policy or advantage of [immigration] taking place in a body (I mean the settling of them in a body) may be much questioned; for, by so doing, they retain the language, habits, and principles (good or bad) which they bring with them. Whereas by an intermixture with our people, they, or their descendants, get assimilated to our customs, measures, and laws: in a word, soon become *one people.*[10]

Benjamin Franklin had worried about the problem of immigrant numbers as an obstacle to assimilation in the 1750s, when a large number of German settlers threatened to transform the character of Pennsylvania:

> Those who come hither are generally of the most ignorant stupid sort of their own nation. . . . Not being used to liberty, they know not how to make a modest use of it. . . . [In elections] they come in droves, and carry all before them, except in one or two counties. . . . In short, unless the stream of their importation could be turned from this to other colonies, . . . they will soon so outnumber us, that all the advantages we have will not in my opinion be able to preserve our language, and even our government will become precarious. . . . Yet I am not for refusing entirely to admit them into our colonies; all that seems to be necessary is to distribute them equally, mix them with the English, establish English schools where they are now too thick settled.

As it happened, restrictions on immigration from Europe did not become necessary. War between Britain and France greatly reduced the influx, and the German population stabilized at about one-third of Pennsylvania. Except for the Amish, whose numbers were too small to affect the character of the state, they gradually took on the ways of the English-speaking majority.[11]

Franklin expressed his cautious view of immigration again in "Information to Those Who Would Remove to America" (1784). When Jefferson was ambassador to France in the late 1780s, he showed his approval of Franklin's pamphlet by reprinting and distributing it. America had evidently gotten a reputation among some Europeans as a place of loose and easy living. Franklin warned them that "America is the land of labor, and by no means what the English call Lubberland, and the French *pays de Cocagne,* where the streets are said to be paved with half-peck loaves, the houses tiled with pancakes, and where the fowls fly about ready roasted, crying, *Come eat me!*" The absence of wealth obliges most Americans "to follow some business for subsistence." "Industry and constant employment are great preservatives of the morals and virtue of a nation."[12] Jefferson and Franklin wanted to discourage would-be immigrants who were not prepared to adopt what is now called the work ethic.

Other leading Founders held opinions similar to those of Washington and Franklin. In a speech in the first Congress of 1790, James Madison welcomed immigrants to citizenship, but "believed it necessary to guard against abuses. They should induce the worthy of mankind to come, the object being to increase the wealth and strength of the country. Those who would weaken it were not wanted." Therefore Madison favored the law, which was soon approved, establishing a residency requirement for foreigners wishing to become citizens.[13]

Three years earlier, at the Constitutional Convention, Madison said, "He wished to maintain the character of liberality which had been professed in all the constitutions and publications of America. He wished to invite foreigners of merit and republican principles among us. America was indebted to emigration for her settlement and prosperity."[14]

Jefferson and Hamilton on Immigration

Historians sometimes place Washington on the conservative and Thomas Jefferson on the liberal end of the Founders' political spectrum. Actually, almost all the prominent men of the founding era agreed on the fundamental principles of natural rights on which America was based, although they often disagreed among themselves on the best way to secure the rights of mankind consistently with government by consent. Washington and Jefferson (along with Franklin and Hamilton) held very similar views of immigration, except for an episode that we will mention shortly.

The need for immigration to fill a sparsely populated land occasioned one of the complaints against the British king that Jefferson included in the Declaration of Independence: "He has endeavored to prevent the population of these states; for that purpose obstructing the laws for naturalization of foreigners; refusing to pass others to encourage their migration hither." But Jefferson did not favor unlimited immigration any more than Washington. In Query 8 of his book, *Notes on Virginia,* Jefferson questioned "[t]he present desire of America . . . to produce rapid population by as great an importation of foreigners as possible." In doing so he gave one of the fullest explanations of the principles shared by the founding generation guiding their thoughts on immigration.

Jefferson's point of departure was his concern for liberty:

> Every species of government has its specific principles. Ours perhaps are more peculiar than those of any other in the universe. It is a composition of the freest principles of the English constitution, with others derived from natural right and natural reason.

"Natural right and natural reason" refer to the "laws of nature and of nature's God" of the Declaration of Independence. These laws, discovered by reason, teach us "truths" that are "self-evident": that "all men are created equal, that they are endowed by their Creator with certain unalienable rights, that among these are life, liberty, and the pursuit of happiness."

Jefferson was saying that America's principles are the principles of the Declaration, combined with only that part of the British tradition which is fully compatible with liberty and equality. Jefferson was not saying that America is defined by its ethnocultural British heritage, as some conservatives now argue. (Russell Kirk went so far as to entitle one of his books *America's British Culture.*)[15] Jefferson was glad that America had repudiated those aristocratic and monarchical parts of its English heritage that are incompatible with political liberty. But this does not mean that America can afford to be indifferent to the character and numbers of its immigrants. He wrote that "nothing can be more opposed" to the principles of American government

> than the maxims of absolute monarchies. Yet, from such, we are to expect the greater number of emigrants. They will bring with them the principles of the governments they leave, imbibed in their early youth; or, if

able to throw them off, it will be in exchange for an unbounded licentiousness, passing, as is usual, from one extreme to another. It would be a
miracle were they to stop precisely at the point of temperate liberty.
These principles, with their language, they will transmit to their children.
In proportion to their numbers, they will share with us the legislation.
They will infuse into it their spirit, warp and bias its direction, and render it a heterogeneous, incoherent, distracted mass.

Jefferson feared that people accustomed to despotism will lack the vigilant
spirit of self-assertion to resist the natural tendency of government toward
oppression, while those whom despots have forbidden to control their own
lives will be licentious when given free rein, lacking the self-control to live
in "temperate liberty." From these reflections, Jefferson did not conclude
that there was any need to restrict immigration; in moderate numbers,
additional population was good for America, especially "useful artificers"
with the right skills. He did think it imprudent to promote it: "If they come
of themselves, they are entitled to all the rights of citizenship: but I doubt
the expediency of inviting them by extraordinary encouragements."[16]

Jefferson changed his mind about immigration, at least temporarily,
after his election to the presidency. However, short-term partisan calcula-
tion, not a principled rethinking of his earlier position, seems to have been
at work. The votes of recent immigrants had been important, perhaps decisive, in the narrow Jefferson-Burr victory of 1800 (as they have generally
been for the Democratic Party ever since). In his First Annual Message to
Congress, Jefferson proposed immediate naturalization of foreigners instead
of the fourteen-year residency then required. He argued that this lengthy
period discouraged desirable immigration; that it refused hospitality to "the
unhappy fugitives from distress"; that a mere declaration of "a *bona fide* purpose of embarking his life and fortunes permanently with us" should be
sufficient for admission to citizenship.

Jefferson's old opponent, Alexander Hamilton, criticized this proposal
in two newspaper editorials. Hamilton was no opponent of immigration
from Europe; he had strongly commended it in his 1791 *Report on Manufactures,* which he had written when he was secretary of the treasury under
President Washington. But Hamilton did not think citizenship should be
given as cheaply as Jefferson recommended in 1801. He quoted at length
the passage from Jefferson's *Notes on Virginia* on the dangers of too rapid an
admixture of foreigners into America. Hamilton then went on to say, in his
own name:

The safety of a republic depends essentially on the energy of a common
national sentiment; on a uniformity of principles and habits; on the

exemption of the citizens from foreign bias and prejudice; and on the love of country which will almost invariably be found to be closely connected with birth, education, and family. The opinion advanced in *Notes on Virginia* is undoubtedly correct, that foreigners will generally be apt to bring with them attachments to the persons they have left behind; to the country of their nativity, and to its particular customs and manners. They will also entertain opinions on government congenial with those under which they have lived; or if they should be led hither from a preference to ours, how extremely unlikely is it that they will bring with them that *temperate love of liberty,* so essential to real republicanism?

In sum, Hamilton wrote:

> In the recommendation to admit indiscriminately foreign emigrants of every description to the privileges of American citizens, on their first entrance into our country, there is an attempt to break down every pale which has been erected for the preservation of a national spirit and a national character; and to let in the most powerful means of perverting and corrupting both the one and the other.[17]

Hamilton, like the earlier Jefferson, was arguing that "real republicanism"—based, as Hamilton said elsewhere, echoing the Declaration, on "the unalienable rights of mankind,"[18] held equally by all—can only be sustained by a "temperate love of liberty." That, in turn, requires that immigrants leave behind their "foreign bias and prejudice" and acquire republican "opinions on government" and republican habits of moderation.

In spite of Jefferson's call for immediate naturalization, Congress, dominated by Jefferson's party, sided with Hamilton (and the earlier Jefferson) against President Jefferson. They voted to return to the pre-1798 requirement of a five-year residency before admission to citizenship.

The Equality Principle and the *Right* to Exclude

None of the Founders gave a theoretical account of the right of a political community to exclude would-be immigrants. That is because such a right was obvious to all as an inference from the general principles they all shared. No one in the early debates in Congress on naturalization laws doubted the government's right to determine exclusionary criteria for citizenship. It is possible, however, to understand the principled basis of the Founders' understanding by reflecting on the equality principle announced in the Declaration of Independence and in the declarations of rights in several of the early state constitutions.

The Declaration of Independence says that "all men are created equal." Virginia and Pennsylvania declared, "All men are by nature equally free and independent." Massachusetts said, "All men are born free and equal." Each of these formulas has the same meaning. All human beings are equal in the sense of possessing the same natural rights to life, liberty, and the pursuit of happiness. But when men live outside of government (in a "state of nature," as Madison calls it in *Federalist* No. 51), "the weaker individual is not secured against the violence of the stronger." Therefore, says the Declaration, "to secure these rights, governments are instituted among men." That happens when one part of mankind, one people, separates itself from the rest and establishes a political community. The government of that community secures the people's life, liberty, and property against those who might threaten them. It does not attempt to secure the inalienable rights of people outside of that community. In the sense of the Declaration, a people is any self-selected group which agrees to live together as a political community. If the government so formed is to be consistent with the natural right to liberty, it must be formed by, and operate by, consent and do its best to secure the natural rights of all citizens. As a practical matter, that means majority rule through a government of elected representatives.

One people can become two peoples (as almost happened in America in the 1860s), and two peoples can become one (as in the former Czechoslovakia). The original draft of the Declaration said, "We might have been a free and a great people together," implying that Americans and British had been, or could have become, one people.[19] But the Declaration called the United States "one people" that is about to "dissolve the political bands which have connected them with another." A people, in the sense of the Declaration, is not defined by a common religion, language, location, or ethnicity, although it usually shares some or all of those things. It is not some organic growth in which a person's individuality is dissolved in the larger unit. It is constituted by the free choice of each member.[20]

The preamble of the Massachusetts Constitution of 1780 expresses the Founders' understanding perfectly: "The body-politic is formed by a voluntary association of individuals: It is a social compact, by which the whole people covenants with each citizen, and each citizen with the whole people, that all shall be governed by certain laws for the common good." If the community does not wish to covenant with a particular individual, or if an individual refuses to covenant with the rest of the community, the condition of citizenship is not met. In other words, one obvious meaning of the right to liberty is that all people are free to associate with—to form a compact with—whomever they wish. Before two persons enter the marriage contract, they are free to marry whomever they please; before individuals enter the social compact, they are free to become fellow citizens with whomever they choose.[21]

The crucial point for the question of a *right to exclude* newcomers from citizenship is this: Once a people forms itself, no one has a right to join it without the consent of those being joined. No outsider has any more right to claim membership in an already existing people than he has a right to intrude himself into a household where he has not been invited.

In accordance with this understanding, Gouverneur Morris observed at the Constitutional Convention of 1787 that "every society from a great nation down to a club had the right of declaring the conditions on which new members should be admitted."[22] The Constitution therefore lays down citizenship requirements for officers of the national government and grants Congress the right "to establish an uniform rule of naturalization." There is no natural right to immigrate or to become a citizen of a country of one's choice where one has not been invited.

Today, however, it is frequently said that it is wrong to deny foreigners the blessings of American liberty. This leads Roger Mahoney, the Catholic cardinal of Los Angeles, to assert, "The right to immigrate is more fundamental than that of nations to control their borders."[23] The Founders would answer: The purpose of government is to secure the rights of the people, that is, the citizens, the people who form the government. The Declaration of Independence was issued "in the name, and by authority of the good people *of these colonies.*" When government fails to secure the rights of the people, it is their right and duty "to alter or abolish it" for the sake of "*their* safety and happiness." "We the people of the United States" established the Constitution of 1787 to "secure the blessings of liberty to *ourselves* and *our* posterity." To say that there is a fundamental right to immigrate is as much as to say that the government of one country is obliged to secure the rights of every person in the world who presents himself and demands it. Such an obligation is by nature both impossible and unjust. It is a violation of the liberty of a people to live with those they choose to associate with, and therefore a violation of the fundamental terms of the social compact. In the Founders' understanding, Americans are no more responsible for securing the rights of Mexicans and Haitians than Mexicans and Haitians are for securing the rights of Americans. Each people must undertake the task of securing its natural rights by and for itself.

This does not mean that Americans may treat foreigners unjustly. In *Federalist* No. 43, Madison touched on the delicate question of what would be the relation of the states that ratify the new Constitution (the new "United States of America") with states that refuse to ratify it. America, he wrote, will have "no political relation" with the nonratifiers (or with other foreign countries). But the "claims of justice, both on one side and on the other, will be in force, and must be fulfilled; the rights of humanity must in all cases be duly and mutually respected." We must not harm foreigners' lives, liberty, or property. But when we refuse to admit foreigners to our community, we do not treat them unjustly or deny them their rights. We simply leave them in the same condition they were in before.

The natural right to liberty also means that individuals are free to emigrate. Otherwise, a child, who does not choose what country he is born in, could never exercise his right to consent to become a member of a people. In his 1774 *Summary View of the Rights of British America,* Jefferson wrote that there is

> a right which nature has given to all men, of departing from the country in which chance, not choice, has placed them, of going in quest of new habitations, and of there establishing new societies, under such laws and regulations as to them shall seem most likely to promote public happiness.

Pennsylvania's 1776 Declaration of Rights made explicit the right to depart from the country of one's birth: "All men have a natural inherent right to emigrate from one state to another that will receive them, or to form a new state in vacant countries, or in such countries as they can purchase, whenever they think that thereby they may promote their own happiness."[24] By implication, this affirms the right of any people to exclude immigrants, because people may emigrate only to an inhabited place "that will receive them."

The Equality Principle and the *Duty* to Exclude

Just because the equality principle permits a people to decide which outsiders should be admitted and which excluded, should this right be exercised? If so, when and how?

The Declaration of Independence states the principles of just government based on the equality principle. First, the purpose of government is to secure the citizens' equal rights to life, liberty, and the pursuit of happiness. Second, government must derive its just powers from the consent of the governed. These two principles were repeated over and over again in the founding era. All of the leading American Founders believed them to be true.

These two requirements of the Declaration are not necessarily in harmony. Government by *consent* does not always secure individual rights. In the course of the Revolutionary War, and even more so afterwards, thoughtful Americans became increasingly aware of how hard it is to reconcile consent with rights. The majority, as Madison wrote in *Federalist* No. 10, may become a faction, violating minority rights. For example, a long recession after the Revolutionary War led to the intentional inflation of the currency by several state governments in order to relieve debtors. In the worst instance, Rhode Island passed laws requiring merchants to accept its almost worthless currency for their goods. The economy came to a standstill as stores were closed throughout the state. Mobs attacked businesses and farmers who refused to sell their goods at a loss. Rhode Islanders had consented to a policy that deprived individuals of their liberty, which includes the right to keep the property they earn through their own efforts.

The Federalist answers this challenge by showing how a sound institutional structure makes it hard for representative democracy to violate the rights of the minority. The Constitution's framers placed much of their trust in these structural devices: a government by elected representatives, spread out over a large country; a two-house legislature; a strong one-man executive; and a judiciary with lifetime appointments. But they also knew that devices alone are not enough. At least a minimally good character is also needed.

In his First Inaugural address, Jefferson pointed to this tension between consent and rights when he spoke of "this sacred principle, that though the will of the majority is in all cases to prevail, that will, to be rightful, must be reasonable; that the minority possess their equal rights, which equal laws must protect, and to violate would be oppression." Jefferson went on to praise the religious and moral convictions of Americans. He implied that they helped to make the will of the people rightful and reasonable. Americans, he said, are "enlightened by a benign religion, professed, indeed, and practiced in various forms, yet all of them inculcating honesty, truth, temperance, gratitude, and the love of man."[25] These qualities, he implied, are necessary for a people to remain free. So also is the belief that God favors liberty over tyranny, so that they will defend their own freedom and respect that of others. In Query 18 of *Notes on Virginia,* Jefferson had written that the "only firm basis" of the liberties of a nation is "a conviction in the minds of the people that these liberties are of the gift of God."

Founders like Jefferson, Madison, Washington, and Adams supported public education for the same reason that they expressed concern about unlimited immigration: A people must have the right character and beliefs if it is to sustain a free government. The purpose of public education, wrote

Jefferson, is to make the people "the safe, as they are the ultimate, guardians of their own liberty. . . . And to render even them safe their minds must be improved to a certain degree. This indeed is not all that is necessary, though it be essentially necessary."[26]

All human beings have a right to be free. But the wrong habits and beliefs can make a particular people, at a particular time, incapable of freedom. Since those who lack the qualities of republican citizenship cannot be "safe . . . guardians of their own liberty," a free society should regulate the admission of new citizens with a view to the danger they might pose to liberty, to the extent that they have not yet acquired the political principles and minimal morality of freedom.

There is no a priori formula that says how many immigrants, from what countries, and with what habits and talents, should be permitted at a given time. That is a matter for sensible statesmen to decide, weighing all the relevant factors.

We conclude that every people has a *right* to exclude aliens that it deems undesirable, and a *duty* to exclude aliens whose excessive numbers or questionable character might endanger the citizens' liberty.

The Virtues of a Free People: Self-Control and Self-Assertion

We have stated the general problem. There are certain virtues, and certain convictions, that are necessary for a people to be free. What are those virtues and convictions?

The Founders understood the term *self-government* in a double sense: (1) governing oneself morally, controlling one's own tendency to indulge the selfish and violent passions unreasonably; and (2) governing oneself politically, through democratic institutions that provide a wide scope for self-governing private associations such as families, churches, private schools, and businesses. The second sense is obvious. The first—self-government as self-control—is indicated in *Federalist* No. 63, where Madison spoke of the Athenian people being dominated by "the tyranny of their passions" when they condemned Socrates to death.

The Founders had to ask themselves what qualities sustain self-government in these two senses. The Northwest Ordinance of 1787 was the first federal law governing the western territories—the future states of Ohio, Michigan, Indiana, Illinois, and Wisconsin. Article 3 provided, "Religion, morality, and knowledge, being necessary to good government and the happiness of mankind, schools and the means of education shall forever be encouraged."[27]

Several state constitutions went into greater detail. Virginia's 1776 Declaration of Rights said: "That no free government, or the blessings of liberty, can be preserved to any people, but by a firm adherence to justice, moderation, temperance, frugality, and virtue, and by frequent recurrence to fundamental principles." The Massachusetts Constitution of 1780 stated: "the happiness of a people, and the good order and preservation of civil government, essentially depend upon piety, religion, and morality." The Massachusetts Constitution particularly encouraged public and private education, to "inculcate the principles of humanity and general benevolence, public and private charity, industry and frugality, honesty and punctuality in their dealings; sincerity, good humor, and all social affections, and generous sentiments among the people." Pennsylvania's 1776 constitution listed the same virtues as Virginia, and further stated: "Laws for the encouragement of virtue, and prevention of vice and immorality, shall be made and constantly kept in force, and provision shall be made for their due execution."[28]

The virtues mentioned in these quotations are the "nice" ones, that is, those qualities that enable fellow citizens to get along with each other in peace and good will. Let us give these virtues the general name of *moderation* or *self-restraint*.

Another set of qualities, less "nice" but more spirited, more noble, is also needed: those that enable free men to establish and defend their liberty against its enemies. These qualities were alluded to by Congress in its Declaration of Causes of Taking Up Arms in 1775:

> Honor, justice, and humanity forbid us tamely to surrender that freedom which we received from our gallant ancestors, and which our innocent posterity have a right to receive from us. We cannot endure the infamy and guilt of resigning succeeding generations to that wretchedness which inevitably awaits them, if we basely entail hereditary bondage upon them. . . . [We are] with one mind resolved to die freemen, rather than to live slaves.[29]

The same noble sense of manly honor was stressed by George Washington in a message to his soldiers on the eve of independence in 1776:

> Our cruel and unrelenting enemy leaves us no choice but a brave resistance, or the most abject submission. This is all we can expect. We have therefore to resolve to conquer or die. Our own country's honor, all call upon us for a vigorous and manly exertion, and if we now shamefully fail, we shall become infamous to the whole world. . . . Let us therefore animate and encourage each other, and show the whole world, that a freeman contending for liberty on his own ground is superior to any slavish mercenary on earth.[30]

The Declaration of Independence concludes with these words, expressing the same choice for honorable freedom over shameful enslavement: "We mutually pledge to each other our lives, our fortunes, and our sacred honor."

Let us give this second set of virtues the general name of *manliness* or *self-assertion*.

These two sets of virtues—moderation or the right kind of self-restraint, and manliness or the right kind of self-assertion—complement each other. They enable citizens to respect each other's rights, to limit their irrational passions in a way that promotes decency in family and private life. They also enable citizens to be tough and feisty where it counts, namely, whenever liberty is threatened, either at home by excesses in the rulers, or abroad by nations who might want to rule Americans without their consent. In our earlier quotation from the *Notes on Virginia,* we saw that Jefferson worried that immigrants would lack both republican self-restraint and republican self-assertion.

The qualities in question have long been discussed by political philosophers. Plato's *Statesman,* for example, concludes by arguing that the great task of statesmanship is to weave moderation and manliness together, in the right proportion, in the souls of the citizens. These are the same two qualities we have seen, under various names, in important documents of the founding era.

In *Federalist* No. 51, Madison writes that a well-constructed government will make use of the passions to control the passions of the people: "Ambition must be made to counteract ambition." Madison calls this the "policy of supplying, by opposite and rival interests, the defect of better motives." However, this policy, while indispensable, has its limits, as he acknowledges in *Federalist* No. 55:

> As there is a degree of depravity in mankind which requires a certain degree of circumspection and distrust, so there are other qualities in human nature which justify a certain portion of esteem and confidence. Republican government presupposes the existence of these qualities in a higher degree than any other form. [If people were as bad as some opponents of the Constitution say they are,] the inference would be that there is not sufficient virtue among men for self-government; and that nothing less than the chains of despotism can restrain them from destroying and devouring one another.

In this passage Madison is speaking of *moderation.* Two papers later he speaks of our complementary virtue, *manliness.* There he writes that freedom can be maintained only by "the vigilant and manly spirit which actuates the people of America." Without this spirit, "the people will be prepared to tolerate anything but liberty."

In his First Annual Address to Congress, Washington too spoke of these twin themes of republican restraint and republican assertiveness: the people must be taught

> to know and to value their own rights; to discern and provide against invasions of them; to distinguish between oppression and the necessary exercise of lawful authority; . . . to discriminate the spirit of liberty from that of licentiousness—cherishing the first, avoiding the last; and uniting a speedy but temperate vigilance against encroachments, with an inviolable respect to the laws.[31]

However cleverly the institutions of government are constructed, republican liberty requires, at least in some degree, the citizen virtues spoken of and praised since antiquity by the philosophers, ancient and modern alike. Thus Madison's desire, noted earlier, that "foreigners of merit and republican principles" be particularly sought out as future citizens.

France in the 1790s: Unfit for Liberty

The failure of the French Revolution gives us a vivid example of why the character of the citizens is a necessary element of liberty.

Gouverneur Morris was a leading framer at the Constitutional Convention of 1787 and a resident of France in the early 1790s. He was named U.S. ambassador in 1792. During these years, Morris kept a diary and wrote frequent letters to his superiors in America. Very early in the French Revolution, Morris saw that its end would not be good for France.

The French, he wrote, were trying to set up "an American constitution . . . without reflecting that they have not American citizens to support that constitution":

> I wish much, very much, the happiness of this inconstant people. I love them. I feel grateful for their efforts in our cause and I consider the establishment of a good constitution here as the principal means, under divine providence, of extending the blessings of freedom to the many millions of my fellow men who groan in bondage on the continent of Europe. But I do not greatly indulge the flattering illusions of hope, because I do not yet perceive that reformation of morals without which liberty is but an empty sound.[32]

Morris's prediction that the French Revolution would fail proved correct. It ended in terror and tyranny.

Morris commented frequently on the French lack of the virtues of self-control:

> Everybody agrees that there is an utter prostration of morals, but this general position can never convey to an American the degree of depravity. It is . . . from such crumbling matter that the great edifice of freedom is to be erected here. . . . [T]here is one fatal principle which pervades all ranks. It is a perfect indifference to the violation of engagements. Inconstancy is so mingled in the blood, marrow, and every essence of this people, that when a man of high rank and importance laughs today at what he seriously asserted yesterday, it is considered as in the natural order of things. . . . The great mass of the common people have no religion but their priests, no law but their superiors, no moral but their interest.[33]

Paris in particular was "perhaps as wicked a spot as exists. Incest, murder, bestiality, fraud, rapine, oppression, baseness, cruelty." A lack of self-control among the politicians made deliberation impossible in the French Assembly. "One half of the time is spent hallowing and bawling," while those who do try to speak are often shouted down by "a continual uproar till the orator leaves the pulpit." The French were constantly "crying down and even ridiculing religion," but Morris believed "that religion is the only solid base of morals and that morals are the only possible support of free governments." In contrast, "America in the worst of times was much better because at least our criminal law was executed, not to mention the mildness of our manners."[34]

Besides their deficiency in self-restraint, the French also lacked, in Morris's view, appropriate self-assertion. That is evident in the following conversation between Morris and a prominent Frenchman, occasioned when the Frenchman "mentioned the necessity of fleets and armies to secure us [America] against invasion."

> Morris: Nothing would be more difficult than to subdue a nation, every individual of which in the pride of freedom thinks himself equal to a king, and if, sir, you should look down on him would say: "I am a man, are you any thing more?"
>   Frenchman: All this is very well, but there must be a difference in ranks, and I should say to one of these people: "You, sir, who are equal to a king, make me a pair of shoes."
>   Morris: Our citizens, sir, have a manner of thinking peculiar to

themselves. This shoemaker would reply: "Sir, I am very glad of the opportunity to make you a pair of shoes. It is my duty to make shoes and I love to do my duty. Does your king do his?"

In his diary, Morris entered this comment: "This manner of thinking and speaking however is too masculine for the climate I am now in." Few French commoners would have spoken in this way. They had too little "pride of freedom" to keep the haughty upper classes in line. When the Revolution began, Morris wrote, "as to public spirit, it cannot exist among a people so lately emancipated." In other words, the French were incapable of the kind of vigilant self-assertion necessary to establish and sustain a free government.[35]

Morris was not claiming any congenital defect in the French race. He thought that one day France might show herself as capable of liberty as America, as he implies in this statement:

In effect, time is needful to bring forward slaves to the enjoyment of liberty. Time. Time. Education. But what is education? It is not learning. It is more the effect of society on the habits and principles of each individual, forming him at an early period of life to act afterwards the part of a good citizen and contribute in his turn to the formation of others. Hence it results that the progress towards freedom must be slow.[36]

Morris's observations, and the reflections of other Founders that we saw earlier, have definite implications for immigration and naturalization policy. Potential citizens should be judged by their "habits and principles," their capacity for republican citizenship, based on national character and other considerations. The deliberation of politicians will decide what precise policy would be best. Perhaps, as in the early republic, no special restrictions would be needed on immigration as long as the character and number of immigrants was such that they could be assimilated into the body of citizens without great difficulty. Limits on naturalization, however, might be useful. Perhaps, as happened later in American history, immigration restrictions would have to be established as well. Whatever the policy, it should be based on an accurate awareness that the character of citizens (and therefore of outsiders who will become citizens) is an indispensable condition of freedom. If the will of the majority is consistently unreasonable, as it must when citizens lack the minimal virtues of republican self-restraint and self-assertion, freedom must eventually give way to despotism.

History of Immigration and Naturalization Policy

By 1776 over a third of American citizens were from countries other than England. In a famous passage of his *Letters from an American Farmer* (1782), Crevecoeur asked, "What then is the American, this new man? . . . Here individuals of all nations are melted into a new race of men." Most new-comers became citizens merely by satisfying a residency requirement. In the first federal naturalization law in 1790, the term was two years. In 1795 it was raised to five years, then to fourteen during the near-war with France in 1798. In 1801 it was set back to five years, where it remains to the present day. In spite of partisan differences contributing to the controversy over these laws, Americans of every party, as historian James Kettner writes, shared the assumption that "the national government had a legitimate interest in con-trolling the character of potential citizens" through naturalization policy.[37]

It should be noted that we speak here of the Founders' policy on nat-uralization (becoming a citizen) rather than immigration (entering the country). The Constitution was silent on the latter, assigning Congress the power "to establish an uniform rule of naturalization." In practice, for the first century of American history, naturalization policy was used to encourage or discourage immigration, as indicated in this typical early argument: "The power to naturalize," said a petition to Congress in 1837, "was given to Congress to add to the physical strength of the United States." Few came to America to stay unless they were eligible for citizen-ship. It is therefore technically correct, but misleading, to say, as is com-monly said, that the United States had an open door policy on immigra-tion before the 1880s.[38]

After the Civil War, American-born children of immigrants began to be granted automatic citizenship as a result of the Fourteenth Amendment ("All persons born . . . in the United States, and subject to the jurisdiction thereof, are citizens"). Those who came to America knew that if they did not become citizens, their children would. Therefore naturalization law gradually became less important as a means to regulate immigration. The first federal law limiting immigration, the Chinese Exclusion Act, was passed in 1882.

It appears, however, that the citizenship clause of the Fourteenth Amendment has long been misunderstood. Edward J. Erler points out that the author of the clause, Senator Jacob Howard, emphatically stated that those "subject to the jurisdiction" of the United States "will not, of course, include persons born in the United States who are foreigners" or "aliens." In other words, the Fourteenth Amendment was never intended to grant automatic citizenship to American-born children of foreigners, and the

Supreme Court erred in 1898 when it ruled otherwise. (The Court has never ruled that American-born children of *illegal* aliens are citizens, although that too is current federal policy.) Senator Howard's reading, endorsed by Senator Lyman Trumbull, chairman of the Senate Judiciary Committee, and by the Supreme Court in the *Slaughter House Cases,* is the only reading of the amendment that is consistent with the equality principle, according to which, as we showed above, no one can justly become a citizen of a nation without its consent.[39]

The nation's first naturalization law of 1790 reflected the Founders' concern for republican character. It required would-be citizens to apply "to any common law court of record in any of the states wherein he shall have resided, . . . and mak[e] proof to the satisfaction of such court that he is a person of good character." (This could ordinarily be done by having a citizen sponsor testify on one's behalf.) They also had to take "the oath or affirmation prescribed by law to support the Constitution of the United States." Most states had similar requirements for state citizenship. Remnants of this concern for the character of newcomers survive today. According to a 1989 government brochure, federal law generally forbids entry to any person who is a "beggar," has "committed a serious crime," is "coming for immoral sexual acts," or is otherwise morally objectionable. Those being naturalized must learn the elementary facts of American government and declare their allegiance to the Constitution.[40]

The law made national origin or race a condition of citizenship through most of American history. The first naturalization law (1790) stated, "That any alien being a free white person, who shall have resided within the limits and under the jurisdiction of the United States for the term of two years, may be admitted to become a citizen thereof on application to any common law court." Naturalization remained limited to whites until 1870, when, in the aftermath of the Civil War, "aliens of African nativity" were also made eligible. Filipinos became eligible after the Spanish-American War. Chinese were made eligible for naturalization only in 1943. It was not until 1952 that all national-origin restrictions on naturalization were removed. (As we noted earlier, however, the American-born children of these excluded groups became citizens at least as early as 1898.)[41]

The growing openness to members of all the world's races was always possible under the terms of the Declaration of Independence, which, as Lincoln noted, made a transracial principle—the equal natural rights of all men—the basis of citizenship. For that reason, America from the beginning was always a multinational and multiracial society. As early as 1776, as we saw in the first chapter, some blacks were citizens, as were many non-British Europeans.

The huge immigration wave of 1880 to 1914 was followed by five decades of very little immigration. A series of laws, culminating in the Immigration Act of 1924, limited total immigration to 150,000 per year, and the actual numbers were usually much less than that. (Between 1881 and 1920, annual immigration had averaged almost 600,000.) Each country was assigned a quota in proportion to its percentage of the American population in 1890. Northern and western Europe received 82 percent of the quota, southern and eastern Europe 16 percent, with 2 percent left for the rest of the world. The last national-origins provisions of American immigration law were repealed in 1965.[42]

Why Was National Origin or Race Considered?

Today this history of exclusion by race and national origin in immigration and naturalization law is considered an embarrassment and an injustice. But if we consider the earlier law charitably, we can see that Americans were struggling, however clumsily, with a real problem: how to maintain a population with the moral and religious qualities to keep itself free.

When Americans used rough categories like national origin to determine who should be eligible for entry or citizenship, they did not believe that every member of a given nation was perfectly suited or absolutely unsuited for citizenship. They were far from believing that every white man was virtuous, or that every black, Indian, or Asian was vicious. They resorted to these crude categories because characteristics shared by *many* (not all) of a given group in the past were judged likely to affect their future capacity, *as a group,* for assimilation and for developing, at least in some measure, the republican qualities of self-control and self-assertion.

From the standpoint of the Founders' principles, the perfect immigration policy would judge people as individuals, not as groups. It would be based on an exact knowledge of the moral and political habits and attitudes of every person who might wish to enter and become an American. The difficulty, as Aristotle observed long ago, is that virtue, unlike beauty, is invisible. In an individual it becomes manifest through his deeds over a long time. Many nonwhites would obviously have qualified in the 1790s and afterwards under a policy that was able to discern individual differences in character. A great many whites would have been excluded. But such knowledge is beyond human capacity. Officials cannot look into the individual souls of thousands of immigrants. They have to make do, as Tocqueville observed, with general categories that "permit human minds to pass judgment quickly on a great number of things." Tocqueville was well aware that when we judge people or things in light of general ideas, "what is gained in extent is always lost in exactitude." But we cannot do without such categories, for "if a human intelligence tried to examine and judge all the particular cases that came his way individually, he would be lost in a wilderness of detail."[43]

To understand why the Founders would write a law limiting naturalization to whites, we do not have to dismiss them as mindless bigots. We need only to recall that in those days white was practically equivalent to European. (In the year following the first naturalization law, Hamilton spoke of the general benefits of "emigration from abroad" in his *Report on Manufactures* (1791), but he mentioned only emigrants "from Europe.")[44] Europe was the realm of what we now call Western civilization. The words we quoted earlier from Washington, Jefferson, and other Founders show that they were thinking of civilization, not whiteness, when they reflected on the positive qualities (such as sensible political convictions, along with the virtues associated with self-assertion and self-restraint) that at least some European immigrants would bring with them to America. Europeans as a group shared with Americans a heritage that made them, in the Founders' view, the most likely candidates for successful assimilation into democratic citizenship.

George Washington paid his respects to this European (not just British) heritage and its importance for the success of America's experiment in self-government when he wrote,

> The foundation of our empire was not laid in the gloomy age of ignorance and superstition, but at an epoch when the rights of mankind were better understood and more clearly defined than at any former period; . . . the free cultivation of letters, the unbounded extension of commerce, the progressive refinement of manners, the growing liberality of sentiment, and above all, the pure and benign light of revelation, have had a meliorating influence on mankind and increased the blessings of society. At this auspicious period, the United States came into existence as a nation.[45]

The Founders' respect for European civilization was not tied to a belief in the superiority of the white race per se. If they had believed in some sort of automatic equation of "white" with "virtue," they would not have worried about whether some Europeans—whether Frenchmen in France or immigrants to America—were capable at that time of living in "temperate liberty." If they had been racists in the sense of believing that some races are destined to be rightfully enslaved by other races, they would not have denounced black slavery and passed laws for its abolition in eight of the original thirteen states during the founding era after it had existed without controversy for a century and a half in colonial America. In fact, as we saw in chapter 1, no Founder believed in racial differences with respect to the natural rights of mankind. Jefferson wrote, "Whatever may be their degree of talent, it is no measure of their rights. Because Sir Isaac Newton was superior to others in understanding, he was not therefore lord of the person or property of others."[46] Human beings of every race are created equal in the sense of the Declaration.

Morris's claim that the French of the 1790s lacked the right "habits and principles" to sustain a regime of liberty was not racist. It was not a claim that every individual Frenchman lacked elementary self-control. Many of them, including the Revolutionary War hero Lafayette, were people of outstanding virtue. Nor was it a *stereotype,* because a stereotype by definition is an image in the mind that is, in the words of Harvard social scientist Thomas Pettigrew, "acquired culturally rather than through personal experience,"[47] and Morris reached his opinion of the French through personal experience, through his own observation and reflection. Mistaken or not, it would have been a reasonable basis for deciding not to admit large numbers of Frenchmen to American citizenship over a short period of time.

Finally, it would be wrong to leave the impression that only high-minded arguments about the moral conditions of liberty were advanced to justify the pre-1965 preference for European immigrants. Benjamin Franklin bluntly stated that he preferred English immigrants because other Europeans "are generally of what we call a swarthy complexion; as are the Germans also, the Saxons alone excepted." Franklin justified his feelings with an all-too-human remark: "But perhaps I am partial to the complexion of my country, for such kind of partiality is natural to mankind."[48] From the point of view of the Declaration of Independence, this kind of preference for one's own, the love of one's own kind, is a permissible and understandable, although not a particularly noble, basis for immigration and citizenship policy.

It is one thing to decide whom to admit to America on the basis of personal preference. It is quite another to deny to Americans already living here the privileges or immunities of citizenship and the equal protection of the laws. In his letter to the Hebrews in Newport, Washington wrote, "Happily the Government of the United States . . . gives to bigotry no sanction, to persecution no assistance." In the Old South, well into the twentieth century, government gave its sanction to bigotry, and its assistance to persecution. This was not a matter of people innocently associating with those of their own choice. Quite the contrary. The laws forced private parties to discriminate even when they preferred not to. In the famous *Plessy* case, the railroad company was compelled by Louisiana law to set up separate cars for whites and blacks. Governments in the South also tacitly allowed private individuals such as the Ku Klux Klan to do violence to innocent blacks and whites who wanted to associate or do business together in unapproved ways. This Jim Crow regime contradicted the principles of the founding. It was abolished by the civil rights acts of the 1960s.[49]

Nor should we equate the innocent preference for one's own with the ugly claim that some races do not possess the rights to life, liberty, and the pursuit of happiness. Before the Civil War, Lincoln complained that Americans both North and South were beginning to argue that the equality of men was a "self-evident lie." Darwinism and German political thought persuaded many American intellectuals after the Civil War to reject the equality principle. In his 1895 presidential address to the American Association for the Advancement of Science, anthropologist Daniel Brinton argued that knowledge of inherited racial differences could "supply the only sure foundations for legislation; not a priori notions of the rights of man." Sociologist John Commons' influential 1909 book on immigration began with an explicit attack on the Declaration of Independence. The Founders would have rejected these views with indignation.[50]

The Moral Conditions of Citizenship

As we saw earlier, the most serious reason for encouraging immigrants from some places and discouraging them from others is to sustain responsible republican citizenship. This purpose, however, is promoted by many policies, only one of which is regulating the character and number of new citizens. Far more important, from the Founders' viewpoint, was the role of law and government in promoting the moral conditions of citizenship among those who already are or will soon become Americans. I mention four examples.

First, public education was considered one of the most effective means to teach both immigrants and native-born Americans the rights and duties of a free people. Two quotations from leading Founders may illustrate the consensus of their generation. Earlier we quoted George Washington's First Annual Address to Congress, in which he spoke of teaching the people respect for the law and avoidance of licentiousness (self-restraint), along with vigilance against invasions of their rights (self-assertion). Washington continued:

> Whether this desirable object will be best promoted by affording aids to
> seminaries of learning already established; by the institution of a nation-
> al university; or by any other expedients, will be well worthy of a place
> in the deliberations of the Legislature.[51]

Sharing Washington's belief in the role of public education in maintaining
freedom, James Madison once wrote:

> The liberal appropriations made by the legislature of Kentucky for a gen-
> eral system of education cannot be too much applauded. . . . Learned
> institutions ought to be the favorite objects with every free people. They
> throw that light over the public mind which is the best security against
> crafty and dangerous encroachments on the public liberty. . . . What
> spectacle can be more edifying than that of liberty and learning, each
> leaning on the other for their mutual and surest support?[52]

Second, government promoted knowledge of and respect for the
moral obligations of free men not only in schools but also through the
speeches of politicians. George Washington's First Inaugural address set an
example that was long followed:

> There exists in the economy and course of nature, an indissoluble union
> between virtue and happiness; between duty and advantage; between
> the genuine maxims of an honest and magnanimous policy, and the solid
> rewards of public prosperity and felicity; since we ought to be no less
> persuaded that the propitious smiles of Heaven can never be expected
> on a nation that disregards the eternal rules of order and right, which
> Heaven itself has ordained.[53]

Third, state and local governments continued to enforce those parts of
the common law, inherited from Britain, that support the virtue and duty
of which Washington spoke. These included laws against public immorality (such as public nudity and prostitution), against licentious speech (vulgar
and obscene publications), in support of enduring marriage (making
divorce rare and discouraging sex outside of marriage), and encouraging
public respect for the prevailing religious opinions of the nation (through
Sunday-closing laws, for example).

Fourth, government used many other laws to promote self-restraint
and self-assertion. Taxes on liquor were intended from the beginning, as
Hamilton wrote in *Federalist* No. 12, to foster "the morals, and . . . the
health of the society." States and towns were careful in their poor laws to

promote decent conduct and discourage laziness and irresponsibility. Welfare was given conditionally and sparingly, so that men would be discouraged from becoming shiftless, women discouraged from bearing children outside of marriage, and both sexes encouraged to get married and stay married. (See chapter 6, on welfare.) As for self-assertion, Congress passed a militia law in 1792 requiring that almost every male citizen between the ages of eighteen and forty-five be enrolled in the militia of his state, and "provide himself with a good musket or firelock" and "not less than twenty-four cartridges." They were also required to "appear, so armed, accoutred and provided, when called out to exercise, or into service."[54]

I mention these four means by which government supported the moral conditions of freedom in order to put immigration and naturalization policy into perspective. That policy is one element, but by no means the most important element, in a free government's indispensable efforts to combine *consent* with *protection of rights*. The Founders aimed to form a body of citizens who would be capable of governing themselves *democratically* through elected representatives, while also governing themselves *reasonably* through policies that secured their own rights while respecting those of others.

Afterword

$\mathcal{O}$n the verge of the twenty-first century, it sometimes seems as if the American Founders have no admirers in America except among those who are relatively uneducated. Leading sophisticates—writers, professors, and journalists, whatever their political persuasion—seem convinced that there was something profoundly wrong with the origins of America.

Liberals

Liberals condemn the Founders because they supposedly did not believe that all human beings are created equal, or because they supposedly betrayed their own stated belief in human equality. "Jefferson didn't mean it when he wrote that all men are created equal," writes historian John Hope Franklin. "We've never meant it. The truth is we're a bigoted people and always have been."[1] We have seen that such falsehoods are incessantly repeated and broadcast by many of today's leading scholars and textbooks. Historian Paul Finkelman writes that Jefferson committed "treason against the hopes of the world" because he failed to do more to abolish slavery.[2] This ungenerous verdict is contradicted by the record of Jefferson and other Founders. It is contradicted above all by the testimony of Abraham Lincoln, who appealed again and again to Jefferson's Declaration of Independence and his eloquent denunciations of slavery in order to build opposition to the expansion of slavery in the Western territories. "This is a world of compensations," Lincoln wrote on the eve of the Civil War:

> and he who would *be* no slave, must consent to *have* no slave. Those who deny freedom to others, deserve it not for themselves; and, under a just God, cannot long retain it. All honor to Jefferson—to the man who, in the concrete pressure of a struggle for national independence by a single people, had the coolness, forecast, and capacity to introduce into a merely revolutionary document, an abstract truth, applicable to all men and all times, and so to embalm it there, that today, and in all coming days, it shall be a rebuke and a stumbling-block to the very harbingers of reappearing tyranny and oppression.[3]

For a hundred years the right to private property has been loudly condemned as oppressive by those who do not understand the political economy of plenty. Yet this right has proved to be the basis of the most successful antipoverty program in world history. Property has also been criticized on the ground that it fosters greed and avarice. Yet the discipline of acquiring property for oneself through hard work and postponement of immediate gratification has been an essential element in the formation of sturdy and independent character in the citizens.

The Founders' legal supports for the family, denounced for three decades as antifeminine and tyrannical, can now be seen more dispassionately as important elements in the stability of marriage. And without lasting marriage, as we are now learning, life is becoming increasingly hard and unhappy for large numbers of Americans.

Finally, the Founders have long been accused of mean-spirited elitism because of their approval of a property requirement for voting. Contrary to this impression, we have shown that they established the most inclusive electorate in a large country in history, and that their principles, as they understood them, were fully compatible not only with their own minor limits on voting rights but also with a broadening of the right to vote to include almost all adult Americans.

In the course of this book, we have seen that these and many other charges against the Founders either have no merit or are wildly exaggerated.

Conservatives

Conservatives, on the other hand, tend to be almost as critical of the founding as liberals, although from a different angle. Robert Bork, for example, thinks the Founders believed in equality too much. In *Slouching towards Gomorrah,* Bork asserts that it is "profoundly unfortunate" that the equality idea in the Declaration of Independence became "the single most powerful and radical ideological force in all of American history." He believes that America's "rage for liberty" and "passion for equality" are responsible for today's problems, including seemingly endless demands for bigger government, higher taxes, and ever more explicit public expression of the most degraded passions.[4] Bork is not anti-democratic; he does not mean to deny that government should protect the equal rights to life, liberty, and property. But his exasperation at liberal excesses committed in the name of equality and liberty tempts him into a condemnation of America's founding principles. Unfortunately, this leaves Bork without a principled basis on which to build his argument for a return to the kinds of policies that he and the Founders would support today.

UCLA political scientist James Q. Wilson agrees with Bork's "slippery slope" view of the principles of the Declaration of Independence. The Enlightenment, Wilson writes in *The Moral Sense*, "made man the measure of all things, and placed individuality and individual consent front and center on the political stage":

> It took a few generations for the principle to be worked out in practice, but when it was, the result was what the legal scholar Mary Ann Glendon calls "rights talk"—the widespread tendency to define the relation of the self to others and to society as a whole in terms of rights. . . . If rights are all that is important, what will become of responsibilities? If the individual man is the measure of all things, what will become of the family. . . ?[5]

Considerations like these lead Leon Kass of the University of Chicago to be "deeply pessimistic" about the future. In an article on the collapse of the family and the derangement in the relations between the sexes, Kass says he fears that the "destructive trends" that have been unleashed by the modern idea of rights are "largely irreversible" because "they spring from the very heart of liberal democratic society and of modernity altogether." Allan Bloom elaborates Kass's point in this way: "in modern political regimes, where rights precede duties, freedom definitely has priority over community, family and even nature."[6]

Bork, Wilson, Kass, and Bloom do not mean to condemn the Founders altogether. Their point is that whatever the merits of the natural rights argument may have been, and however noble the motives of the men who made America, they imposed on succeeding generations a doctrine that has proved to be a sort of time bomb that went off in the twentieth century. In this view, we today live amidst the moral rubble of that explosion.

Here too we have shown that the critics misunderstand the Founders, who rejected the amoral understanding of liberty and rights so common today. For the Founders, "freedom" could never have "priority over . . . nature," because nature—the nature of man as a rational creature, subject to the "laws of nature and of nature's God"—was itself the ground of freedom. The Founders therefore distinguished liberty from license and encouraged responsibility toward family and community. They promoted "religion, morality, and knowledge" as "necessary for good government and the happiness of mankind," in the phrase of the Northwest Ordinance of 1787. They were far from taking for granted the moral character of the people. As we saw in the chapters on property, women, welfare, and immigration and the moral conditions of citizenship, the Founders devised a variety of

policies to support the morality of republican self-control and self-assertion.

The problem that the conservatives are addressing, then, does not
spring from the mistaken principles of the founding. It springs from the
mistaken twentieth-century rejection or distortion of those principles.

The Founders

The liberal and the conservative critics of the founding both tend to over-
look a central theme in the Founders' reflections on political liberty. The
Declaration of Independence speaks of two requirements that follow from
the natural equality of all men: government must be by consent of the governed (that is, it must be democratic), and government must protect the
rights of all. These two requirements can be, but are not necessarily, in harmony with each other. The threat of what Madison in *Federalist* No. 10
called "majority faction"—the violation by the majority of the rights of the
minority or of the common good—is an ever-present danger.

Liberals (and libertarians) often forget that in order for democracy to
protect the equal rights of all, citizens need to have the right kind of character and convictions about justice. They must be enlightened as to the
rights of mankind. They must be vigilant in defense of those rights for
themselves. They must be respectful of those rights in others. That means
government must promote manly independence, moral restraint, strong
families, and limits on self-indulgence and irresponsible self-expression.

Liberals (but not libertarians) also tend to forget that the right to
acquire property, rightly enforced and protected, favors the interests of the
poor no less than of the wealthy. When government protects the fruits of
one's honest industry, it eventually enables the large majority of the poor to
become self-sufficient by their own efforts. Liberals sometimes fail to note
that antipoverty programs can easily have a corrupting effect if they are not
set up in a way that promotes rather than breaks down the morality of self-
restraint and self-assertion that is a necessary foundation of what Jefferson
called "temperate liberty."

Conservatives do not give the Founders the credit they deserve for
understanding the tension between consent and protection of rights, and
for doing something about it. We have seen examples of that in almost
every chapter. The Founders knew that institutional restraints on selfish
passions are indispensable, but that they are not a sufficient guard by themselves against unreason in the majority. The Founders devoted considerable
thought and energy to providing for the right kind of citizen character.

They established public schools and universities in several states. They refined but also continued in force the laws supporting responsibility in sexual and family relations. They fostered a manly assertiveness in the population through laws promoting gun ownership and protecting property rights. They taught citizens to respect "the laws of nature and of nature's God" through speeches, laws, and the good example of their own statesmanship. Because of these concerns, although they favored immigration, they were cautious about the kinds and numbers of newcomers who would be admitted, many of whom lacked the character and principles that sustain republican citizenship.

Liberals need to recognize that the language of equality in the Declaration of Independence was sincere and that the Founders implemented its principles to the best of their ability. The lot of women, blacks, and the poor improved substantially in the founding era and afterwards. Conservatives need to recognize that there is no need to go beyond the Declaration, or to reject the Founders' principles, in order to justify limits on the abuse of liberty. The idea of liberty in the Declaration contains its own limitation, for the natural right to liberty is not a right to licentious or destructive conduct. As Lincoln said in his debates with Douglas, one "cannot logically say that anybody has a right to do wrong."[7]

Although America has not always lived up to her own best principles, she has a great and noble heritage. It would be a shame if that heritage were to be squandered because of misunderstandings and distortions of the Founders' principles by today's intellectuals. Our task as scholars and teachers is to recover the truth about the founding, to discern its strengths, to acknowledge its defects, and to pass that knowledge along to future generations. This book is my contribution to that effort.

Notes

Preface

1. Conor Cruise O'Brien, *The Long Affair: Thomas Jefferson and the French Revolution, 1785–1800* (Chicago: University of Chicago Press, 1996), 319. Thurgood Marshall, "Reflections on the Bicentennial of the U.S. Constitution," *Harvard Law Review* 101 (November 1987): 4. John M. Blum, *Liberty, Justice, Order: Essays on Past Politics* (New York: Norton, 1993), 25; to illustrate the Founders' understanding, Blum attributes this view (incorrectly) to John Locke, "to whom," he correctly says, "so many American political theorists repaired" during that era. Richard N. Current et al., *American History: A Survey,* 7th ed. (New York: Knopf, 1987), 142. Karen O'Connor and Larry J. Sabato, *American Government: Roots and Reform* (New York: Macmillan, 1993), 133. Rogers Smith, "The 'American Creed' and American Identity: The Limits of Liberal Citizenship in the United States," *Western Political Quarterly* 41 (1988): 245. Joan Hoff Wilson, "The Illusion of Change," in *The American Revlution: Explorations in the History of American Radicalism,* ed. Alfred F. Young (Dekalb: Northern Illinois University Press, 1976), 387.

2. George Washington, To the Roman Catholics in the United States, 15 March 1790, in *George Washington: A Collection,* ed. W. B. Allen (Indianapolis: Liberty Classics, 1988), 547. In my quotations from the Founders in this book, I have sometimes modernized spelling, capitalization, and punctuation for the sake of readability.

3. Thomas G. West, "Was the American Founding Unjust? The Case of Slavery," *Principles,* Spring/Summer 1992, 1–12. "Was the American Founding Unjust? The Case of Women," *Principles,* Winter 1993, 1–12. "Was the American Founding Unjust? The Case of Voting Rights," *Principles,* Spring/Summer 1993, 1–12.

Chapter 1

1. Peter Kolchin, *American Slavery, 1619–1877* (New York: Hill & Wang, 1993), 3, 4, 63. Abraham Lincoln, Gettysburg Address (1863). Thurgood Marshall, "Reflections on the Bicentennial of the U.S. Constitution," *Harvard Law Review* 101 (November 1987): 2.

2. Marshall, "Reflections," 4 (quoting with approval Chief Justice Taney's words in the infamous 1857 *Dred Scott* decision). Conor Cruise O'Brien, *The Long Affair: Thomas Jefferson and the French Revolution, 1785–1800* (Chicago: University

of Chicago Press, 1996), 319. Forrest McDonald, *Novus Ordo Seclorum: The Intellectual Origins of the Constitution* (Lawrence: University Press of Kansas, 1985), 53.

3. Richard L. Bushman, "Declaration of Independence," in *The Readers' Companion to American History,* ed. Eric Foner and John A. Garraty (Boston: Houghton Mifflin, 1991), 272.

4. John Blum et al., *The National Experience: A History of the United States,* 8th ed. (Fort Worth: Harcourt Brace Jovanovich College Publishers, 1993), 130; Paul Finkelman, *Slavery and the Founders: Race and Liberty in the Age of Jefferson* (Armonk, N.Y.: M. E. Sharpe, 1996), 105.

5. Samuel Eliot Morison, *Oxford History of the American People* (1965; reprint, New York: Mentor, New American Library, 1972), 1: 295. Thomas Jefferson, *Writings,* ed. Merrill D. Peterson (New York: Library of America, 1984), 22.

6. Donald Robinson, *Slavery in the Structure of American Politics, 1765–1820* (New York: Norton, 1979), 379. Jefferson, "A Bill concerning Slaves" (1779), in *Papers of Thomas Jefferson,* ed. Julian P. Boyd (Princeton: Princeton University Press, 1950–), 2:470–72. Jefferson, *Notes on the State of Virginia* (1787), Query 18, in *Writings,* 288–89. Jefferson, "Sixth Annual Message" (1806), in *Writings,* 528. Ralph Lerner, *The Thinking Revolutionary: Principle and Practice in the New Republic* (Ithaca: Cornell University Press, 1987), 67.

7. Gordon S. Wood, "Equality and Social Conflict in the American Revolution," *William and Mary Quarterly* 51 (1994): 707.

8. Jack P. Greene, *Imperatives, Behaviors, and Identities: Essays in Early American Cultural History* (Charlottesville: University Press of Virginia, 1992), 265. See also David B. Davis, *The Problem of Slavery in the Age of Revolution, 1770–1823* (Ithaca: Cornell University Press, 1975), 257. Like Greene, Davis argues that the Revolution did not necessarily point to the end of slavery. It supposedly defined liberty as a reward for righteous struggle, not as a natural right possessed by all. Therefore, Davis believes, it must be earned.

9. John A. Garraty, *The Story of America: Beginnings to 1877* (Austin, Texas: Holt, Rinehart, & Harcourt Brace, 1992), 163, my emphasis. See also Lorna C. Mason et al., *History of the United States,* vol. 1, *Beginnings to 1877* (Boston: Houghton Mifflin, 1992), 188: "When Jefferson spoke of 'the people,' however, he meant only free white men. In Jefferson's time it was commonly believed that some people should rule and others should be ruled." Both textbooks are Texas-approved for eighth grade.

10. George Washington to Morris, 12 April 1786, in *George Washington: A Collection,* ed. W. B. Allen (Indianapolis: Liberty Classics, 1989), 319. John Adams to Evans, 8 June 1819, in *Selected Writings of John and John Quincy Adams,* ed. Adrienne Koch and William Peden (New York: Knopf, 1946), 209. Benjamin Franklin, "An Address to the Public from the Pennsylvania Society for Promoting the Abolition of Slavery" (1789), in *Writings,* ed. J. A. Leo Lemay (New York: Library of America, 1987), 1154. Hamilton, *Philo Camillus* No. 2 (1795), in *Papers of Alexander Hamilton,* ed. Harold C. Syrett (New York: Columbia University Press, 1961–79), 19:101–2. James Madison, speech at Constitutional Convention, 6 June 1787, in *The Records of the Federal Convention of 1787,* ed. Max Farrand (New Haven: Yale University Press, 1937), 1:135.

11. Bushman, "Declaration of Independence," in *Readers' Companion,* ed. Foner and Garraty, 272.

12. John Jay to the President of the Society for the Manumission of Slaves, June 1788, in *The Founders' Constitution,* vol. 1, *Major Themes,* ed. Philip B. Kurland and Ralph Lerner (Chicago: University of Chicago Press, 1987), 550.

13. John Dickinson, *Letters from a Farmer* (1768), Letter 7, end, in *The Political Writings of John Dickinson, 1764–1774,* ed. Paul L. Ford (New York: Da Capo, 1970), 356. Congress, "Declaration of Causes of Taking Up Arms, July 6, 1775," in *Sources and Documents Illustrating the American Revolution,* ed. Samuel Eliot Morison (New York: Oxford University Press, 1923), 144–45.

14. Resolutions of the House of Representatives of Massachusetts, 29 October 1765, in *Founders' Constitution,* ed. Kurland and Lerner, 1:629.

15. James Otis, *The Rights of the British Colonies* (1764), in *Pamphlets of the American Revolution,* ed. Bernard Bailyn (Cambridge: Harvard University Press, 1965), 1:439. Jay to Price, 27 September 1785, in *Founders' Constitution,* ed. Kurland and Lerner, 1:538; Leon F. Litwack, *North of Slavery: The Negro in the Free States, 1790–1860* (Chicago: University of Chicago Press, 1961), 9.

16. Kenneth Coleman, *The American Revolution in Georgia, 1763–1789* (Athens: University of Georgia Press, 1958), 45–46. Gary Nash, *Race and Revolution* (Madison, Wis.: Madison House, 1990), 15.

17. Slave Petition to the Province of Massachusetts, 25 May 1774, in *Founders' Constitution,* ed. Kurland and Lerner, 1:435. Other slave petitions: Nash, *Race and Revolution,* 171–76; Benjamin Quarles, *The Negro in the American Revolution* (Chapel Hill: University of North Carolina Press, 1961), 39–40. David B. Davis, "American Slavery and the American Revolution," in *Slavery and Freedom in the Age of the American Revolution,* ed. Ira Berlin and Ronald Hoffman (Charlottesville: University Press of Virginia, 1983), 279.

18. Garraty, *Story of America,* 163.

19. Franklin to Waring, 17 December 1763, in *Writings,* 800. Hamilton to Jay, 14 March 1779, *Papers of Alexander Hamilton,* 2:18. Benjamin Rush agreed; see "Address . . . upon Slave-Keeping" and "Vindication of the Address" (both Philadelphia, 1773), in *Am I Not a Man and a Brother: The Antislavery Crusades of Revolutionary America, 1688–1788,* ed. Roger Bruns (New York: Chelsea House, 1977), 224–25. St. George Tucker, a Virginia professor of law, said that there was not enough evidence to resolve the debate over black inferiority; see "On the State of Slavery in America," in Tucker's edition of William Blackstone's *Commentaries* (1803; reprint, New York: Augustus Kelley, 1969), vol. 2, appendix, p. 75 n. H.

20. Jefferson, *Notes on Virginia,* Queries 14, 18, in *Writings,* 269–70, 289. Jefferson to Gregoire, 25 February 1809, in *Writings,* 1202. Rush, "Vindication of the Address" (Philadelphia, 1773), 240. Lincoln makes the same point as Jefferson and Rush in his "Fragment on Slavery," 1 July 1854 (?), in *Collected Works of Abraham Lincoln,* ed. Roy T. Basler (New Brunswick: Rutgers University Press, 1953), 2:223.

21. Edmund Randolph, *History of Virginia,* ed. Arthur H. Shaffer (written about 1810; Charlottesville: University Press of Virginia, 1970), 96. Edmund S. Morgan, *American Slavery, American Freedom: The Ordeal of Colonial Virginia* (New York: Norton, 1975), 4, 380–81, 385. Morgan quotes the "unbounded love of

liberty" remark from an English diplomat with whom he expresses his agreement.

22. Robinson, *Slavery in the Structure of American Politics*, 297.

23. Arthur Zilversmit, *The First Emancipation: The Abolition of Slavery in the North* (Chicago: University of Chicago Press, 1967), 116–24, 131, 181, 193, 222. On Massachusetts, Davis, *Problem of Slavery*, 319.

24. Zilversmit, *First Emancipation*, 181–82. The authorship of the Pennsylvania preamble has been attributed to Thomas Paine; see Moncure Conway, ed., *Writings of Thomas Paine* (1902; reprint New York: Burt Franklin, 1969), where it is printed at 2:29.

25. Nash, *Race and Revolution*, 43; Zilversmit, *First Emancipation*, 155; James H. Kettner, *The Development of American Citizenship, 1608–1870* (Chapel Hill: University of North Carolina Press, 1984), 302; Ira Berlin, *Slaves without Masters: The Free Negro in the Antebellum South* (1974; reprint, New York: Oxford, 1981), 46–50, 396. Benjamin Quarles, *The Negro and the American Revolution* (Chapel Hill: University of North Carolina Press, 1961), chaps. 4–6. Paul A. Finkelman, ed., *Slavery, Revolutionary America, and the New Nation* (New York: Garland, 1989), xii.

26. Hamilton to Jay, 14 March 1779, *Papers of Alexander Hamilton*, 2:18.

27. William M. Wiecek, *Sources of Antislavery Constitutionalism in America, 1760–1848* (Ithaca: Cornell University Press, 1977), 102–3.

28. *Harry v. Decker & Hopkins* (1818); *Mississippi v. Jones* (1820); Paul Finkelman, *The Law of Freedom and Bondage: A Casebook* (New York: Oceana Publications, 1986), 171, 249 (other courts: 169). Kettner, *Development of American Citizenship*, 305. Robert M. Cover, *Justice Accused: Antislavery and the Judicial Process* (New Haven: Yale University Press, 1975), 95–99. Herbert J. Storing, "Slavery and the Moral Foundations of the American Republic," in *The Moral Foundations of the American Republic*, ed. Robert H. Horwitz, 3d ed. (Charlottesville: University Press of Virginia, 1986), 316–18.

29. Lawrence M. Friedman, *Crime and Punishment in American History* (New York: Basic Books, 1993), 90–91, emphasis added.

30. Adams to Belknap, 21 March 1795, in *Founders' Constitution,* ed. Kurland and Lerner, 1:559. There are many scholars whose research supports the "logic of revolution" argument presented here, including Zilversmit, *First Emancipation*; Davis, "American Slavery," 262–80; Bernard Bailyn, *The Ideological Origins of the American Revolution*, enlarged ed.(Cambridge: Harvard University Press, 1992), 232–36; Duncan J. MacLeod, *Slavery, Race, and the American Revolution* (Cambridge: Cambridge University Press, 1974); Nash, *Race and Revolution*, 3–23.

31. Kolchin, *American Slavery*, 4.

32. Finkelman, *Slavery and the Founders*, 1. Marshall, "Reflections," 2.

33. Morris, 8 August, in *Records of the Convention*, ed. Farrand, 2:222.

34. Madison, 14 June, in *Records of the Convention*, ed. Farrand, 2:10; Davie, 12 June, in ibid., 1:594; Pinckney, 23 July, in ibid., 2:95; Rutledge and Pinckney, 21 August, in ibid., 2:364; Pinckney, Baldwin, Williamson, 22 August 1787, in ibid., 2:371–73. Finkelman, *Slavery and the Founders*, 16, 27.

35. "Circular to the States" (1783), in *George Washington: A Collection*, 241.

36. Frederick Douglass, "The Constitution of the United States: Is It Pro-Slavery or Anti-Slavery?" (1860) in *The Life and Writings of Frederick Douglass,* ed. Philip S. Foner (New York: International Publishers, 1950), 2:478.

37. Kenneth L. Karst, *Belonging to America: Equal Citizenship and the Constitution* (New Haven: Yale University Press, 1989), 48. Pinckney, 6 July; Gouverneur Morris, 11 July; in *Records of the Convention*, ed. Farrand, 1:542, 588.

38. Pinckney, 29 August, with Madison's footnote, in *Records of the Convention*, ed. Farrand, 2:449. Wiecek, *Sources of Antislavery Constitutionalism*, 117–18. Walter Berns, "The Constitution and the Migration of Slaves," *Yale Law Journal* 78 (1968): 198–228, makes an excellent case for this antislavery reading of the commerce and migration clauses.

39. Speech at Pennsylvania Ratifying Convention, 3 December 1787, in *Documentary History of the Ratification of the Constitution,* ed. Merrill Jensen (Madison: State Historical Society of Wisconsin, 1976–), 463.

40. See *Records of the Convention*, ed. Farrand, 2:417 (25 August); 601 (report of Committee of Style); 628 (15 September).

41. Karen O'Connor and Larry J. Sabato, *American Government: Roots and Reform* (New York: Macmillan, 1993), 37.

42. Frederick Douglass, quoted by William Wiecek, "The Witch at the Christening," in *The Framing and Ratification of the Constitution,* ed. Leonard W. Levy and Dennis J. Mahoney (New York: Macmillan, 1987), 181.

43. Alexander Hamilton et al., *The Federalist* (New York: New American Library, 1961), No. 39, 240; No. 40, 253; No. 43, 279–80. This question is ably explored by Harry V. Jaffa, *Original Intent and the Framers of the Constitution: A Disputed Question* (Washington: Regnery Gateway, 1994).

44. Luther Martin, *Genuine Information* (1788), in *The Complete Anti-Federalist,* ed. Herbert J. Storing (Chicago: University of Chicago Press, 1981), 2:62. Jefferson, *Notes on Virginia*, Query 18, in *Writings,* 288. Mason, 22 August, in *Records of the Convention*, ed. Farrand, 2:370.

45. Ralph David Abernathy, *And the Walls Came Tumbling Down: An Autobiography* (New York: Harper Perennial, 1990), 17.

46. For further support of my argument, see Storing, "Slavery and the Moral Foundations"; John Alvis, "The Slavery Provisions of the U.S. Constitution: Means for Emancipation," *Political Science Reviewer* 17 (1987): 241–65; Bernard Bailyn, *Faces of Revolution* (New York: Knopf, 1990), 222–23; Paul Rahe, *Republics Ancient and Modern* (Chapel Hill: University of North Carolina Press, 1992), 625–37.

47. O'Connor and Sabato, *American Government,* 132.

48. Robinson, *Slavery in the Structure of American Politics*, 88.

49. Lincoln, "Perpetuation of Our Political Institutions" (1838), in *Collected Works,* ed. Basler, 1:108.

50. William Lloyd Garrison, *Liberator*, 15 December 1837 and 1 January 1831, in *Slavery Attacked: The Abolitionist Crusade,* ed. John L. Thomas (Englewood Cliffs, N.J.: Prentice-Hall, 1965), 77, and George M. Frederickson, ed., *William Lloyd Garrison* (Englewood Cliffs, N.J.: Prentice-Hall, 1968), 23. William Lloyd Garrison, *Thoughts on Colonization* (1832; reprint, New York: Arno, 1968), 9. Aileen S. Kraditor, *Means and Ends in Abolitionism: Garrison and His Critics on Strategy and Tactics, 1834–1850* (New York: Pantheon, 1969). Harry V. Jaffa, *Crisis of the House Divided* (1959; reprint, Seattle: University of Washington Press, 1973), 261, 270–72. Thomas G. West and Sanderson Schaub, *Marx and the Gulag: Two Essays* (Montclair, Calif.:

Claremont Institute, 1988). Charles L. Griswold Jr., "Rights and Wrongs: Jefferson, Slavery, and Philosophical Quandaries," in *A Culture of Rights,* ed. Michael J. Lacey et al. (Cambridge: Cambridge University Press, 1991), 189–214.

51. Jefferson to Richard Price, 7 August 1785, in Thomas Jefferson, *Life and Selected Writings,* ed. Adrienne Koch and William Peden (New York: Modern Library, 1944), 368. Jay to Society for the Manumission of Slaves, June 1788, *Founders' Constitution,* ed. Kurland and Lerner, 1:550. Lincoln, Speech at Chicago, 10 July 1858, in *Collected Works,* ed. Basler, 2:500.

52. 22 August, *Records of the Convention,* ed. Farrand, 2:371, 373. Rawlins Loundes, South Carolina ratifying convention, 1788, in Jonathan Elliot, *The Debates in the Several State Conventions on the Adoption of the Constitution* (Philadelphia: Lippincott, 1937), 4:272. Madison to Rush, 10 March 1790, *Founders' Constitution,* ed. Kurland and Lerner, 1:555.

53. Petitions to Virginia legislature from six counties (1785), Robert E. Brown and B. Katherine Brown, *Virginia, 1705–1786: Aristocracy or Democracy?* (East Lansing: Michigan State University Press, 1964), 285.

54. Storing, "Moral Foundations," 324–25. John Henry to Pleasants, 18 January 1773, in *Founders' Constitution,* ed. Kurland and Lerner, 1:517. Henry quoted in Elliot, *Debates,* 3:590. Jefferson to Holmes, 22 April 1820; Jefferson, *Notes on Virginia,* Query 14, both in *Writings,* 1434, 264 (emphasis added).

55. Finkelman, *Slavery and the Founders,* chap. 5. Alexis de Tocqueville, *Democracy in America,* ed. J. P. Mayer (New York: Harper & Row, 1988), 357–60. James Fenimore Cooper, *The American Democrat* (1838; reprint, Indianapolis: Liberty Classics, 1981), 222. St. George Tucker, who opposed slavery, also feared that a general emancipation would lead to a race war ending in "the extermination of one party or the other"; Tucker to Belknap, 29 June 1795, *Founders' Constitution,* ed. Kurland and Lerner, 1:559.

56. Alfred N. Hunt, *Haiti's Influence on Antebellum America* (Baton Rouge: Louisiana State University Press, 1988), 21–22, 39–40.

57. Jefferson, *Notes on Virginia,* Query 18, *Writings,* 289.

58. Harry V. Jaffa, *The Conditions of Freedom: Essays in Political Philosophy* (Baltimore: Johns Hopkins University Press, 1975), 244.

59. Jefferson to Bancroft, 26 January 1788, *Papers,* 14:492. James Madison, "Memorandum on an African Colony for Freed Slaves" (1789), in *Founders' Constitution,* ed. Kurland and Lerner, 1:552. Frederick Law Olmsted, *The Cotton Kingdom* (1861; reprint, New York: Modern Library, 1984), 464. St. George Tucker to Belknap, 29 June 1795, *Founders' Constitution,* ed. Kurland and Lerner, 1:559. Washington to Lafayette, 10 May 1786, in *George Washington: A Collection,* ed. Allen, 322.

60. Litwack, *North of Slavery,* 66.

61. Winthrop P. Jordan, *White over Black: American Attitudes toward the Negro, 1550–1812* (Chapel Hill: University of North Carolina Press, 1968), 411–12. Kettner, *Development of American Citizenship,* 236, 319, 330. Robert J. Dinkin, *Voting in Revolutionary America: A Study of Elections in the Original Thirteen States, 1776–1789* (Westport, Conn.: Greenwood, 1982), 41–42. Kirk H. Porter, *A History of Suffrage in the United States* (1918; reprint, New York: AMS Press, 1971), 80–85, 90. "An Act

. . . Establishing an Uniform Militia," 8 May 1792, in *Annals of Congress*, ed. Joseph Gales and William W. Seaton (Washington, D.C.: Gales and Seaton, 1834–56), 1:1392.

62. Kruman, "Suffrage," in *Reader's Companion*, ed. Foner and Garraty, 1044. Litwack, *North of Slavery*, 94, 79, 90, 174. Cf. MacLeod, *Slavery, Race*, 168–69. Douglass, "What Are the Colored People Doing for Themselves?" (1848), in *What Country Have I? Political Writings by Black Americans*, ed. Herbert J. Storing (New York: St. Martin's, 1970), 45–46.

63. Litwack, *North of Slavery*, 66.

64. Jefferson to Holmes, 22 April 1820, *Writings*, 1434; *Notes on Virginia*, Query 14, *Writings*, 264.

65. Jordan, *White over Black*, 548, 567. Lincoln to Caleb Smith, 23 October 1861, in *Collected Works*, ed. Basler, 4:561; Abraham Lincoln, Annual Message to Congress, 3 December 1861, in ibid., 5:48; Appeal to Border State Representatives, 12 July 1862, in ibid., 5:318; Address on Colonization to a Deputation of Negroes, 14 August 1862, in ibid., 373; Annual Message to Congress, 1 December 1862, in ibid., 5:530, 534–35.

66. Washington, "Circular to the States" (1783), in *George Washington: A Collection*, 240. Jefferson to Weightman, 24 June 1826; *Notes on Virginia*, Query 18, both in *Writings*, 1517, 289. Madison to Rush, 20 March 1790, in *Founders' Constitution*, ed. Kurland and Lerner, 555.

67. "An Address to the Public from the Pennsylvania Society for Promoting the Abolition of Slavery" (1789), in Franklin, *Writings*, 1154.

68. Hamilton, *Federalist* No. 6, p. 59.

69. Daniel Webster, *Effects of Slavery, on Morals and Industry* (1791), quoted in David B. Davis, *Slavery and Human Progress* (New York: Oxford University Press, 1984), 159. Devereaux Jarrett quoted in Larry E. Tise, *Proslavery: 1701–1840* (Athens: University of Georgia Press, 1987), 37.

70. 22 August, in *Records of the Convention*, ed. Farrand, 2:369–72.

71. Lincoln, speech at Springfield on Dred Scott, 26 June 1857, in *Collected Works*, 2:403–4. Rahe, *Republics Ancient and Modern*, 641–50. The "saddles on their backs" reference is to Jefferson's famous letter to Weightman, 24 June 1826, in *Writings*, 1517.

72. Abraham Lincoln, Speech at Alton, 15 October 1858, in *The Lincoln-Douglas Debates of 1858*, ed. Robert W. Johannsen (New York: Oxford University Press, 1965), 319. On the permanent conflict between good and evil in the soul, see Aleksandr Solzhenitsyn, *The Gulag Archipelago* (New York: Harper & Row, 1974), 1:168; 2: 615.

73. Bailyn, *Faces of Revolution*, 222–23.

74. Lincoln, Speech at Alton, 15 October 1858, in *Lincoln-Douglas Debates*, 311–12.

75. Harry V. Jaffa, *How to Think about the American Revolution* (Durham: Carolina Academic Press, 1978), 53.

76. Jefferson, *Writings*, 22, 18.

77. John C. Calhoun, Senate speech of 10 January 1838, in *Slavery Defended*, ed. Eric L. McKitrick (Englewood Cliffs, N.J.: Prentice Hall, 1963), 18. Calhoun,

Senate speeches, 6 February 1837 and 19 February 1847, in *Union and Liberty: The Political Philosophy of John C. Calhoun,* ed. Ross M. Lence (Indianapolis: Liberty Fund, 1992), 474, 518. Harry V. Jaffa, *Defenders of the Constitution: Calhoun vs. Madison* (Irving: University of Dallas, 1987). *George (a slave) v. The State* (Mississippi, 1859), in Finkelman, *Law of Freedom,* 261. John C. Calhoun, *A Disquisition on Government* (1853), in *Union and Liberty,* ed. Lence, 44. George Fitzhugh, "Southern Thought" (1857), in *The Ideology of Slavery,* ed. Drew G. Faust (Baton Rouge: Louisiana State University Press, 1981), 279.

78. *Sociology for the South* (1854), in *Slavery Defended,* ed. McKitrick, 38, 44. Compare Karl Marx, *On the Jewish Question,* in *The Marx-Engels Reader,* ed. Robert C. Tucker, 2d ed. (New York: Norton, 1978), 24–51.

79. Alexander Stephens, "Corner-Stone Speech," 21 March 1861, in Henry Cleveland, *Alexander H. Stephens* (Philadelphia: National Publishing, 1866), 721.

80. Lincoln, Speeches at Galesburg, 7 October 1858, *Lincoln-Douglas Debates,* 215–16, 219–20. Jefferson's statement is from *Notes on Virginia,* Query 18, in *Writings,* 289.

81. Lincoln, Gettysburg Address, 19 November 1863.

Chapter 2

1. John Dickinson, *Letters from a Farmer* (1768), Letter 7, end, in *The Political Writings of John Dickinson, 1764–1774,* ed. Paul L. Ford (New York: Da Capo, 1970), 356. Thomas Jefferson, *A Summary View,* in *Writings,* ed. Merrill D. Peterson (New York: Library of America, 1984), 121–22, emphasis added.

2. Letter to Milligan, 6 April 1816, in *Writings of Thomas Jefferson,* ed. Albert E. Bergh (Washington: Thomas Jefferson Memorial Association, 1904), 14:466.

3. Alexander Hamilton, "The Defence of the Funding System" (July 1795), in *Papers of Alexander Hamilton,* ed. Harold C. Syrett (New York: Columbia University Press, 1961–79), 19:52. *Vanhorne's Lessee v. Dorrance,* 2 Dallas 304, 310, in *The Founders' Constitution,* vol. 1, *Major Themes,* ed. Philip B. Kurland and Ralph Lerner (Chicago: University of Chicago Press, 1987), 599.

4. Vernon L. Parrington, *Main Currents in American Thought* (1927; reprint, New York: Harvest Book, Harcourt, Brace, 1954), 1:350. Garry Wills, *Inventing America: Jefferson's Declaration of Independence* (Garden City, N.Y.: Doubleday, 1978), 250–51, 255. Gordon S. Wood, *The Creation of the American Republic* (New York: Norton, 1969), 61, 64, 418. On Wood's misunderstanding, Gary J. Schmitt and Robert H. Webking, "Revolutionaries, Antifederalists, and Federalists: Comments on Gordon Wood's Understanding of the American Founding," *Political Science Reviewer* 9 (1979):195–229.

5. Jefferson, First Inaugural Address (1801), in *Writings,* 494.

6. Virginia Declaration of Rights (1776), in *Founders' Constitution,* ed. Kurland and Lerner, 1:6.

7. Seventh Lincoln-Douglas debate, 15 October 1858; speech at Springfield, 26 June 1857; in Abraham Lincoln, *Collected Works,* ed. Roy P. Basler (New

Brunswick: Rutgers University Press, 1953), 3:315; 2:405.

8. James Madison, "Note to His Speech on the Right of Suffrage," in *Records of the Federal Convention of 1787,* ed. Max Farrand, (New Haven: Yale University Press, 1937), 3:450. Edward J. Erler, "The Great Fence to Liberty: The Right to Property in the American Founding," in *Liberty, Property, and the Foundations of the American Constitution,* ed. Ellen F. Paul et al. (Albany: State University of New York Press, 1988), 43.

9. Thomas G. West, "The Decline of Free Speech in Twentieth-Century America: The View from the Founding," in *Liberty under Law: American Constitutionalism Yesterday, Today, and Tomorrow,* ed. Kenneth L. Grasso and Cecilia Rodriguez Castillo (Lanham, Md.: University Press of America, 1997), 160.

10. Robert Lerner et al., *Molding the Good Citizen: The Politics of High School History Texts* (Westport, Conn.: Praeger, 1995), 102–5. Gary B. Nash, *American Odyssey: The United States in the Twentieth Century,* teacher's ed. (New York: Glencoe/McGraw Hill, 1994), 121, 126, 170–71. (Nash mentions Carnegie as one "of the robber barons who . . . supported the spirit of charity.") David E. Shi, *Matthew Josephson: Bourgeois Bohemian* (New Haven: Yale University Press, 1981). Burton W. Folsom Jr., *The Myth of the Robber Barons,* 3d ed. (Herndon, Va.: Young America's Foundation, 1996).

11. Nash, *American Odyssey,* p. 763.

12. Alexander Hamilton et al., *The Federalist* (New York: New American Library, Mentor, 1961), No. 10, p. 78; and No. 51, p. 324.

13. Michael Parenti, "The Constitution as an Elitist Document," in *How Democratic Is the Constitution?* ed. Robert A. Goldwin and William A. Schambra (Washington: American Enterprise Institute, 1980), 52–53.

14. Kenneth L. Karst, *Belonging to America: Equal Citizenship and the Constitution* (New Haven: Yale University Press, 1989), 179. Arthur S. Miller, quoted by Michael Les Benedict, "Laissez-Faire and Liberty: A Re-Evaluation of the Meaning and Origins of Laissez-Faire Constitutionalism," *Law and History Review* 3 (Fall 1985): 293.

15. Jefferson, *Autobiography,* in *Writings,* 32.

16. Cass Sunstein, *The Partial Constitution* (Cambridge: Harvard University Press, 1993), 40–67, 138.

17. This is proved beyond a reasonable doubt by Steven M. Dworetz, *The Unvarnished Doctrine: Locke, Liberalism, and the American Revolution* (Durham: Duke University Press, 1990).

18. Thomas G. West, "The Classical Spirit of the Founding," in *The American Founding: Essays on the Formation of the Constitution,* ed. J. Jackson Barlow, Leonard W. Levy, and Ken Masugi (Westport, Conn.: Greenwood Press, 1988), 4. Locke, *Second Treatise,* in *Two Treatises of Government,* ed. Peter Laslett, student ed. (Cambridge: Cambridge University Press, 1988), secs. 44–45, my emphasis.

19. Locke, *Second Treatise,* secs. 34, 41, 42. Far from being only of rhetorical use, as some scholars suggest, Locke's account of the origin of property rights (labor) remains effective in society, where money and contract law enable producers to keep the monetized fruits of their labor. Cf. Abram N. Shulsky, "The Concept of Private Property in the History of Political Economy," in *From Political Economy to Economics—And Back?* ed. James H. Nichols Jr. and Colin Wright (San Francisco: ICS Press, 1990), 25–26.

20. Locke, *Second Treatise*, secs. 43, 41.

21. Jefferson, *Autobiography*, in *Writings*, 32. John Stuart Mill, *Principles of Political Economy*, quoted by Marc Plattner, "Natural Right and the Moral Presuppositions of Political Economy," in *From Political Economy to Economics*, ed. Nichols and Wright, 48. Locke, *Second Treatise*, sec. 37.

22. Quoted by Robert E. Brown and B. Katherine Brown, *Virginia 1705–1786: Aristocracy or Democracy?* (East Lansing: Michigan State University Press, 1964), 8.

23. Richard L. Bushman, "Social and Cultural Change," in *The Readers' Companion to American History*, ed. Eric Foner and John A. Garraty (Boston: Houghton Mifflin, 1991), 943. On today's incomprehension of "laissez-faire," see Benedict, "Laissez-Faire and Liberty," and James L. Huston, "The American Revolutionaries, the Political Economy of Aristocracy, and the American Concept of the Distribution of Wealth, 1765–1900," *American Historical Review* 98 (1993): 1079–1105.

24. Abraham Lincoln, Speech at New Haven, 6 March 1860, *Collected Works*, 4:24.

25. Locke, *Second Treatise*, sec. 42.

26. Jefferson, letter to Madison, 6 September 1789, in *Writings*, 963–64.

27. Robert Matthews, Charles Wiltse, and Staughton Lynd make this mistake about Jefferson. See Jean Yarbrough, "Jefferson and Property Rights," in *Liberty, Property*, ed. Paul, 70, 81.

28. Jefferson, letter to Rev. James Madison, 28 October 1785, in *Writings*, 841–42, emphasis added.

29. Jefferson, *Autobiography*, in *Writings*, 32.

30. Willi Paul Adams, *The First American Constitutions: Republican Ideology and the Making of the State Constitutions in the Revolutionary Era* (Chapel Hill: University of North Carolina Press, 1980), 193.

31. *Alexander Hamilton, The Vindication* No. 3 (1792), in *Papers*, ed. Syrett, 11:472.

32. Gordon S. Wood, *The Radicalism of the American Revolution* (New York: Knopf, 1992), 183.

33. Jefferson, *Autobiography*, in *Writings*, 32.

34. Willard S. Randall, *Thomas Jefferson: A Life* (New York: Henry Holt, 1993), 288.

35. Jefferson, *Autobiography*, in *Writings*, 32–33.

36. Alexis de Tocqueville, *Democracy in America*, ed. J. P. Mayer (New York: Harper & Row, 1988), 52, 54.

37. Nathaniel Chipman, *Sketches of the Principles of Government* (Rutland, Vt.: J. Lyon, 1793), 178. The passage is reprinted in *Founders' Constitution*, ed. Kurland and Lerner, 1:557.

38. Maryland in *The Federal and State Constitutions*, ed. Francis N. Thorpe (Washington: Government Printing Office, 1909), 3:1690. Massachusetts in *Founders' Constitution*, ed. Kurland and Lerner, 1:12, emphasis added.

39. In postcommunist Russia during the 1990s, property rights were, if anything, even less secure than they were under communism. In this Russian "state of nature," property was protected only by private force; see Stephen Handelman, *Comrade Criminal: Russia's New Mafiya* (New Haven: Yale University Press, 1995).

40. L. Ray Gunn, *The Decline of Authority: Public Economic Policy and Political Development in New York, 1800–1860* (Ithaca: Cornell University Press, 1988), 226. Wood, *Radicalism*, 321.

41. William E. Nelson, *The Americanization of the Common Law: The Impact of Legal Change on Massachusetts Society, 1760–1830* (Cambridge: Harvard University Press, 1975), 121. Morton Horwitz, *The Transformation of American Law, 1780–1860* (Cambridge: Harvard University Press, 1977), 31. Advisory Commission on Regulatory Barriers to Affordable Housing, *"Not in My Back Yard": Removing Barriers to Affordable Housing* (Washington: Department of Housing and Urban Development, 1991).

42. Horwitz, *Transformation of American Law*, 31–32. Horwitz does not agree with my view that the new law of property favored the poor, but his facts support it, as Stephen B. Presser shows in "Revising the American Tradition," in *Law in the American Revolution,* ed. Hendrick Hartog (New York: New York University Press, 1981), 139–40. James Willard Hurst, *Law and the Conditions of Freedom in the Nineteenth-Century United States* (Madison: University of Wisconsin Press, 1956), 24.

43. Horwitz, *Transformation of American Law,* 37, emphasis added.

44. Jeff L. Lewin, "*Boomer* and the American Law of Nuisance: Past, Present, and Future," *Albany Law Review* 54 (1990): 189–299 (quotation on 210). Robert G. Bone, "Normative Theory and Legal Doctrine in American Nuisance Law: 1850 to 1920," *Southern California Law Review* 59 (1986): 1101–226 (quotation on 1224).

45. Thomas Sowell, *Markets and Minorities* (New York: Basic Books, 1981), 8.

46. Wood, *Radicalism*, 184–85. Note on Madison's speech of 7 August 1787, ca. 1821, in *Mind of the Founder: Sources of the Political Thought of James Madison*, ed. Marvin Meyers, rev. ed. (Hanover, N.H.: University Press of New England, 1981), 396.

47. Jon Greenwood, letter to the editor, *Wall Street Journal*, 16 January 1996, A19.

48. Dennis J. Coyle, "Feudalism and Liberalism," in *Property Rights and the Constitution: Shaping Society through Land Use Regulation* (Albany: State University of New York Press, 1993), 217, quoting Philbrick, "Changing Conceptions of Property in Law," *University of Pennsylvania Law Review* 86 (1938): 691, 710; and John Cribbet, "Changing Concepts in the Law of Land Use," *Iowa Law Review* 50 (1965): 245, 247.

49. Many of these practices are detailed in Coyle, *Property Rights*, and in Clint Bolick, *Grassroots Tyranny: The Limits of Federalism* (Washington: Cato Institute, 1993).

50. Hernando de Soto, *The Other Path: The Invisible Revolution in the Third World* (New York: Harper & Row, 1989), 18, 134, 201.

51. Richard Hofstadter, *The American Political Tradition* (New York: Vintage, 1948), 16. Marc Plattner, "Natural Rights and the Moral Presuppositions of Political Economy," in *From Political Economy to Economics*, ed. Nichols and Wright, 41.

52. J. Allen Smith, *The Spirit of American Government* (1907; reprint, Cambridge: Harvard University Press, 1965), 297–98.

53. Charles Beard, *An Economic Interpretation of the Constitution of the United*

States (1913; reprint, New York: Free Press, 1941), 324.

54. Franklin D. Roosevelt, Acceptance of Renomination for the Presidency, 27 June 1936, *Public Papers and Addresses,* ed. Samuel I. Rosenman (New York: Harper, 1938–50), 5:230–36. Mark Leff, *The Limits of Symbolic Reform: The New Deal and Taxation* (New York: Cambridge University Press, 1984), vi (thanks to Burt Folsom for this reference).

55. John Dewey, *Liberalism and Social Action* (1935; reprint, New York: Perigree Books, 1980), 26.

56. Dewey, *Liberalism and Social Action,* 17, 36, 54–55, 62, 92.

57. Dewey, *Liberalism and Social Action,* 33. John Dewey, *Reconstruction in Philosophy* (1948; reprint, Boston: Beacon, 1957), 193–94. Jean-Jacques Rousseau, *Discourse on Inequality,* in *The First and Second Discourses,* ed. Roger D. Masters (New York: St. Martin's 1984), 114–15.

58. Dewey, *Reconstruction in Philosophy,* 194, 22–23; Dewey, *Liberalism and Social Action,* 26.

59. Dewey, *Liberalism and Social Action,* 48.

60. Harvey C. Mansfield Jr., "Responsibility versus Self-Expression," in *Old Rights and New,* ed. Robert Licht (Washington: American Enterprise Institute Press, 1993), 105–6.

61. Jennifer Nedelsky, *Private Property and the Limits of American Constitutionalism* (Chicago: University of Chicago Press, 1990), 262, 273.

62. *Harris v. McRae,* 448 U.S. 297 (1980).

63. Nedelsky, *Private Property,* 263.

64. Henry Shue, "Subsistence Rights: Shall We Secure *These* Rights?" in *How Does the Constitution Secure Rights?* ed. Robert A. Goldwin and William A. Schambra (Washington: American Enterprise Institute, 1985), 93.

65. John Rawls, *A Theory of Justice* (Cambridge: Harvard University Press, 1971), 74, 101–2. On the arguments of Rawls and other New Liberals, see John Marini, *The Politics of Budget Control: Congress, the Presidency, and the Growth of the Administrative State* (New York: Crane Russak, 1992), 88–92.

66. Jonathan K. Van Patten, "Judicial Independence and the Rule of Law," *Benchmark* 2 (May/August, 1986): 125; John A. Wettergreen, "The Bird Court on the Law of Torts," ibid., 132.

67. Franklin D. Roosevelt, State of the Union Message, 11 January 1944, *Public Papers and Addresses,* 13:41.

68. Harvey C. Mansfield Jr., *America's Constitutional Soul* (Baltimore: Johns Hopkins University Press, 1991), 94.

69. James Madison, "Property," 29 March 1792, in *Founders' Constitution,* ed. Kurland and Lerner, 1:598.

70. Jefferson, *Autobiography,* in *Writings,* 74.

71. James Madison, "Note to His Speech on the Right of Suffrage," in *Records of the Federal Convention of 1787,* ed. Max Farrand (New Haven: Yale University Press, 1937), 3:450. James Wilson, "Lectures on Law" (1790–91), in *Works of James Wilson,* ed. Robert G. McCloskey (Cambridge: Harvard University Press, 1967), 2:718–19.

72. Hamilton, *Federalist* No. 12, p. 91.

73. John Adams, *Thoughts on Government* (1776), in *American Political Writing during the Founding Era*, ed. Charles S. Hyneman and Donald S. Lutz (Indianapolis: Liberty Press, 1983), 1:408. John Adams, Letter to Mercy Warren, 8 January 1776, *Selected Writings of John and John Quincy Adams*, ed. Adrienne Koch and William Peden (New York: Knopf, 1946), 49. For a more critical view of the effect of commerce on character than that of the Founders, see Ralph Lerner, *The Thinking Revolutionary: Principle and Practice in the New Republic* (Ithaca: Cornell University Press, 1987), chap. 6; and Thomas L. Pangle, *The Spirit of Modern Republicanism: The Moral Vision of the American Founders and the Philosophy of Locke* (Chicago: University of Chicago Press, 1988), chap. 9.

74. Benjamin Franklin, "Information to Those Who Would Remove to America" (1784), *Writings*, ed. J. A. Leo Lemay (New York: Library of America, 1987), 982.

75. Jefferson, *Notes on Virginia*, Query 17, in *Writings*, 287. Adams to Jefferson, 21 December 1819, *The Adams-Jefferson Letters*, ed. Lester J. Cappon (New York: Simon & Schuster, 1959), 551.

76. Hamilton, "Defence of the Funding System," in *Papers*, ed. Syrett, 19:52.

77. Wilson, "Lectures on Law," 719. Aristotle, *Politics*, 1263b.

78. Jefferson, *Notes on Virginia*, Query 19, in *Writings*, 290. Jefferson, letter to Washington, 14 August 1787, quoted in Yarbrough, "Jefferson and Property Rights," 76.

79. Quoted in Yarbrough, "Jefferson and Property Rights," 78. See also Harry V. Jaffa, "The Virtue of a Nation of Cities: On the Jeffersonian Paradoxes," in *The Conditions of Freedom: Essays in Political Philosophy* (Baltimore: Johns Hopkins University Press, 1975), 99–110.

80. Tocqueville, *Democracy in America*, 511.

81. Howard Husok, "The Folly of Public Housing," *Wall Street Journal*, 28 September 1993, A18.

82. Alexander Hamilton, "Report on Manufactures," in *Selected Writings and Speeches of Alexander Hamilton*, ed. Morton J. Frisch (Washington: American Enterprise Institute Press, 1985), 288, 290.

83. Hamilton, *Federalist* No. 11, pp. 85–88. Rudyard Kipling shows the noble side of the spirit of enterprise in *Captains Courageous*. Stephen E. Ambrose, *D-Day, June 6, 1944: The Climactic Battle of World War II* (New York: Simon & Schuster, 1994), 344–45; also 49, 52, 275.

Chapter 3

1. Joan Hoff Wilson, "The Illusion of Change: Women and the American Revolution," in *The American Revolution: Explorations in the History of American Radicalism*, ed. Alfred F. Young (DeKalb: Northern Illinois University Press, 1976), 387.

2. Lorna C. Mason et al., *History of the United States*, vol. 1, *Beginnings to 1877* (Boston: Houghton Mifflin, 1992), 188. Milton C. Cummings and David Wise, *Democracy under Pressure: An Introduction to the American Political System*, 7th ed. (Fort Worth: Harcourt Brace, 1993), 45.

3. Linda Kerber, *Women of the Republic: Intellect and Ideology in Revolutionary America* (Chapel Hill: University of North Carolina Press, 1980), xii.

4. Richard L. Bushman, "Revolution," in *The Reader's Companion to American History,* ed. Eric Foner and John A. Garraty (Boston: Houghton Mifflin, 1991), 944.

5. Abraham Lincoln, letter to Pierce, 6 April 1859, in *Collected Works,* ed. Roy T. Basler (New Brunswick: Rutgers University Press, 1953), 3:375–76. On historicism: Leo Strauss, *What Is Political Philosophy?* (Glencoe, Ill.: Free Press, 1959), chaps. 1, 2.

6. Gordon S. Wood, *The Radicalism of the American Revolution* (New York: Knopf, 1992), 7.

7. Gordon S. Wood, "Equality and Social Conflict in the American Revolution," *William and Mary Quarterly* 51 (October 1994): 707. James MacGregor Burns et al., *Government by the People,* 15th ed. (Englewood Cliffs, N.J.: Prentice Hall, 1993), 117.

8. "Men" and "mankind" in "Address to the People of Great Britain" (1774): Worthington C. Ford, ed., *Journals of the Continental Congress* (Washington: Government Printing Office, 1904–37), 1:82, 89. "Man" and "humanity" in "Manifesto," October 1778: Ford, *Journals,* 12:1080, 1082. "Human nature" in David Ramsay, *History of the American Revolution* (1789; reprint, Indianapolis: Liberty Classics, 1990), 1:29. "Human rights" in John Jay, Letter to President of Manumission Society, June 1788, in Philip B. Kurland and Ralph Lerner, ed., *The Founders' Constitution,* vol 1., *Major Themes* (Chicago: University of Chicago Press, 1987), 550. "Rights of nature" in John Adams, *Novanglus* (1774–75), in *Works of John Adams,* ed. Charles F. Adams (Boston: Little, Brown, 1854), 4:124. Hamilton quotation in Alexander Hamilton, *The Farmer Refuted* (1775), in *Papers of Alexander Hamilton,* ed. Harold C. Syrett (New York: Columbia University Press, 1961–79), 1:104.

9. Thomas Jefferson, *Notes on the State of Virginia* (1783), Query 6, in *Writings,* ed. Merrill D. Peterson (New York: Library of America, 1984), 185–86. Francis Parkman, *France and England in North America* (1865–92; reprint, New York: Library of America, 1983), 1:358.

10. John M. Blum, Kenneth Stampp, et al., *The National Experience: A History of the United States,* 8th ed. (Fort Worth: Harcourt Brace, 1993), 266.

11. Karen O'Connor and Larry Sabato, *American Government: Roots and Reform* (New York: Macmillan, 1993), 132.

12. Northwest Ordinance, sec. 9; Massachusetts Constitution, chap. 1, sec. 3, art. 4; in *Founders' Constitution,* ed. Kurland and Lerner, 1:27, 16. See also Jan Lewis, "'Of Every Age Sex and Condition': The Representation of Women in the Constitution," *Journal of the Early Republic* 15 (1995): 359–87.

13. Several of the points made in this section are from Robert Goldwin, *Why Blacks, Women, and Jews Are Not Mentioned in the Constitution, and Other Unorthodox Views* (Washington: American Enterprise Institute Press, 1990), 16–18. See also Herman Belz, "Liberty and Equality for Whom? How to Think Inclusively about the Constitution and the Bill of Rights," *History Teacher* 25 (May 1992): 263–77.

14. Burns et al., *Government by the People,* 325. Robert A. Divine et al., *America: The People and the Dream,* vol. 1, *The Early Years* (Glenview, Ill.: Scott, Foresman, 1992), 196.

15. A good summary is Judith A. Klinghoffer and Lois Elkis, "'The Petticoat Electors': Women's Suffrage in New Jersey, 1776–1807," *Journal of the Early Republic* 12 (1992): 159–93. See also Edward R. Turner, "Women's Suffrage in New Jersey, 1790–1807," *Smith College Studies in History* 1 (1916): 165–87; Richard P. McCormick, *History of Voting in New Jersey* (New Brunswick: Rutgers University Press, 1953); Mary Philbrook, "Woman's Suffrage in New Jersey prior to 1807," *Proceedings of the New Jersey Historical Society* 57 (1939): 87–98; J. R. Pole, "The Suffrage in New Jersey, 1790–1807," *Proceedings of the New Jersey Historical Society* 71 (1953): 39–61; William A. Whitehead, "A Brief Statement of the Facts Connected with Female Suffrage," *Proceedings of the New Jersey Historical Society* 8 (1859): 101–5.

16. Turner, "Women's Suffrage," 169–70.

17. Klinghoffer and Elkis, "'The Petticoat Electors,'" 162, 171–72, 192.

18. McCormick, *Voting in New Jersey*, 78.

19. Turner, "Women's Suffrage," 178; McCormick, *Voting in New Jersey*, 77–78.

20. Philbrook, "Woman's Suffrage in New Jersey," 93; Whitehead, "Brief Statement of Facts," 103.

21. Turner, "Women's Suffrage," 182; McCormick, *Voting in New Jersey*, 204 n. 63.

22. William Griffith, *Eumenes* (Trenton, 1799), quoted by Philbrook, "Woman's Suffrage in New Jersey," 92.

23. Robert J. Dinkin, *Voting in Provincial America* (Westport, Conn.: Greenwood Press, 1977), 30.

24. Turner, "Women's Suffrage," 185. Sandra L. Bartky, *Femininity and Domination: Studies in the Phenomenology of Oppression* (New York: Routledge, 1990), 2.

25. Carol M. Mueller, "The Empowerment of Women," in *The Politics of the Gender Gap: The Social Construction of Political Influence,* ed. Mueller (Newbury Park, Calif.: Sage, 1988), 35. Arthur Miller, "Gender and the Vote: 1984," in ibid., 259. Henry C. Kenski, "The Gender Factor in a Changing Electorate," in ibid., 43. Data for 1996 is from *New York Times*, 10 November 1996, 16Y.

26. "The Marriage Gap," unsigned editorial, *Wall Street Journal*, 15 November 1996, A14.

27. U.S. Bureau of the Census, *Statistical Abstract of the United States: 1996* (Washington: Government Printing Office, 1996), 54.

28. James Otis, *The Rights of the British Colonies* (1764), in *Pamphlets of the American Revolution,* ed. Bernard Bailyn (Cambridge: Harvard University Press, 1965), 420–21.

29. Kerber, *Women of the Republic*, 31.

30. Hamilton, *Farmer Refuted*, 106, quoting William Blackstone, *Commentaries,* (1765–69; reprint, Chicago: University of Chicago Press, 1979) bk. 1, chap. 2, emphasis added.

31. Adams to James Sullivan, 26 May 1776, in *Works*, 9:377.

32. Daniel Dulany, *Considerations on the Propriety of Imposing Taxes in the British Colonies* (1765), in *Pamphlets,* ed. Bailyn, 614.

33. William Blackstone, *Commentaries,* ed. Tucker (1765–69; reprint, Chicago: University of Chicago Press, 1979), 2:445.

34. Richard Henry Lee to Hannah Corbin, 17 March 1778, in *Founders' Constitution*, ed. Kurland and Lerner, 1:396. Carol Berkin and Leonard Wood, *Land of Promise: A History of the United States to 1877* (Glenview, Ill.: Scott, Foresman, 1986), 215.

35. Howard V. Hayghe, "Working Wives' Contributions to Family Incomes," *Monthly Labor Review*, U.S. Department of Labor, Bureau of Labor Statistics, August 1993, 43. U.S. Bureau of the Census, *Statistical Abstract of the United States: 1996*, 390, 405, 479. George Gilder, *Men and Marriage* (Gretna, La.: Pelican, 1992), 141.

36. Adams to Sullivan, 26 May 1776, *Works*, 9:375–76. Theophilus Parsons, *The Essex Result* (1778), in *American Political Writing during the Founding Era*, ed. Charles S. Hyneman and Donald S. Lutz (Indianapolis: Liberty Press, 1983), 1:497.

Chapter 4

1. David J. Ayers, "My Days and Nights in the Academic Wilderness," *Heterodoxy*, January 1993, 1, 12–13.

2. Morton White, *The Philosophy of the American Revolution* (New York: Oxford University Press, 1978), 261. Betty Wood, "The Impact of the Revolution on the Role, Status, and Experience of Women," in *The Blackwell Encyclopedia of the American Revolution*, ed. Jack P. Greene and J. R. Pole (Oxford: Basil Blackwell, 1991), 402. Lorna C. Mason et al., *History of the United States*, vol. 1, *Beginnings to 1877* (Boston: Houghton Mifflin, 1992), 188. Marc W. Kruman, "Suffrage," in *The Reader's Companion to American History*, ed. Eric Foner and John A. Garraty (Boston: Houghton Mifflin, 1991), 1044.

3. James Wilson, "Lectures on Law" (1790–91), *Works of James Wilson*, ed. Robert G. McCloskey (Cambridge: Harvard University Press, 1967), 87. Ann Moir and David Jessel, *Brain Sex* (New York: Dell/Laurel, 1989), 42–49, 88–98, 110, 140; Steven Goldberg, *Why Men Rule: A Theory of Male Dominance* (Chicago: Open Court, 1993), 197–219; Michael Levin, *Feminism and Freedom* (New Brunswick, N.J.: Transaction, 1987), 82–87.

4. Adams to Sullivan, 26 May 1776, in *Works of John Adams*, ed. Charles F. Adams (Boston: Little, Brown, 1854), 9:375–76.

5. Theophilus Parsons, *The Essex Result* (1778), in *American Political Writing during the Founding Era*, ed. Charles S. Hyneman and Donald S. Lutz (Indianapolis: Liberty Press, 1983), 1:497.

6. Alexander Hamilton et al., *The Federalist* (New York: Mentor Books, 1961), No. 57, p. 353; No. 46, p. 299. Washington to James Warren, 7 October 1785, in *George Washington: A Collection*, ed. W. B. Allen (Indianapolis: Liberty Classics, 1988), 313. John Adams, *Thoughts on Government* (1776), in *American Political Writing*, ed. Hyneman and Lutz, 401–9.

7. Edward L. Kain, *The Myth of Family Decline: Understanding Families in a World of Rapid Social Change* (Lexington, Mass.: Lexington Books, 1990), 112. Judith Lorber and Susan A. Farrell, eds., *The Social Construction of Gender* (Newbury Park, Calif.: Sage, 1991).

8. Carl N. Degler, *In Search of Human Nature: The Decline and Revival of Darwinism in American Social Thought* (New York: Oxford University Press, 1991), 134, 139, 187–89, 293–309.

9. Eleanor E. Maccoby and Carol N. Jacklin, *The Psychology of Sex Differences* (Stanford: Stanford University Press, 1974), 242–43, 352. Besides *Brain Sex,* see James Q. Wilson, *The Moral Sense* (New York: Free Press, 1993), 165–90.

10. John Money and Anke E. Ehrhardt, *Man and Woman, Boy and Girl: The Differentiation and Dimorphism of Gender Identity from Conception to Maturity* (Baltimore: Johns Hopkins University Press, 1972), 98–105. Criticisms of this study, and further confirmation of its results, are discussed in Levin, *Feminism and Freedom,* 79–82.

11. Melford E. Spiro, *Gender and Culture: Kibbutz Women Revisited* (Durham: Duke University Press, 1979), 106.

12. Presidential Commission on the Assignment of Women in the Armed Forces, *Report to the President* (Washington: Government Printing Office, 1992), 5, 9, 19, C4, C8, C9.

13. Margaret Hennig and Anne Jardim, *The Managerial Woman* (Garden City: Doubleday Anchor, 1977), 76–93.

14. Page Smith, *Daughters of the Promised Land: Women in American History* (Boston: Little, Brown, 1970), 54.

15. David Gelernter, response to critics, *Commentary,* June 1996, 6.

16. Mohammedreza Hojat, "The World Declaration of the Rights of the Child: Anticipated Challenges," *Psychological Reports* 72 (1993): 1017.

17. Benjamin Rush, "Thoughts on Female Education" (1787), in *Essays on Education in the Early Republic,* ed. Frederick Rudolph (Cambridge: Harvard University Press, 1965), 35. Mark E. Kann, *On the Man Question: Gender and Civic Virtue in America* (Philadelphia: Temple University Press, 1991).

18. Murray Straus, "Explaining Family Violence," in *Marriage and Family in a Changing Society,* ed. James M. Henslin (New York: Free Press, 1989), 351–53. Alice Miller, *For Your Own Good: Hidden Cruelty in Child-Rearing and the Roots of Violence* (New York: Farrar Straus Giroux, 1983), 4, 70, 146. John Bradshaw, *The Family: A Revolutionary Way of Self-Discovery* (Deerfield Beach, Fla.: Health Communications, 1988). Stephanie Coontz, *The Way We Never Were: American Families and the Nostalgia Trap* (New York: Basic Books, 1992), 35. Dana Mack, "Are Parents Bad for Children?" *Commentary,* March 1994, 30–35, criticizes some of these authors. See also Dana Mack, *The Assault on Parenthood: How Our Culture Undermines the Family* (New York: Simon & Schuster, 1997).

19. U.S. Department of Justice, Bureau of Justice Statistics, *Violence against Women: Estimates from the Redesigned Survey* (Washington: U.S. Department of Justice, Bureau of Justice Statistics, 1995), tables 4, 6. Jan E. Stets, "Cohabiting and Marital Aggression," *Journal of Marriage and the Family* 53 (1991): 674.

20. Gwat-Yong Lie and Sabrina Gentlewarrior, "Intimate Violence in Lesbian Relationships," *Journal of Social Service Research* 15 (1991): 46. Gwat-Yong Lie et al., "Lesbians in Currently Aggressive Relationships: How Frequently Do They Report Aggressive Past Relationships?" *Violence and Victims* 6 (1991): 125–26. Lettie L. Lockhart et al., "Letting Out the Secret: Violence in Lesbian Relationships,"

Journal of Interpersonal Violence 9 (1994): 470. See also Claire M. Renzetti, *Violent Betrayal: Partner Abuse in Lesbian Relationships* (Newbury Park, Calif.: Sage, 1992), 115. Donald G. Dutton et al. competently discuss this research in "Patriarchy and Wife Assault: The Ecological Fallacy," *Violence and Victims* 9 (1994): 167–78.

21. Dutton, "Patriarchy and Wife Assault," 174. David Blankenhorn, *Fatherless America: Confronting Our Most Urgent Social Problem* (New York: Basic Books, 1995), 26–39. Andrew P. Thomas, *Crime and the Sacking of America: The Roots of Chaos* (Washington: Brassey's, 1994), 166.

22. Jan Lewis, "The Republican Wife: Virtue and Seduction in the Early Republic," *William and Mary Quarterly* 44(1987): 707. Jefferson to Mary Eppes, 1 January 1799 and 26 October 1801, *The Family Letters of Thomas Jefferson,* ed. Edwin M. Betts and James A. Bear Jr. (Columbia: University of Missouri Press, 1966), 170, 210. Jan Lewis discusses Jefferson's view of the family in "The Blessings of Domestic Society," in *Jeffersonian Legacies,* ed. Peter Onuf (Charlottesville: University Press of Virginia, 1993), 109–46. Abigail to John Adams, 20 June 1783, in *The Book of Abigail and John: Selected Letters of the Adams Family, 1762–1784* (Cambridge: Harvard University Press, 1975), 354.

23. Atlee L. Stroup et al., "Economic Consequences of Marital Dissolution," *Journal of Divorce and Remarriage* 22 (1994): 37–54. Diane Medved, *The Case against Divorce* (New York: D. I. Fine, 1989). Quotations are from Judith S. Wallerstein and Sandra Blakeslee, *Second Chances: Men, Women, and Children a Decade after Divorce* (New York: Ticknor & Fields, 1989), 27, 29.

24. Blankenhorn, *Fatherless America,* 219–20. On male-female differences in raising children, see also Wilson, *The Moral Sense,* 176–82; Moir and Jessel, *Brain Sex,* 145. Adams, "Diary" (1778), *Works,* 3:171.

25. Nicholas Zill and Charlotte Schoenborn, "Developmental, Learning, and Emotional Problems," Advance Data, no. 190 (Washington: National Center for Health Statistics, U.S. Department of Health and Human Services, 16 November 1990), 9. Judith S. Wallerstein and Joan B. Kelly, *Surviving the Breakup: How Children and Parents Cope with Divorce* (New York: Basic Books, 1980), ix, 35–95, 198. Wallerstein and Blakeslee, *Second Chances.* Thomas M. Achenbach et al., "Six-Year Predictors of Problems in a National Sample of Children and Youth: I. Cross-Informant Syndromes," *Journal of the American Academy of Child and Adolescent Psychology* 34 (1995): 336–46 (divorce is the leading predictor of behavioral and psychological problems). Allan Bloom, *The Closing of the American Mind* (New York: Simon & Schuster, 1987), 117–21. Leon Kass, "The End of Courtship," *The Public Interest,* Winter 1997, 47. Andre P. Derdeyn, "Discussion of 'Parental Separation, Adolescent Psychopathology, and Problem Behaviors,'" *Journal of the American Academy of Child and Adolescent Psychology* 33 (1994): 1132.

26. Wallerstein and Kelly, *Surviving the Breakup,* ix, 35–95, 198. Frank F. Furstenberg and Andrew J. Cherlin, *Divided Families: What Happens to Children When Parents Part* (Cambridge: Harvard University Press, 1991). For a popular overview of current research on the harmful effects of divorce and single motherhood on children, Barbara D. Whitehead, "Dan Quayle Was Right," *Atlantic Monthly,* April 1993, 47–84.

27. John Demos, "Child Abuse in Context," in *Past, Present, and Personal: The*

Family and the Life Course in American History (New York: Oxford, 1986), 68–91.

28. Andrea J. Sedlak et al., *Executive Summary of the Third National Incidence Study of Child Abuse and Neglect* (Washington: U.S. Department of Health and Human Services, 1996), 8.

29. Martin Daly and Margo Wilson, "Child Abuse and Other Risks of Not Living with Both Parents," *Ethology and Sociobiology* 6 (1985): 202, 205–6.

30. Daly and Wilson, "Child Abuse," 205–6. Leslie Margolin, "Child Abuse by Mothers' Boyfriends: Why the Overrepresentation?" *Child Abuse and Neglect* 16 (1992): 541–51. Richard J. Gelles, "Child Abuse and Violence in Single-Parent Families: Parental Absence and Economic Deprivation," *American Journal of Orthopsychiatry* 59 (1989): 496, 499.

31. David Finkelhor et al., "Sexual Abuse in a National Survey," *Child Abuse and Neglect* 14 (1990): 24–25. Leslie Margolin and John L. Craft, "Child Sexual Abuse by Caretakers," *Family Relations* 38 (1989): 452.

32. Jay Belsky, "The 'Effects' of Infant Day Care Reconsidered," *Early Childhood Research Quarterly* 3 (1988): 253, 255, 257. Deborah L. Vandell and Mary A. Corasaniti, "Variations in Early Child Care: Do They Predict Social, Emotional, and Cognitive Differences?" *Early Childhood Research Quarterly* 5 (1990): 569. See also Jay Belsky and David Eggebeen, "Early and Extensive Maternal Employment and Young Children's Socioemotional Development: Children of the National Longitudinal Survey of Youth," *Journal of Marriage and the Family* 53 (1991): 1083–110. Both Belsky articles discuss the intense pressure in the field of day-care research to reach "politically correct" (pro-day care) results.

33. Blankenhorn, *Fatherless America,* 26–39. Thomas, *Crime and the Sacking of America,* 166.

34. John to Abigail Adams, 30 September 1764, *Book of Abigail and John,* ed. Butterfield, 45. George Gilder, *Men and Marriage* (Gretna, La.: Pelican, 1992), 61–68. George Gilder, *Naked Nomads: Unmarried Men in America* (New York: Quadrangle/New York Times Book Co., 1974).

35. Aristotle discusses the family in bk. 1 of the *Politics* and bks. 8 and 9 of the *Nicomachean Ethics.* See Darrell Dobbs, "Family Matters: Aristotle's Appreciation of Women and the Plural Structure of Society," *American Political Science Review* 90 (1996): 74–89.

36. James Kent, *Commentaries on American Law* (1826–30; reprint, New York: Da Capo, 1971), 2:159–60.

37. John Adams, *Discourses on Davila,* no. 4, in *Works,* 6:243, 246.

38. *Reynolds v. U.S.,* 998 U.S. 244 (1879).

39. Kent, *Commentaries on American Law,* 2:86. Wilson, "Lectures on Law," *Works,* 603.

40. Wilson, "Lectures on Law," *Works,* 604. Richard Wexler, *Wounded Innocents: The Real Victims of the War against Child Abuse* (Buffalo: Prometheus Press, 1990), 15–18, 95–134.

41. Thomas Jefferson, "A Bill for Support of the Poor," in *Papers of Thomas Jefferson,* ed. Julian P. Boyd (Princeton: Princeton University Press, 1950–), 2:422. Michael Grossberg, *Governing the Hearth: Law and the Family in Nineteenth-Century America* (Chapel Hill: University of North Carolina Press, 1985).

42. Wilson, "Lectures on Law," *Works,* 602. Linda Kerber, *Women of the Republic: Intellect and Ideology in Revolutionary America* (Chapel Hill: University of North Carolina Press, 1980), 141.

43. Wilson, "Lectures on Law," *Works,* 599–600.

44. Abigail Adams to John Adams, 31 March 1776; John Adams to Abigail Adams, 14 April 1776, *Adams Family Correspondence,* ed. L. H. Butterfield (Cambridge: Harvard University Press, 1963), 1:370, 382. Camille Paglia, *Sex, Art, and American Culture* (New York: Vintage, 1992), 62. Anthony Rotundo, *American Manhood: Transformations in Masculinity from the Revolution to the Modern Era* (New York: Basic Books, 1993), 104, 107. The philosopher Friedrich Nietzsche writes, persuasively, that the emancipation of modern women has led to their losing power over men: *Beyond Good and Evil,* no. 239. Blankenhorn, *Fatherless America,* 216–17. Gilder, *Men and Marriage,* 27, 40–47. Goldberg, *Why Men Rule;* and Steven Goldberg, "Can Women Beat Men at Their Own Game?" *National Review,* 27 December 1993, 30–36. David M. Buss, *The Evolution of Desire: Strategies of Human Mating* (New York: Basic Books, 1994), 19–72, 168–82. Philip Blumstein and Pepper Schwartz, *American Couples: Money, Work, Sex* (New York: William Morrow, 1983), 311–12.

45. Jan Lewis, "The Republican Wife," 689. Merril D. Smith, *Breaking the Bonds: Marital Discord in Pennsylvania, 1730–1830* (New York: New York University Press, 1991), 5. Abigail Adams to Elizabeth Peabody, 19 July 1799, quoted by Page Smith, *John Adams* (Garden City, N.Y.: Doubleday, 1962), 2:1006. See also Kann, *On the Man Question;* Carl N. Degler, *At Odds: Women and the Family in America from the Revolution to the Present* (New York: Oxford University Press, 1980), 8–19, 26–30; Nancy Cott, *The Bonds of Womanhood: Women's Sphere in New England, 1780–1835* (New Haven: Yale University Press, 1976).

46. Quoted by Lewis, "The Republican Wife," 700. Kerber, *Women of the Republic,* 283.

47. Alexis de Tocqueville, *Democracy in America,* ed. J. P. Mayer (New York: Harper & Row, 1988), 600–603. Jay Fliegelman, *Prodigals and Pilgrims: The American Revolution against Patriarchal Authority, 1750–1800* (Cambridge: Cambridge University Press, 1982), 10.

48. Marylynn Salmon, *Women and the Law of Property in Early America* (Chapel Hill: University of North Carolina Press, 1986), 189–91. Willard S. Randall, *Thomas Jefferson: A Life* (New York: Henry Holt, 1993), 162–67. Smith, *Breaking the Bonds,* 22–24. Bruce H. Mann, "The Evolutionary Revolution in American Law," *William and Mary Quarterly* 50 (1993): 168–80. On the connection between the American Revolution and the reformation of divorce law, Norman Basch, "From the Bonds of Empire to the Bonds of Matrimony," in *Devising Liberty: Preserving and Creating Freedom in the New American Republic,* ed. David T. Konig (Stanford: Stanford University Press, 1995), 217–42.

49. Abigail to John Adams, 31 March 1776, *Adams Family Correspondence,* 1:370.

50. Joan B. Kelly, "How Adults React to Divorce," in *Marriage and Family,* ed. Henslin, 411.

51. On the transformation of opinion among American elites in the 1960s, see Myron Magnet, *The Dream and the Nightmare: The Sixties' Legacy to the Underclass*

(New York: Morrow, 1993), chap. 1. *Statistical Abstract of the United States: 1996* (Washington: Government Printing Office, 1996), 54, 79, 65. Rickie Solinger, *Wake Up Little Susie: Single Pregnancy and Race before* Roe v. Wade (New York: Routledge, 1994).

52. Barbara Ehrenreich, "The Bright Side of Overpopulation," *Time,* 26 September 1994, 86.

53. Barbara D. Whitehead et al., "Man, Woman, and Public Policy," *First Things,* August 1991, 31.

54. Gilder, *Men and Marriage,* 57, 76–77, citing studies by anthropologists George P. Murdock, Edward Westermarck, and George Devereux. William Tucker, "The New Polygamy," *St. Croix Review* 21 (February 1988): 26–31. Carol Gilligan, *In a Different Voice: Psychological Theory and Women's Development* (Cambridge: Harvard University Press, 1982), 130–32 (celebrating adultery).

55. Norman Dennis and George Erdos, *Families without Fatherhood,* 2d ed. (London: IEA Health and Welfare Unit, 1993), 5, 106.

56. See the lyrics of "KKK Bitch," "Evil Dick," and "Momma's Gotta Die Tonight" on *Body Count.* See also Lawrence A. Stanley, ed., *Rap: The Lyrics* (New York: Penguin, 1992); and Dinesh D'Souza, *The End of Racism: Principles for a Multiracial Society* (New York: Free Press, 1995), 511–14.

57. Wilson, "Lectures on Law," *Works,* 599.

58. Thomas Jefferson, "Memorandums on a Tour from Paris to Amsterdam" (1788), *Writings,* 651–52. Thomas Paine, "Reflections on Unhappy Marriages"; Thomas Paine, "An Occasional Letter on the Female Sex" (from *Pennsylvania Magazine,* June and August, 1775), in *Writings of Thomas Paine,* ed. Moncure D. Conway (1902; reprint, New York: Burt Franklin, 1969), 53, 60, 63. Francis Parkman, *France and England in North America* (1865–92; reprint, New York: Library of America, 1983), 1:358.

Chapter 5

1. Gordon S. Wood, "Democracy and the Constitution," in *How Democratic Is the Constitution?* ed., Robert A. Goldwin and William A. Schambra (Washington: American Enterprise Institute Press, 1980), 2. Charles A. Beard, *An Economic Interpretation of the Constitution of the United States* (1913; reprint, New York: Free Press, 1941), 324. Richard Hofstadter, *The Progressive Historians: Turner, Beard, Parrington* (New York: Vintage, 1970), 190–95. J. Allen Smith, *The Spirit of American Government* (1907; reprint, Cambridge: Harvard University Press, 1965), 369.

2. Michael Parenti, "The Constitution as an Elitist Document," in *How Democratic Is the Constitution?* ed. Goldwin and Schambra, 41. Larry Berman and Bruce A. Murphy, *Approaching Democracy* (Upper Saddle River, N.J.: Prentice Hall, 1996), 15–16. Karen O'Connor and Larry J. Sabato, *American Government: Roots and Reform* (New York: Macmillan, 1993), 133. Robert A. Divine et al., *America: The People and the Dream,* vol. 1, *The Early Years* (Glenview, Ill.: Scott, Foresman, 1992), 198.

3. Discussed by John Adams, *Defense of the Constitutions,* in *Works of John Adams,* ed. Charles F. Adams (Boston: Little, Brown, 1854), 4:303–27.

4. Jackson Turner Main, "Government by the People: The American Revolution and the Democratization of the Legislatures," in *The Revolution in the States,* ed. Peter Onuf (New York: Garland, 1991), 1–17. The quotation is from a Boston newspaper in 1786.

5. State and federal constitutions and laws. Kirk H. Porter, *A History of Suffrage in the United States* (1918; reprint, New York: AMS Press, 1971). On presidential elections: Neal R. Peirce and Lawrence D. Longley, *The People's President: The Electoral College in American History,* rev. ed. (New Haven: Yale University Press, 1981), 32, 247. Pre–1776 percentage: my estimate, based on Robert J. Dinkin, *Voting in Revolutionary America: A Study of Elections in the Original Thirteen States, 1776–1789* (Westport, Conn.: Greenwood, 1982), 39. The electorate in the "late provincial period" had "a range of 50 to 80 percent." Dinkin's full account is in his *Voting in Provincial America: A Study of the Elections in the Thirteen Colonies, 1689–1776* (Westport, Conn.: Greenwood, 1977). New Jersey percentage: based on Dinkin, *Voting in Revolutionary America,* 37 ("close to 90 percent" in the 1770s); and on Chilton Williamson, *American Suffrage from Property to Democracy, 1760–1860* (Princeton: Princeton University Press, 1960), 121: "By 1798, . . . the qualification was not enforced 'from a conviction of its repugnance to the principles of republicanism, and from the impracticality of its observance.'" Georgia and Delaware: based on Williamson, *American Suffrage,* 136: "In New Hampshire, Delaware, Georgia, and North Carolina all adult males were subject to a poll tax or its equivalent. With taxation of adult males almost universal, a taxpaying suffrage was almost universal suffrage." Massachusetts: J. R. Pole, *Political Representation in England and the Origins of the American Republic* (New York: St. Martin's, 1966), 209: "Such disenfranchisement as was intended by the Constitution of 1780 soon proved to be insignificant in practice. Within a very few years, the property qualifications were ignored and it appeared to be the custom to allow every man who had a settled residence and paid a poll tax to vote. In 1786 it was noted that 'estate to the value of sixty pounds, or the yearly value of three pounds' was commonly construed to mean any man who could earn 3 pounds a year." Lax enforcement of property requirements in Massachusetts may go back to colonial times, as John Adams implies: "Our people have never been very rigid in scrutinizing into the qualifications of voters, and I presume they will not now begin to be so." Letter to Sullivan, 26 May 1776, *Works,* 9:377. Pennsylvania: Dinkin, *Voting in Revolutionary America,* 36, says that "about 90 percent of the adult white males were now taxpaying freemen" in 1787; however, that estimate does not take into account disqualification by residency (a requirement excluded in this table). South Carolina: based on Williamson, *American Suffrage,* 136: "It would appear, however, that in practice anyone who tendered 3 shillings to a tax collector could vote." North Carolina: for House figure, see source on Georgia. Senate figure is based on rural Massachusetts, Delaware, and South Carolina in the 1770s: Dinkin, *Voting in Revolutionary America,* 36–37. Maryland: Dinkin, *Voting in Revolutionary America,* 39. The number may have been higher at important elections because of nonenforcement of the requirement; see Williamson, *American Suffrage,* 139–40. Virginia, Rhode Island, and

Connecticut: Dinkin, *Voting in Revolutionary America,* 38–39. New York: The lower numbers are from Dinkin, *Voting in Revolutionary America,* 38. For the higher numbers, see Merrill D. Peterson, ed., *Democracy, Liberty, and Property: The State Constitutional Conventions of the 1820s* (Indianapolis: Bobbs Merrill, 1966), 135. Willi Paul Adams, *The First American Constitutions* (Chapel Hill: University of North Carolina Press, 1980), 204–5, estimates 33 percent for senate and governor; and "in 1790, in New York City, at least, just about every white adult male could vote. In rural areas, the number of those unable to vote seems to have been . . . about 35 percent." Combining these two numbers, I estimate 70 percent for house elections. Northwest Ordinance: In 1792 hardly anyone except Indians lived in the Northwest Territory. What proportion of the frontier settlers had clear title to their land is unknown. U.S. Constitution: My estimate of males eligible to vote for House of Representatives, based on above numbers.

6. Resolutions of the House of Representatives of Massachusetts, 29 October 1765, in *The Founders' Constitution,* vol. 1, *Major Themes,* ed. Philip B. Kurland and Ralph Lerner (Chicago: University of Chicago Press, 1987), 629.

7. Return of the town of Richmond on the Massachusetts constitution of 1780; Return of Dorchester on the proposed constitution of 1778; Return of Mansfield on the constitution of 1780; in *The Popular Sources of Political Authority: Documents on the Massachusetts Constitution of 1780,* ed. Oscar Handlin and Mary Handlin (Cambridge: Harvard University Press, 1966), 487, 254, 520.

8. Remonstrance of Salem County Freemen to Second Provincial Congress, New Jersey, 1776, in *History of Voting in New Jersey,* by Richard P. McCormick, (New Brunswick: Rutgers University Press, 1953), 67. Return of Dorchester on the Massachusetts constitution of 1780, in *Popular Sources,* ed. Handlin and Handlin, 778.

9. Marc W. Kruman, "Suffrage," in *The Reader's Companion to American History,* ed. Eric Foner and John A. Garraty (Boston: Houghton Mifflin, 1991), 1044.

10. Edmund Pendleton to Thomas Jefferson, 10 August 1776, *The Papers of Thomas Jefferson,* ed. Julian P. Boyd (Princeton: Princeton University Press, 1950–), 1:489–90; Jefferson to Pendleton, 26 August 1776, *Papers,* 1:504.

11. The state declarations of rights are in Bernard Schwartz, ed., *The Roots of the Bill of Rights* (New York: Chelsea House, 1980), vol. 2.

12. Daniel J. Boorstin, *A History of the United States* (Lexington, Mass.: Ginn, 1986), 185. Stanley N. Katz, "Constitutional Equality," *This Constitution,* no. 18 (Spring/Summer 1988): 32.

13. "A Reliable Predictor," *Forbes,* 23 November 1992, 26. Letter from Weekly Reader Corporation to author, 10 February 1994.

14. Alexander Hamilton, *The Farmer Refuted,* in *Papers of Alexander Hamilton,* ed. Harold C. Syrett (New York: Columbia University Press, 1961–79), 1:106, quoting Blackstone, *Commentaries,* bk. 1, ch. 2.

15. Note During the Convention for Amending the Constitution of Virginia (1829), in *The Mind of the Founder: Sources of the Political Thought of James Madison,* ed. Marvin Meyers, rev. ed. (Hanover, N.H.: University Press of New England, 1981), 407, emphasis added.

16. Adams to Sullivan, 26 May 1776, in *Works,* 9:377. Adams published the same argument to the world in his 1787 *Defense of the Constitutions:* "At present a

husbandman, merchant, or artificer [craftsman], provided he has any small property, by which he may be supposed to have a judgment and will of his own, instead of depending for his daily bread on some patron or master, is a sufficient judge of the qualifications of a person to represent him in the legislature." *Works,* 5:456.

17. Speeches of 7 August, *Records of the Federal Convention of 1787,* ed. Max Farrand, rev. ed.(New Haven:Yale University Press, 1966), 2:202–4.

18. Gordon S. Wood, *The Radicalism of the American Revolution* (New York: Knopf, 1992), 178.

19. Thomas Paine,"A Serious Address to the People of Pennsylvania" (1777), in *Complete Writings of Thomas Paine,* ed. Philip S. Foner (New York: Citadel Press, 1945), 2:287.

20. David Hackett Fischer, *The Revolution of American Conservatism* (Chicago: University of Chicago Press, 1965), 14–16, 217.

21. Edmund Randolph, *History of Virginia,* ed. Arthur H. Shaffer (Charlottesville: University Press of Virginia, 1970), 256, emphasis added.

22. Address of the Massachusetts Convention to their Constituents, March 1780, *Popular Sources,* ed. Handlin and Handlin, 437.

23. Speech of August 7, in *Records of the Convention,* ed. Farrand, 2:202.

24. John Adams, *Novanglus,* no. 5, in *Works,* ed. Adams, 4:79.

25. Alexander Hamilton et al., *The Federalist,* ed. Clinton Rossiter (New York: New American Library, 1961), No. 9, p. 72; Letter of Washington to Jay, 15 August 1786, in *George Washington: A Collection,* ed. W. B. Allen (Indianapolis: Liberty Classics, 1988), 334.

26. Speech of 19 June 1787, *Records of the Convention,* ed. Farrand, 1:318.

27. Madison, *Federalist* No. 10, pp. 82–84; No. 51, p. 322.

28. Notes on Madison's speech of 6 June, *Records of the Convention,* ed. Farrand, 1:146.

29. Remarks on Mr. Jefferson's Draft of a Constitution for Kentucky, ca. 15 October 1788, in *Mind of the Founder,* ed. Meyers, 36. Speech of 7 August 1787, and Madison's Note on that speech, in *Records of the Convention,* ed. Farrand, 2:203–4.

30. Quotations since the last note are drawn from three statements in which Madison expounded the same argument: Note on Madison's speech of 7 August 1787, ca. 1821; Note during the Convention for Amending the Constitution of Virginia (1829); both in *Mind of the Founder,* ed. Meyers, 396–99, 406; and Note to Speech of J. Madison of 7 August 1787 in *Records of the Convention,* ed. Farrand, 2:204.

31. Speech of Adams at the Massachusetts Constitutional Convention of 1820–21, in *Democracy, Liberty, and Property,* ed. Peterson, 75–77. Madison, Note during the Convention for Amending the Constitution of Virginia (1829), in *Mind of the Founder,* ed. Meyers, 407.

32. Madison's 1821 notes on his Convention speech of 7 August 1787, in *Mind of the Founder,* ed. Meyers, 504.

33. James Wilson, "Considerations on . . . Parliament" (1774); "Lectures on Law" (1790–91), emphasis added, in *Works of James Wilson,* ed. Robert G. McCloskey (Cambridge: Harvard University Press, 1967), 2:725; 1:411, emphasis added.

34. Madison, "Republican Distribution of Citizens" (1792), in *Mind of the Founder,* ed. Meyers, 184–86; Jefferson, *Notes on the State of Virginia,* Query 19, in *Writings,* ed. Merrill D. Peterson (New York: Library of America, 1984), 290–91. Wood, *Radicalism,* 185.

35. George Gilder, *Wealth and Poverty* (New York: Bantam, 1981), shows the truth of this observation in today's economy.

36. *Federalist* No. 10, p. 79.

Chapter 6

1. James MacGregor Burns et al., *Government by the People,* 15th ed. (Englewood Cliffs: Prentice Hall, 1993), 196, 199–200. Larry Berman and Bruce A. Murphy, *Approaching Democracy* (Upper Saddle River, N.J.: Prentice Hall, 1996), 568.

2. Barry Goldwater, *Conscience of a Conservative* (1960; reprint, Washington: Regnery Gateway, 1990), 68.

3. Michael B. Katz, *In the Shadow of the Poorhouse: A Social History of Welfare in America* (New York: Basic, 1986), 3. Walter I. Trattner, *From Poor Law to Welfare State: A History of Social Welfare in America,* 5th ed. (New York: Free Press, 1994), 55–56, 387–95.

4. Thomas Jefferson, *Notes on the State of Virginia* (1787), Query 14, in *Writings,* ed. Merrill D. Peterson (New York: Library of America, 1984), 259. Thomas Jefferson, "A Bill for Support of the Poor" and "A Bill Concerning . . . Apprentices," in *The Papers of Thomas Jefferson,* ed. Julian P. Boyd (Princeton: Princeton University Press, 1950–), 2:422, 487. Marcus W. Jernegan, *Laboring and Dependent Classes in Colonial America, 1607–1783* (1931; reprint, New York: Frederick Ungar, 1960), 188. Ralph Lerner, *The Thinking Revolutionary: Principle and Practice in the New Republic* (Ithaca: Cornell University Press, 1987), 65–66, on Jefferson's poor law.

5. Thomas Jefferson, letter to John Adams, 28 October 1813, *Writings,* 1307–9.

6. Benjamin Franklin, "On the Price of Corn, and Management of the Poor," *London Chronicle* (November 1766), in *Writings,* ed. J. A. Leo Lemay (New York: Library of America, 1987), 587–88.

7. Myron Magnet, *The Dream and the Nightmare: The Sixties' Legacy to the Underclass* (New York: William Morrow, 1993), 47–49. Seventh Lincoln-Douglas debate, 15 October 1858, in *Collected Works of Abraham Lincoln,* ed. Roy T. Basler (New Brunswick: Rutgers University Press, 1953), 3:315.

8. Thomas Jefferson, letter to Milligan, 6 April 1816, in *Writings of Thomas Jefferson,* ed. Albert E. Bergh (Washington: Thomas Jefferson Memorial Association, 1904), 14:466.

9. Richard A. Epstein, *Takings: Private Property and the Power of Eminent Domain* (Cambridge: Harvard University Press, 1985), 316–22. Locke, *Second Treatise,* in *Two Treatises of Government,* ed. Peter Laslett, student ed. (Cambridge: Cambridge University Press, 1988), sec. 6.

10. Quotations in this section are from Trattner, *From Poor Law to Welfare State,*

28, 59, 62–63, and 37; and Robert E. Cray Jr., *Paupers and Poor Relief in New York City and Its Rural Environs, 1700–1830* (Philadelphia: Temple University Press, 1988), 199. Trattner's first seventy-five pages tell the story of welfare in early America; see also Katz, *In the Shadow;* and Benjamin J. Klebaner, *Public Poor Relief in America, 1790–1860* (1952; reprint, New York: Arno, 1976). Marvin Olasky, "The Early American Model of Compassion," in *The Tragedy of American Compassion* (Washington: Regnery Gateway, 1992), chap. 1.

11. The 59 percent figure is from U.S. Department of Commerce, *Survey of Current Business,* vol. 44, no. 4 (April 1964), 11 (percent of American families with less than $3,000 annual income in 1954 dollars). This figure is comparable to the "below poverty level" numbers that the government began to report in 1947, because the below-$3,000 percentage in 1947 was 35, close to the 32 percent officially reported poor in that year. *Economic Report of the President* (Washington: Government Printing Office, 1965), 210. *Statistical Abstract of the United States: 1996* (Washington: Government Printing Office, 1996), 472.

12. Quotations are from Trattner, *From Poor Law to Welfare State,* 102–4. See also Robert H. Bremner, *The Discovery of Poverty in the United States* (1956; reprint, New Brunswick: Transaction Publishers, 1992), chap. 2; Olasky, *Tragedy of American Compassion,* 116–50.

13. Christopher Jencks, *Rethinking Social Policy: Race, Poverty, and the Underclass* (Cambridge: Harvard University Press, 1992), 2. Robert B. Stevens, *Statutory History of the United States: Income Security* (New York: Chelsea House, 1970), 152. Katie Louchheim, ed., *The Making of the New Deal: The Insiders Speak* (Cambridge: Harvard University Press, 1983), 175. George W. Liebmann discusses AFDC, unwed motherhood, and the case for maternity homes in "The AFDC Conundrum: A New Look at an Old Institution," *Social Work* 38 (January 1993): 36–43.

14. Craig Flournoy, "Man Sues City over Order to Raze Home," *Dallas Morning News,* 2 March 1995, 25A, 27A.

15. George Gilder, *Men and Marriage* (Gretna, La.: Pelican, 1992), 80.

16. Robert Rector and William F. Lauber, *America's Failed $5.4 Trillion War on Poverty* (Washington: Heritage Foundation, 1995), 94, 19, 20, 5, 25. Michael Tanner, Stephen Moore, and David Hartman, "Work vs. Welfare Tradeoff," Cato Foundation Policy Analysis, 19 September 1995, 22, 25, 49. Charles Murray, *Losing Ground: American Social Policy from 1950 to 1980* (New York: Basic, 1984), 162.

17. Franklin, *Writings,* 588.

Chapter 7

1. Abraham Lincoln, Speech at Chicago, 10 July 1858; Lincoln, letter to Pierce, 6 April 1859; in *Collected Works of Abraham Lincoln,* ed. Roy T. Basler (New Brunswick, N.J.: Rutgers University Press, 1953), 2:499; 3:376.

2. U.S. Bureau of the Census, *Statistical Abstract of the United States: 1996* (Washington: Government Printing Office, 1996), 10. Lawrence E. Harrison, *Who Prospers? How Cultural Values Shape Economic and Political Success* (New York: Basic

Books, 1992), 180. Peter Brimelow, *Alien Nation: Common Sense about America's Immigration Disaster* (New York: Random House, 1995), 26–27, 283. Linda Chavez, *Out of the Barrio: Toward a New Politics of Hispanic Assimilation* (New York: Basic Books, 1991), 122. Linda Chavez, "What to Do about Immigration," *Commentary*, March 1995, 29. David LaGesse, "INS Believes 5 Million in U.S. Illegally," *Dallas Morning News*, 8 February 1997, 1 A.

3. Rodolfo O. de la Garza et al., *Latino Voices: Mexican, Puerto Rican, and Cuban Perspectives on American Politics* (Boulder, Colo.: Westview Press, 1992), 101. Robert Pear, "Panel to Urge Immigration Cut," *Dallas Morning News*, 5 June 1995, 1A.

4. Rogers Smith, "The 'American Creed' and American Identity: The Limits of Liberal Citizenship in the U.S.," *Western Political Quarterly* 41 (1988): 245. "Sometimes the Door Slams Shut," *Time*, Special Issue, Fall 1993, 33.

5. George J. Borjas, *Friends or Strangers: The Impact of Immigrants on the U.S. Economy* (New York: Basic Books, 1990). Peter Brimelow, *Alien Nation*, 178, 206–11. M. E. Bradford, *Remembering Who We Are: Observations of a Southern Conservative* (Athens: University of Georgia Press, 1985), 118. John O'Sullivan, "America's Identity Crisis," *National Review*, 21 November 1994, 36–45, 76.

6. George Washington to the Volunteer Association of Ireland, December 2, 1783, in *Writings of George Washington*, ed. John C. Fitzpatrick (Washington: Government Printing Office, 1931–44), 27:254. George Washington, "To the Hebrew Congregation in Newport" (1790), in *George Washington, A Collection*, ed. W. B. Allen (Indianapolis: Liberty Classics, 1988), 548. On the Founders' views, see also Matthew Spalding, "From Pluribus to Unum: Immigration and the Founding Fathers," *Policy Review*, Winter 1994, 35–41.

7. Continental Congress, "Appeal to the Inhabitants of Quebec" (1774), in *American Political Writing during the Founding Era, 1760–1805*, ed. Charles S. Hyneman and Donald S. Lutz (Indianapolis: Liberty Press, 1983), 1:235–8. See Thomas G. West, "Religious Liberty: The View from the Founding," in *On Faith and Free Government*, ed. Daniel Palm (Lanham, Md.: Rowman & Littlefield, 1997).

8. Washington to the Volunteer Association of Ireland, 2 December 1783, *Writings*, 27:254.

9. Washington to Jefferson, 1 January 1788, *Writings*, 29:351. Washington to Rev. Francis Vanderkemp, 28 May 1788, in *George Washington: A Collection*, 395–96.

10. Washington to the Vice President, 15 November 1794, *Writings*, 34:23, emphasis added. On assimilation, see also Washington to Congress, 8 February 1785, in *George Washington: A Collection*, 299.

11. Benjamin Franklin to Collinson, 9 May 1753, *Writings*, ed. J. A. Leo Lemay (New York: Library of America, 1987), 472–73. Kathleen Conzen, "Germans," in *Harvard Encyclopedia of American Ethnic Groups*, ed. Stephan Thernstrom (Cambridge: Harvard University Press, 1980), 407. Lawrence H. Fuchs, *The American Kaleidoscope: Race, Ethnicity, and the Civic Culture* (Hanover, N.H.: Wesleyan University Press, 1990), 19–23. Thomas Sowell, *Ethnic America: A History* (New York: Basic Books, 1981), 51.

12. Franklin, "Information to Those Who Would Remove to America" (1784), *Writings*, 978, 982.

13. The quotation is Frank B. Franklin's paraphrase of Madison, in *The Legislative History of Naturalization in the United States* (1906; reprint, New York: Arno, 1969), 40, 23.

14. 13 August, in *Records of the Federal Convention of 1787,* ed. Max Farrand (New Haven: Yale University Press, 1966), 2:268.

15. Russell Kirk, *America's British Culture* (New Brunswick, N.J.: Transaction, 1993).

16. Jefferson, *Notes on Virginia* (1787), Query 8, *Writings,* 210–12.

17. Jefferson, "First Annual Message" (1801), *Writings,* ed. Merrill D. Peterson (New York: Library of America, 1984), 508. Hamilton, *Report on Manufactures* (1791), in *Selected Writings and Speeches of Alexander Hamilton,* ed. Morton Frisch (Washington: American Enterprise Institute, 1985), 290–91. Hamilton, "The Examination," nos. 7–9 (1802), *Papers of Alexander Hamilton,* ed. Harold C. Syrett et al. (New York: Columbia University Press, 1961–79), 25:491–501.

18. Hamilton, Speech in New York Ratifying Convention, 28 June 1788, in *Selected Writings,* ed. Frisch, 238.

19. Jefferson, "A Declaration," *Writings,* 23.

20. The emergence of the idea of "volitional citizenship" in the founding era is traced by James H. Kettner, *The Development of American Citizenship, 1608–1870* (Chapel Hill: University of North Carolina Press, 1978), chap. 7.

21. Philip B. Kurland and Ralph Lerner, eds., *The Founders' Constitution,* vol. 1: *Major Themes* (Chicago: University of Chicago Press, 1987), 11.

22. August 9, in *Records of the Convention,* ed. Farrand, 2:238.

23. Roger Mahoney, "Roman Catholics Should Work for Liberal Immigration Policies," in *Immigration Policy,* ed. Scott Barbour (San Diego: Greenhaven Press, 1995), 97.

24. Thomas Jefferson, *Summary View of the Rights of British America* (1774), in *Writings,* 105. Pennsylvania Declaration of Rights, in *Sources and Documents Illustrating the American Revolution,* ed. Samuel Eliot Morison (New York: Oxford, 1923), 164.

25. Thomas Jefferson, First Inaugural Address (1801), *Writings,* 492–94.

26. Jefferson, *Notes on Virginia,* Query 14, *Writings,* 274.

27. Northwest Ordinance of 1787, art. 3, in *Founders' Constitution,* ed. Kurland and Lerner, 1:28.

28. Kurland and Lerner, eds, *Founders' Constitution,* 1:7 (Virginia), 1:12, 21 (Massachusetts). Morison, *Sources and Documents,* 164, 175 (Pennsylvania).

29. Morison, *Sources and Documents,* 144–45.

30. George Washington, General Orders, 2 July 1776, in *George Washington: A Collection,* 71.

31. George Washington, First Annual Address to Congress, in *George Washington: A Collection,* 469.

32. Gouverneur Morris, *A Diary of the French Revolution,* ed. Beatrix C. Davenport (Boston: Houghton Mifflin, 1939), 1:136 (to Carmichael, 4 July 1789); 2:581 (to Pinckney, 3 December 1792). Most of the passages quoted here from Morris are discussed in George Anastaplo, "American Constitutionalism and the Virtue of Prudence," in *Abraham Lincoln, the Gettysburg Address, and American Constitutionalism,* ed.

Leo Paul S. de Alvarez (Irving: University of Dallas Press, 1976), 94–106.

33. Morris, *Diary,* 1:61 (to Washington, 29 April 1789).

34. Morris, *Diary,* 1:266 (diary, 21 October 1789); 1:382 (to Washington, January 24, 1790); 2:564 (to Jefferson, 23 October 1792); 2:452 (to Gordon, 28 June 1792); 2:333–34 (to Washington, 27 December 1791).

35. Morris, *Diary,* 1:2 (diary, 1 March 1789), 1:283 (diary, 3 November 1789).

36. Morris, *Diary,* 2:387.

37. Hector St. John de Crevecoeur, *Letters from an American Farmer* (1782; reprint, New York: Dutton, 1957), 39. Reed Ueda, "Naturalization and Citizenship," in *Harvard Encyclopedia of American Ethnic Groups,* 737. Kettner, *Development of American Citizenship,* 235–47 (quotation on 241).

38. Franklin, *Legislative History,* 93 (paraphrasing the petition). William S. Bernard, "Immigration: History of U.S. Policy," and Ueda, "Naturalization and Citizenship," in *Harvard Encylcopedia of American Ethnic Groups,* 486–95, 734–48. Bernard uses the phrase "Open Door Era" on 488. A useful recent account is Roger Daniels, *Coming to America: A History of Immigration and Ethnicity in American Life* (New York: Harper Collins, 1990).

39. Edward J. Erler, "Immigration and Citizenship," in *Loyalty Misplaced: Misdirected Virtue and Social Disintegration,* ed. Gerald Frost (London: Social Affairs Unit, 1997), 71–89. *Slaughter House Cases,* 83 U.S. 36, 73 (1873); *U.S. v. Wong Kim Ark,* 169 U.S. 649 (1898).

40. Naturalization Act, 26 March 1790, *Documentary History of the First Federal Congress,* vol. 6, ed. Charlene B. Bickford et al. (Baltimore: Johns Hopkins University Press, 1986), 1516. Ueda, "Naturalization and Citizenship," 736. U.S. Department of Justice, Immigration and Naturalization Service, "United States Immigration Laws: General Information," publication M-50 (Washington: Government Printing Office, 1989), 10–11. On state citizenship, Kettner, *Development of American Citizenship,* chaps. 8–9.

41. Naturalization Act, 26 March 1790, *First Federal Congress,* 6:1516. Ueda, "Naturalization and Citizenship," 739, 746. Daniels, *Coming to America,* gives a more detailed account.

42. Daniels, *Coming to America,* 124, 271, 278–84, 338. Bernard, "Immigration: History of U.S. Policy," 490–95.

43. Alexis de Tocqueville, *Democracy in America,* ed. J. P. Mayer (1835; trans., New York: Harper & Row, 1988), 437.

44. Alexander Hamilton, *Report on Manufactures,* in *Selected Writings,* 291.

45. George Washington, "Circular to the States" (1783), in *George Washington: A Collection,* 240–41.

46. Jefferson to Gregoire, 25 February 1809; *Writings,* 1202.

47. Thomas F. Pettigrew, "Prejudice," in *Harvard Encyclopedia of American Ethnic Groups,* 822.

48. Benjamin Franklin, "Observations Concerning the Increase of Mankind, Peopling of Countries, etc." (1751), *Writings,* 374.

49. Richard A. Epstein, *Forbidden Grounds: The Case against Employment Discrimination Laws* (Cambridge: Harvard University Press, 1992), 91–97. *Plessy v. Ferguson,* 164 U.S. 537 (1896).

50. Abraham Lincoln, Speech at Peoria, 16 October 1854, *Collected Works of Abraham Lincoln,* ed. Roy P. Basler (New Brunswick: Rutgers University Press, 1953), 2:275. Rogers M. Smith, "Beyond Tocqueville, Myrdal, and Hartz: The Multiple Traditions in America," *American Political Science Review* 87 (1993): 559 (quoting Brinton). John Higham, *Strangers in the Land: Patterns of American Nativism, 1860–1925* (New York: Atheneum, 1985), 117 (Commons) and chaps. 10–11.

51. Washington, First Annual Message (1790), in *George Washington: A Collection,* 469.

52. James Madison, Letter to Barry, 4 August 1822, in *Mind of the Founder: Sources of the Political Thought of James Madison,* ed. Marvin Meyers, rev. ed. (Hanover, N.H.: University Press of New England, 1981), 343–46.

53. George Washington, First Inaugural Address, in *George Washington: A Collection,* 462.

54. "An Act . . . Establishing an Uniform Militia," 8 May 1792, in *Annals of Congress,* ed. Joseph Gales and William W. Seaton (Washington, D.C.: Gales and Seaton, 1834–56), 1:392.

Afterword

1. John Hope Franklin, "The Moral Legacy of the Founding Fathers," *University of Chicago Magazine,* Summer 1975, 10–13.

2. Paul Finkleman, *Slavery and the Founders: Race and Liberty in the Age of Jefferson* (Armonk, N.Y.: M. E. Sharpe, 1996), chap. 5.

3. Abraham Lincoln, letter to Henry Pierce and others, 6 April 1859, in *Collected Works of Abraham Lincoln,* ed. Roy T. Basler (New Brunswick, N.J.: Rutgers University Press, 1953), 3:376.

4. Robert Bork, *Slouching towards Gomorrah: Modern Liberalism and American Decline* (New York: Regan Books, 1996), 56, 66.

5. James Q. Wilson, *The Moral Sense* (New York: Free Press, 1993), 245.

6. Leon Kass, "The End of Courtship," *The Public Interest,* Winter 1997, 43–44. Allan Bloom, *The Closing of the American Mind* (New York: Simon & Schuster, 1987), 113.

7. Abraham Lincoln, Fifth debate at Galesburg, Illinois, 7 October 1858, in *Collected Works,* 3:226.

Index

Abernathy, Ralph, 19, 21–22
abuse: of children, 92, 95–97, 100, 105, 109, 142; lesbian, 92–93; of women, 73–74, 91–93, 97, 101–2, 104–9, 142, 144
Adams, Abigail, 94, 97, 102–4
Adams, John, 124, 131, 135, 137, 151, 159; and commerce, 66–67; and the property requirement for voting, 122–23, 128; and reason and passion, 99; and slavery, xiii, 5, 13; and women, 80, 83, 86–87, 94, 97, 102
Adams, Samuel, 20
Adams, Willi Paul, 49
Africa, Africans, 3, 8–10, 14, 22, 34, 99, 167. *See also* blacks
Alabama, 12
aristocracy, 42, 50, 64, 66, 115, 126, 136, 153
Aristotle, 68, 97, 168
Asia, Asians, 54, 99, 168

Bailyn, Bernard, 32
Baldwin, Abraham, 31
Bartky, Sandra, 78
Beard, Charles, 58, 111–12
Berkin, Carol, 81
Berman, Larry, 112, 131
Bible, the, 67, 104. *See also* Christianity; Judaism; religion
Bill of Rights, 75
blacks, 141, 179; and citizenship, 25–28, 167–69, 171; and slavery, xi–xv, 1–36, 39–40, 46, 60, 71, 73; and voting rights, 75, 77, 113
Blankenhorn, David, 94
Bloom, Allan, 95, 177

Bone, Robert, 53
Boorstin, Daniel, 121
Bork, Robert, 176–77
Bradford, M. E., 148
Bradshaw, John, 92
Brennan, William, 61–62
Brinton, Daniel, 171
Britain, 44, 127, 152; and the American Revolution, 3, 6–7, 15, 55, 72, 81–82, 117, 124, 156; and British tradition, 72, 153, 169, 172; and property rights, 52; and slavery, 12; as source of American immigration, 150–52, 166, 170; and voting rights, 81, 115; and welfare policy, 107, 133, 135, 143, 145
Burns, James MacGregor, 73, 75, 131, 137
Bushman, Richard, 2, 5–6, 45, 72

Calhoun, John C., 10, 33
California, 143, 148
capitalism, 40, 46, 57, 127–28
Carnegie, Andrew, 40
Catholicism, 150, 157. *See also* Christianity
Central America, 29
China, Chinese, 151, 166–67
Chipman, Nathaniel, 51
Christianity, 13, 102–4. *See also* Bible; Catholicism; Protestantism; religion
Churchill, Winston, xv
citizenship, xii, xiv, 4, 25–29, 67–68, 112, 121, 147–73, 177, 179
Civil War, xiv, 10–12, 14, 16, 19, 24–29, 32–36, 45, 147, 166–67, 171, 175

Paglia, Camille, 102
Paine, Thomas, 108, 123
Parenti, Michael, 41–42, 112
Parkman, Francis, 74, 108
Parrington, Vernon, 38
patriarchalism, xii, 72, 101–5
Pendleton, Edmund, 120, 121
Pennsylvania, 9, 114; Constitution of
    1776, 161; Declaration of Rights
    (1776), 118, 156, 158; divorce law
    in, 104; immigration and, 151–52;
    and slavery, 11, 26–28; voting rights
    in, 116, 121
Perkins, Frances, 141
Peru, 56
Pettigrew, Thomas, 170
Pinckney, Charles Cotesworth, 22
Plato, 68, 162
Plessy v. Ferguson, 171
Plutarch, 114
polygamy, 99, 106
poverty, xi–xv, 4, 179; as a disqualifica-
    tion from voting, 111–30; and fami-
    ly breakdown, 94–95, 99, 105;
    among pre–Civil War blacks, 27;
    and property rights, 36–70, 178; and
    voting rights, 80; and welfare,
    131–45
primogeniture, 49, 51, 55, 104, 135
Progressives, Progressivism, 40, 55, 58,
    111, 119, 140
Protestantism, 54, 150. *See also* Chris-
    tianity
prudence, 65, 100, 125, 154; and slav-
    ery, 5, 19–21, 23

Quebec, 150

race, xi–xv, 60, 88; and immigration
    and citizenship, 113, 149, 165–71;
    and slavery, 1–36, 46, 73
Randall, Willard, 50
Randolph, Edmund, 9, 10, 123
Rawls, John, 62
Rector, Robert, 144
religion, xii, xiv, 26, 39, 47, 57, 60, 64,

72, 95, 99, 115, 132, 134, 138–39,
    147, 149–51, 156, 159, 161, 164,
    168, 172, 177. *See also* Christianity,
    Judaism, God
Report on Manufactures (Hamilton), 70,
    154, 169
Rhode Island, 11, 114, 117, 159
rights, human, 3, 9, 30, 33, 59, 73
rights, inalienable, 4, 24, 38, 118, 136,
    153, 155–56
right(s), natural, 4, 6–9, 12, 23, 25,
    38–39, 42, 48, 50–51, 53–54, 61, 63,
    74, 79, 118, 120, 136–37, 148–50,
    152–53, 156–58, 167, 170, 177, 179.
    See also law(s) of nature
rights of human nature, 63, 73
rights of humanity, xii, 18, 23, 72–73,
    158
rights of man, of mankind, xiv, 6–7,
    30, 38, 64, 73, 125, 130, 151, 153,
    155, 169, 171, 178
rights of men, 73
rights of nature, 73
Robinson, Donald, 20
Rome, Romans, 101–2, 127–28
Roosevelt, Franklin D., 55, 58, 60, 63,
    131, 141
Rousseau, Jean-Jacques, 59
Rush, Benjamin, 9, 91
Russian Revolution, 30
Rutledge, John, 22

Sabato, Larry, 17, 19–20, 112
self-assertion, 26, 54, 60, 70, 140, 154,
    160–65, 168–73, 178–79
self-control, 26, 60–61, 69, 95, 97, 109,
    130, 140, 154, 160–65, 168–72, 178
self-interest, 65, 125–26, 162, 164; as
    danger to virtue, 66–67;
    in marriage, 98, 105; of property
    owners, 40–41, 45, 57–58, 69, 111;
    and slavery, xii, 13–15, 17, 19–23,
    31; as support of virtue, 65–70
Seneca Falls Convention on Women's
    Rights, 72

About the Author

Thomas G. West is a director and senior fellow at the Claremont Institute and professor of politics at the University of Dallas, where he started teaching in 1974. He received his B.A. from Cornell University and his Ph.D. from Claremont Graduate School. He served in Vietnam as a lieutenant in the U.S. Army. He has been Bradley Resident Scholar at the Heritage Foundation (1988–89) and Salvatori Visiting Scholar at Claremont McKenna College (1990–92).

West has contributed chapters on American politics to several books, including "Misunderstanding the American Founding," in *Interpreting Tocqueville's* Democracy in America (edited by Ken Masugi); "The Decline of Free Speech in Twentieth-Century America," in *Liberty under Law* (edited by Kenneth Grasso and Cecilia Castillo); and "Religious Liberty: The View from the Founding," in *On Faith and Free Government* (edited by Daniel Palm), all published by Rowman & Littlefield. He is also the author of *Plato's Apology of Socrates: An Interpretation, with a New Translation* and cotranslator (with Grace West) of *Four Texts on Socrates: Plato's Euthyphro, Apology, Crito, and Aristophanes' Clouds,* both published by Cornell University Press.